The Beauty of GOD

for a BROKEN WORLD

Reflections on the Goodness of the God of the Bible

Charles - may our Lord give you
a fresh glimpse of His beauty
Psalm 27:4

Dr. John K. La Shell

Oct. 2010

John K. LaShell

The Beauty of GOD for a BROKEN WORLD

Reflections on the Goodness of the God of the Bible

PUBLICATIONS

Fort Washington, PA 19034

Published by CLC Publications

U.S.A.
P.O. Box 1449, Fort Washington, PA 19034

GREAT BRITAIN
51 The Dean, Alresford, Hants. SO24 9BJ

AUSTRALIA
P.O. Box 469, Kippa-Ring QLD 4021

NEW ZEALAND
118 King Street, Palmerston North 4410

Printed in the United States of America
18   17   16   15   14   13   12   11   10   1 2 3 4 5 6

ISBN-13: 978-1-936143-06-1

TABLE OF CONTENTS

FOREWORD

One of the primary purposes of a foreword is to suggest briefly why a book should be read. With John LaShell's *The Beauty of God for a Broken World*, that is a very easy task. In fact, you should speed-read this foreword in order to get quickly to the book itself.

John perceptively, graciously and accurately describes questions we all—whether Christian or not—have about the world in which we live:

- If God is so good and loving, why did He command the ethnic cleansing of Canaan?
- Was God asleep when the December 2004 tsunami wiped out over a hundred thousand people, or when an earthquake in Haiti killed or injured hundreds of thousands more?
- Is He on vacation every time a frustrated mother drowns her children?

These are uncomfortable questions, but they are also real, and John superbly crafts his book to show responsible, Christ-honoring answers. He utilizes the biblical and theological insights of America's (and perhaps the world's) greatest theologian—Jonathan Edwards—in building toward those answers. The result is a remarkably practical book.

Edwards's discussions of the beauty and the love of God, while profound and biblical and directly relevant to the questions mentioned above, can seem dauntingly theoretical to many readers. But John has made Edwards plain, and he has done so without distorting what Edwards taught (and lived).

One of the best aspects of this book is the way in which John offers multiple examples to help us understand the complex matters involved. Algebra, romantic love, human blood, a toddler banging on a piano, monarch butterflies, September 11, twins named Bart and Brent, John's childhood telephone number in California and many other such examples bring "giraffe food" down to the place where rabbits can feast. And what a feast it is!

Beginning with the hard questions of everyday life, John moves smoothly through the complex theology of Edwards and brings us to see the beautiful and loving God whom both Jonathan and John would want us to worship. At the very end, after quoting a magnificent passage in Habakkuk 3:17–19, John concludes with these words:

> God granted Habakkuk such a vision of His greatness, goodness and glory that his aching heart was satisfied—no, more than satisfied. To skip like a deer on the mountains when all you hold dear on this earth has been taken away is incomprehensible to the heart that has not seen the Lord. . . . Pray earnestly, *Lord, show me your beauty.*

This book shows the beauty of the Lord.

Dr. Samuel T. Logan Jr.
International Director, The World Reformed Fellowship
Special Counsel to the President, Biblical Seminary

ACKNOWLEDGMENTS

I am grateful for the patient proofreading of my wife Heather, my daughter Bethany S. LeBedz and my friends Ken Oates and Eric Woro. I greatly appreciate Becca Anderson, who edited the manuscript for CLC Publications; she frequently challenged me to clarify my thoughts. Grace Palmer and Khouri McGrann at CLC took care of many final proofreading and editorial details. Special thanks to Becky English at CLC Publications, without whose encouragement this book would never have seen the light of day.

Dr. Samuel T. Logan's course on Jonathan Edwards at Westminster Seminary introduced me to the major ideas and writings of America's first great theologian and philosopher. Dr. Logan also supervised my PhD dissertation, which explored Edwards's understanding of the visions some people experienced during the Great Awakening. Without his teaching this book would never have been written. Therefore, I was very pleased when he agreed to write the foreword.

Scripture quotations are generally taken from the New American Standard Bible. In keeping with the format of the NASB, I have capitalized personal pronouns referring to deity. I have also capitalized such pronouns in Jonathan Edwards's quotations for the sake of consistency. The only exceptions are in quotations or paraphrases of people hostile to Christianity, who may not capitalize the word "God."

The glorious excellencies and beauty of God will be what will for ever entertain the minds of the saints, and the love of God will be their everlasting feast.

—Jonathan Edwards

Introduction

The Challenge

I loved him. I love him still. Today he describes himself as an ex-Christian, and my heart aches.

I remember his eager attentiveness as I led discussions in a college and career study group. What joy when I baptized the lovely girl who later became his bride! I walked with them through the first few difficult years of marriage, but when they moved away, we lost contact. Later, I learned that my friend had begun spending time on atheistic Web sites and in chat rooms in an attempt to win unbelievers to Christ. They won him instead.

Now he echoes the complaints of a growing cadre of former believers who are hostile to Christianity: "The god of the Bible is ugly. If such a god existed, he would not be worthy of worship. We should despise and hate such a monster." The people who write and say such things used to be called apostates. I will use the term ex-Christians, which some of them seem to prefer.

Is God Ugly?

That ex-Christians vigorously attack the Bible is not new, but their criticisms seem to have become more open and vitriolic in recent years. To reflect their complaints accurately, I will attempt to express them with a measure of the passion I have encountered. (They often do not capitalize God.)

- If god is so good and loving, why did he command the ethnic cleansing of Canaan? He ordered the slaughter of men, women and innocent children—thousands of them. That's horrible! He's worse than Stalin or Pol Pot.

- I can understand how someone like Hitler might deserve to be sent to hell forever, but according to the Bible, god will send billions of ordinary people to hell for little sins that none of us can help doing.

- The whole idea of salvation by faith is repulsive. It's immoral. How can it ever be right to punish one person for someone else's sins, or even worse, for the sins of the whole world? Substitution is not just a silly doctrine; it is also irresponsible because it makes people think it doesn't matter how they live.

- The doctrine of predestination provides another proof of the ugliness of god. He supposedly tells us to be fair, but he arbitrarily decides to hate some people and love others. The people he hates don't have a chance. There's nothing they can do to change god's mind.

- Why should I believe in a good, "omni-max" god? The world is a mess. Was god asleep in December 2004 when a tsunami wiped out over a hundred thousand people? Is he on vacation every time a frustrated mother drowns her children? Are you telling me this is the best of all possible worlds? I don't know much, but if I had all power, I could do better than god.

While not the exact words of any one person, these comments are the true voices of many ex-Christians. Such people are not biblically illiterate. Unlike the average agnostic, they have read the Bible, listened to sermons and have a basic understanding of Christian teaching.

People who wrestle with issues like these need more than the standard proofs for God's existence. It is not so much the existence of God that bothers them, but rather specific characteristics of the God of the Bible. Buddhism, Wicca or atheism may seem more attractive to them.

You may think of yourself as an ex-Christian, or simply as an interested, thoughtful outsider to the Christian faith. Maybe some hopeful, eager believer has placed this book in your hands.

This book is not an attempt to prove that God exists. Others have made that argument from the perspectives of science, philosophy, Christian experience and fulfilled prophecy. Neither am I attempting to defend the general historical reliability of the Bible. Again, others have ably marshaled evidence for that.

All this book attempts to do is explain the attractiveness of God in terms of the Bible's own worldview. This may be helpful for Christians who want to know God better and for thoughtful outsiders to the faith. I have written for two kinds of readers: those who suspect that God is unlovely and those who want to love Him more.

The Beauty of God in the Old Testament

The words "beauty," "glory," "majesty" and "holy" are currently much in vogue in contemporary Christian music. When they are undefined, as is often the case, the words may only produce a temporary emotional or hypnotic effect. They mean little more than the repetitive chant of an eastern mystic. According to the Bible, the true and living God is the most beautiful Being and the source of all real beauty in the world. To see His beauty more clearly is to love Him more passionately.

The writer who has helped me most appreciate the Bible's teaching on God's beauty is Jonathan Edwards (1703–1758). Edwards was America's first great philosopher, and his preaching lit the flame of religious revival known as the Great Awakening. His most famous sermon is "Sinners in the Hands of an Angry God." Unfortunately, those who know Edwards only through that sermon have a terribly unbalanced view of him.

One of the settled convictions of modern ignorance is that the God of the Old Testament is cruel, while the God of the

New Testament is loving. Phyllis McGinley's description of the God of Jonathan Edwards sums up this attitude nicely:

> Abraham's God, the wrathful One,
> Intolerant of error—
> Not God the Father or the Son
> But God the Holy Terror.[1]

The irony is that few theologians have had as clear an understanding of God's love, coupled with a strongly emotional experience of God's beauty, as Jonathan Edwards. Studying Edwards has stimulated my own passion for the beauty of God, and it was Edwards who furnished the basic definition of beauty I have used throughout the book.

The God of Abraham and Jonathan Edwards is as much a God of love as is the Father of Jesus Christ. In fact, some of the Bible's most tender testimonies to divine beauty occur in the Old Testament.

Psalm 27 begins with King David's description of armed enemies who have set up their camps around him. Later in the psalm he says his father and mother have forsaken him. In such dire straits, what is his greatest desire? "One thing I have asked from the LORD, that I shall seek: That I may dwell in the house of the LORD all the days of my life, to behold the beauty of the LORD and to meditate in His temple" (27:4).

David longed to be in the house of the Lord because the temple was the center of Old Testament devotion. That is where the people met God, and they were deeply conscious of His presence there. "For all the gods of the peoples are idols, but the LORD made the heavens. Splendor and majesty are before Him, strength and beauty are in His sanctuary" (96:5–6).

Beauty was in the temple because God was there. For Old Testament believers the Lord was not an object of terror. The people thoroughly enjoyed Him. "You will make known to me the path of life; in Your presence is fullness of joy; in Your right hand there are pleasures forever" (16:11).

The delight of Old Testament saints in their God was not based on simple jingoism ("I rejoice in the Lord because He loves Israel and hates everybody else"). Naturally, they praised the Lord for vanquishing their enemies. Yet even when their enemies had the victory, they continued to love Him. After God informed Habakkuk that the Chaldeans were going to devastate his homeland and massacre his people, the prophet responded with these amazing words:

> Though the fig tree should not blossom
>> And there be no fruit on the vines,
>
> Though the yield of the olive should fail
>> And the fields produce no food,
>
> Though the flock should be cut off from the fold
>> And there be no cattle in the stalls,
>
> Yet I will exult in the LORD,
>> I will rejoice in the God of my salvation.
>
> The Lord GOD is my strength,
>> And He has made my feet like hinds' feet,
>> And makes me walk on my high places.
>
> (Hab. 3:17–19)

The Hebrew prophets and psalmists found their gladness in God, and they used all the words at their disposal to describe what they saw in Him. They spoke of His splendor, majesty, beauty and glory. Although there is a great deal of overlap between these terms, it is helpful to understand the basic distinction between two of them: beauty and glory.

Beauty and Glory

The most common Hebrew word for "glory" is *kavōd*. This noun is related to an adjective *kavēd*, which means "heavy," and to a verb *kavēd*, meaning "to be heavy." Eli is an old man and heavy (*kavēd*, 1 Sam. 4:18). Abraham is also *kavēd*, not because he is fat, but because he is rich (Gen. 13:2). He is heavy (or loaded) with possessions. In general, the Hebrew language can use *kavēd* for anything that is heavy or impressive, in a literal or figurative sense. Children are commanded to honor (kavēd) their parents (Ex. 20:12). That is, they are to treat them as weighty or impressive people. When we glorify the Lord, the word used is again "kavēd." The noun kavōd always means "glory" or "honor," but the underlying thought is that God is weighty or impressive. In Hebrew, glory is a heavy word.

Even though the apostle Paul wrote in Greek, the heaviness of glory in Hebrew was no doubt on his mind when he wrote, "For momentary, light affliction is producing for us an eternal weight of glory far beyond all comparison, while we look not at the things which are seen, but at the things which are not seen; for the things which are seen are temporal, but the things which are not seen are eternal" (2 Cor. 4:17–18).

All God's attributes are glorious, but when we consider them individually, some do not appear beautiful to us. For example, Ezekiel 39 speaks of a great battle in which God destroys the rebellious armies of the earth. At the end of the battle, the Lord invites the birds of the air to come and "eat the flesh of mighty men and drink the blood of the princes of the earth. . . . So you will be glutted at My table with horses and charioteers, with mighty men and all the men of war" (39:18–20). That is not a pretty picture, but in the next verse the Lord declares, "And I will set My glory among the nations; and all the nations will see My judgment which I have executed and My hand which I have laid on them" (39:21). God's just judgment is impressive; it is an expression of His glorious holiness and wrath, but considered by itself it is not attractive. God's judgment is only attractive when we view it in the context of all His perfections and intentions.

So, who is calling God beautiful? Christians who happily sing "I am so glad that Jesus loves me" find it easy to see the beauty of God. God has been gracious to them, so they love Him. But what about those who have not (or not yet) benefited from God's salvation? Is there anything in God that ought to appear attractive to an outsider?

If you are a Christian, I encourage you to set aside, for a

time, the benefits you have received from believing in Christ. Try looking at God from an interested non-Christian's point of view. Can you see God's beauty apart from the fact that He has saved you? Is God beautiful in Himself? The more clearly you see the beauty of God, the more you will love Him for Himself.

The basic distinction between "glory" and "beauty" is that God's glory is what makes Him *impressive*; His beauty is what makes Him *attractive*. The sum of all God's attributes is both glorious and beautiful.

My Challenge to You

A familiar proverb says that beauty is in the eye of the beholder. Some people find the God of the Bible immensely attractive, while others see only ugliness. Millions of Christians continue to love and praise God even while they are enduring unimaginable sufferings. What do they see in Him that others do not?

When people do not find the God of the Bible attractive, sometimes they are looking at Him from their own perspective. They think, *If I were God, I certainly would not act like the God of the Bible!* We have the same problem when we try to understand people from other cultures. I have a friend who lives in another country. If he invites five people for dinner at seven o'clock, they may start showing up at seven thirty. By nine o'clock there may be ten guests in his house, and they won't leave until one in the morning. Most Americans would be irritated by such a situation, but in that country it is normal and quite acceptable.

If understanding another contemporary culture is difficult, understanding God would be impossible unless He made a special effort to reveal what He is like. That is what the Bible claims to be: a revelation from God to us. The words and sentences in the Bible are clear for the most part, but the truths of Scripture are sometimes hard to grasp. People assume God ought to be easy to understand, but why should that be so?

The world around us is simple in some ways and complex in

others. People of limited intelligence can walk home, eat hamburgers and enjoy a pretty butterfly; their world is simple. If you look more deeply, the world is very complicated. It would take many volumes to describe what physicists have learned about the universe in the past one hundred years. In the same way, the simplest believer can enjoy the God of the Bible, but people who ask penetrating questions ought to be prepared to do some careful thinking.

As you read, be prepared to set aside your normal conceptions of how God ought to act. Try to see Him within the context of the Bible's worldview. It is only from that perspective that He will appear beautiful. This suspension of the natural mindset may be as necessary for a Christian who wants to know God better as it is for a thoughtful outsider. The goal is to see God and His purposes more clearly apart from any personal benefits we may receive from Him. When we do, we realize He—not His gifts—is our highest good and greatest joy.

Part 1

The Beauty *of* God the CREATOR

For as God is infinitely the greatest Being, so He is allowed to be infinitely the most beautiful and excellent: and all the beauty to be found throughout the whole creation, is but the reflection of the diffused beams of that Being who hath an infinite fulness of brightness and glory.

—Jonathan Edwards

1   Why Did God Create the World?

I was very good in mathematics at one time. Algebra was fun; so was calculus. As a consequence, I have sometimes been asked to help struggling students. I remember one boy who was taking first-year algebra in the decelerated program—using two years to complete the first year's course. His parents were so proud because he was getting an A in the class. However, he needed help with one small problem for the rapidly approaching examination. He understood how to solve the equation $x + 5 = 7$, but he did not know how to approach the far more difficult matter of $5 + x = 7$. That really was his question!

I was caught between strangled laughter and horrified disbelief. The boy had learned one rule. I had him memorize another because he seemed incapable of grasping the general principle.

In life as in mathematics, few things are more important than grasping the general principles and foundational concepts on which everything else depends. All the proofs in geometry fall back on Euclid's ten axioms. If a student goes wrong at the beginning of a problem, he can only get the right answer by accident. They say that even a blind squirrel finds a few nuts, but I suspect blind squirrels often starve. In order to see clearly in life, one must stick close to the basics—the general principles and the big ideas.

What's the Big Idea?

As a foundation for the weighty questions in the following chapters, here are the big ideas on which this book is based:

- Virtuous love is the highest kind of beauty.
- Because God is love, God is the most beautiful being.
- God is beautiful because the three Persons of the Trinity exist in a perfect harmony of love.
- This divine harmony is the fountain from which all created harmonies—all created beauties—flow.
- God's love is the beautiful motivation behind all He does.

I specify *virtuous* love because some kinds of love are unhealthy. The smothering mother's love that keeps a thirty-year-old man from making any independent decisions is not virtuous love. Neither is the unrestrained passion between a man and his neighbor's wife—a passion that leaves two families distraught, disoriented and permanently damaged.

True friendship between people who love goodness is a beautiful thing. The ancient Greek philosopher Aristotle counted such friendship one of the highest goods and one of the chief sources of human happiness.[1] In Scripture David's lament for his best friend Jonathan reflects the beauty of friendship-love:

Saul and Jonathan, beloved and pleasant in their life,
   And in their death they were not parted;
   They were swifter than eagles,
   They were stronger than lions. . . .
How have the mighty fallen in the midst of the battle!
Jonathan is slain on your high places.
I am distressed for you, my brother Jonathan;
   You have been very pleasant to me.
   Your love to me was more wonderful
   Than the love of women.
How have the mighty fallen,
   And the weapons of war perished!

               (2 Sam. 1:23, 25–27)

Friendship is a beautiful kind of love, but there is a love that is even more attractive. Truly beautiful people are not the glamorous and wealthy, but those who are kind, generous, gentle and faithful. The beautiful people overflow with goodness, both toward those dear to them and those who are outside their friendship and kinship circles (Matt. 5:43–48; Luke 14:1–14). That is virtuous love.

Divine love is far beyond any human affection. One of the simplest yet most profound statements in the Bible is "God is love" (1 John 4:8, 16). God's love is, of necessity, a virtuous love: "For the Lord is righteous, He loves righteousness" (Ps. 11:7). God's love is the model for the highest human affection because it is not restricted to His friends. "But God demonstrates His own love toward us, in that while we were yet sinners, Christ died for us. Much more then, having now been justified by His blood, we shall be saved from the wrath of God through Him. For if while we were enemies we were reconciled to God through the death of His Son, much more, having been reconciled, we shall be saved by His life" (Rom. 5:8–10).

In a more general sense, God's love overflows to everything He has made. "The Lord is gracious and merciful; slow to anger and great in lovingkindness. The Lord is good to all, and His mercies are over all His works" (Ps. 145:8–9). God's good gifts of rain, sunshine and fruitful seasons are the result of His love for all of His creation (Matt. 5:45; Acts 14:17).

Distinctions in God's Love

Though God's love is infinite, it is not stupidly indiscriminate. He loves each creature in exactly the measure that is appropriate for it. He shows His kindness to the cattle by giving them grass (Ps. 104:14) and His liking for the lions by giving them the cattle (104:21). Since God is love, many people assume He must express it uniformly toward all individuals. That is neither true nor reasonable.

The Bible says, "The one who loves violence His soul hates," and, "The Lord abhors the man of bloodshed and deceit" (Ps. 11:5; 5:6). On one hand, God hates, in some sense, evil people to whom He is still good and kind. On the other hand, Jesus said, "He who has My commandments and keeps them, he it is who loves Me; and he who loves Me will be loved by My Father, and I will love him and will disclose Myself to him" (John 14:21). Those who love Jesus Christ enjoy a special relationship with God the Father, so Scripture clearly indicates that God's affection is not exactly the same toward every human being.

It is not even reasonable to expect God to love all people in the same way. While some human love is blind, God is not. He sees our hearts, and He knows the plans He has for each individual human being. God's love is necessarily wise and intelligent.

When we realize that God's love is discriminating, the next natural question is this: What or whom does God love the most? The answer goes against all modern (and postmodern) sensibilities: *the chief object of God's love is His eternal Son.*

Americans seem driven to state their philosophies across their chests and on their bumpers. Among the blasphemies, the beer commercials and the "I'm with stupid" mottos, one T-shirt sums up the spirit of our age: "I ♥ Me." What our self-centered culture ignores is that God's chief concern is not to give us stress-free, fun-filled lives. We are not the focus of His affection. To put it bluntly, God loves His eternal Son far more than He loves you.

Those who put their faith and trust in Jesus Christ are God's adopted sons and daughters. Although God's love is infinite, He does not love us in exactly the same way and to the same degree as He loves Christ. If the Father loved any creature exactly as He loves His Son, He would be placing the value of that creature on a par with the value of God. Though God's love for His adopted children is infinite, Georg Cantor has shown that some infinities are larger than others. For example, there are more points on a line one inch long than there are integers.[2] Therefore, even if the Father's love for His adopted children is infinite, it is not a contradition to say that His love for His eternal Son is even greater.

Why are we here, if we are not the main attraction? Why did God make us? God's love for His Son is the reason He created the world. The bond of love between the Father and the Son is the bedrock on which creation, redemption, judgment and final glory ultimately rest. This divine love is the primary beauty; all beauty we experience in the world around us is a secondary variety that depends on and reflects the beauty of God.[3]

There are two astonishing corollaries to the concept that God loves His Son far more than He loves us. First, God created us because He loved His Son; second, He loves us because He loves His Son.

Two aspects of love are *delight* and *benevolence*.[4] Delight is the pleasure we have in another person; benevolence is the active good will that causes us to seek another's welfare. Delight looks at the beloved and smiles; benevolence looks at the beloved and gives. Both kinds of love have a place in God's decision to create the world.

Creation and God's Delight in His Son

Proverbs 8 personifies God's eternal wisdom as a woman who is crying out in the streets for fools to turn from their folly. To reinforce the importance of heeding her words, wisdom claims that she was with the Lord when He created the world. "Then I was beside Him, as a master workman; and I was daily His delight, rejoicing always before Him" (8:30).

In the context of Proverbs, the literary device "wisdom" is the antithesis of the woman of folly, who is also calling out to men passing by in the streets (9:13–18). The New Testament, however, suggests that the creative wisdom in Proverbs is Jesus Christ, because He is the eternal Word through whom all things were made: "In the beginning was the Word, and the Word was with God, and the Word was God. He was in the beginning with God. All things came into being through Him, and apart from Him nothing came into being that has come into being" (John 1:1–3).

The Greek word *logos* is translated as "Word" in this text. It indicates more than a single spoken or written word; it is an expression of the reason and thought of the speaker. Jesus is the complete expression of who God is—His eternal Word. In Christ "are hidden all the treasures of wisdom and knowledge" (Col. 2:3). Considering these passages together, many expositors and theologians have concluded that the creative wisdom in Proverbs 8 is the pre-incarnate Son of God. God delighted in His wisdom, His Son, before the foundation of the world.

Scripture frequently highlights the Father's delight in Jesus. Seven hundred years before Christ was born, God said, "Behold, My Servant, whom I uphold; My chosen one in whom My soul delights. I have put My Spirit upon Him; He will bring forth justice to the nations" (Isa. 42:1).

When John the Baptist baptized Jesus in the Jordan River before Jesus began His public ministry, God's voice came from heaven saying, "This is My beloved Son, in whom I am well-pleased" (Matt. 3:17). God repeated His approval of Jesus using the same words when He stood on the Mount of Transfiguration shining in heavenly glory (17:5).[5]

God's pleasure in His Son helps us to understand why He created the people He planned to redeem. Creation is Christ-centered in the following four ways:

The Father created the redeemed in Christ. According to Ephesians 2:8–10, those who are saved by God's grace through faith are "His workmanship, created in Christ Jesus for good works, which God prepared beforehand so that we would walk in them." The redeemed are "created in Christ" in two ways. First, Christ created believers, body and soul, along with the rest of the world (John 1:1–3; Col. 1:15–16). But then they undergo a second creation: "If any man is in Christ, he is a new creature" (2 Cor. 5:17). "In Christ" is one of the apostle Paul's favorite phrases. It expresses the living union that exists between Christ and His people. To be a new creature "in Christ" is to be united with the Son whom God loves. God's purpose in making people was to bring at least some of them into a special relationship with Christ.

The Father will fashion the redeemed into the image of Christ. Parents have different responses to their children. Sometimes when they have a baby they say, "Whoa! One is definitely enough. We don't want to go through colic and the terrible twos ever again." Other parents may say, "Wow! Being parents is the most wonderful thing in the world. We want to have as many as we can afford."

God is in the second category. He passionately delighted in His eternal, uncreated Son. Although He could not have another Son who completely shares His divine nature, He wanted a multitude of sons and daughters who would be as much like Jesus as a created being can be. The way He decided to accomplish this was to create men and women whom He would adopt and then transform into the image of Christ. "For those whom [God] foreknew, He also predestined to become conformed to the image of His Son, so that He would be the first-born among many brethren" (Rom. 8:29).

Every human being bears the image of the first man, Adam. Jesus Christ is called the "last Adam," and all who belong to Him will eventually bear His image (1 Cor. 15:45–49). When this transformation is complete, God's design for His people will be fulfilled.

The Father will delight in the redeemed because of Christ. The latter chapters of Isaiah describe the glory and beauty of God's redeemed people. Although the prophecy is couched in terms of Israel being restored to the land of Canaan, the sentiment applies to all the people of God:

> You will also be a crown of beauty in the hand of the LORD,
>   And a royal diadem in the hand of your God.
> It will no longer be said to you, "Forsaken,"
>   Nor to your land will it any longer be said, "Desolate";
>   But you will be called, "My delight is in her,"
>   And your land, "Married";

For the LORD delights in you,
And to Him your land will be married.
For as a young man marries a virgin,
So your sons will marry you;
And as the bridegroom rejoices over the bride,
So your God will rejoice over you.

(Isa. 62:3–5)

In the same vein the prophet Zephaniah sings, "The LORD your God is in your midst, a victorious warrior. He will exult over you with joy, He will be quiet in His love, He will rejoice over you with shouts of joy" (3:17). God will delight in the people He saves because they will resemble His beloved Son. He creates people anew in Christ in order to transform them into the image of Christ. The result is that He rejoices over them.

The Father will be glorified through Christ in the redeemed. The first question in the *Westminster Shorter Catechism* asks "What is the chief end of man?" The justly famous reply is "Man's chief end is to glorify God, and to enjoy Him forever." All of Scripture reinforces the lesson that God made us for His glory.[6] The Lord says,

I will say to the north, "Give them up!"
And to the south, "Do not hold them back."
Bring My sons from afar
And My daughters from the ends of the earth—
Everyone who is called by My name,
And whom I have created for My glory,
Whom I have formed, even whom I have made.

(Isa. 43:6–7)

Since we were created for God's glory, we are called to live for His glory: "Whether, then, you eat or drink or whatever you do, do all to the glory of God" (1 Cor. 10:31). Holy lives glorify God because they reflect the character of Christ, and Christ is the "radiance of [God's] glory and the exact representation of His nature" (Heb. 1:3). We can only glorify God—display His glory—as God conforms us to the image of His Son. Therefore, the Father "chose us in [Christ] before the foundation of the world, that we would be holy and blameless before Him. In love He predestined us to adoption as sons through Jesus Christ to Himself, according to the kind intention of His will, to the praise of the glory of His grace, which He freely bestowed on us in the Beloved" (Eph. 1:4–6).

Before the foundation of the world, a beautiful relationship of mutual love existed between God the Father and God the Son. The Father was so delighted with His Son that He planned to create men and women, to adopt them and to make them like His Son so they could be united with the Father and the Son in their glorious bond of love (John 17:20–26). That is the big picture of what God is doing in the world.[7]

Creation and God's Benevolence toward His Son

Lovers enjoy giving to each other. Boy meets girl. Boy thinks girl is the most beautiful creature God has ever made, so he is eager to spend every cent he has in order to please her. It is the nature of love to give. Since God is love, it is God's nature to give. Before the world began, giving and receiving took place within the Trinity. After creation the divine giving and receiving included all of the living creatures God had made. God's benevolence—His gracious, giving love—is evident in many ways.

The Father gave Himself to His Son. John 17 contains the most magnificent prayer in the Bible. The night before His crucifixion, Jesus prayed for the disciples He was leaving behind and for the disciples of all ages who would believe because of their testimony. He also prayed for Himself, and in the process He gave us a glimpse into His relationship with the Father:

> Now, Father, glorify Me together with Yourself, with the glory which I had with You before the world was. . . . The glory which You have given Me I have given to them, that they may be one, just as We are one; I in them and You in Me, that they may be perfected in unity, so that the world may know that

You sent Me, and loved them, even as You have loved Me. Father, I desire that they also, whom You have given Me, be with Me where I am, so that they may see My glory which You have given Me, for You loved Me before the foundation of the world. (17:5, 22–24)

The Father gave His glory to the Son before the world began. In this prayer Jesus asks the Father to restore the outward display of His eternal glory. God's people will begin to share in His glory at some point in the future, but Jesus shared the glory of the Father throughout eternity past.

After the creation of the world, God's glory could refer to His fame or His praise, but before time began there were no angels or men to sing His praise. God's glory was entirely within Himself. The Father and Son shared the same glorious, divine nature. They were equally glorious because They were equally God.

The Persons of the Trinity do not live in isolation from each other. The unity between the Father and the Son is one of the grand themes of the Gospel of John. They live in each other; they share the same life, so they, together with the Holy Spirit, are one God. Jesus said, "I am in the Father and the Father is in Me" (John 14:10–11; 10:38).

There is, however, an ordering among the Persons of the Trinity. As a human son is dependent on his father, so the Son of God has an eternally dependent relationship with the Father. "For just as the Father has life in Himself, even so He gave to the Son also to have life in Himself" (John 5:26). God gives us life in an entirely different way. We do not have a self-sufficient and self-sustaining life; that is what the Father gave to Jesus Christ alone. God's self-sustaining life and eternal glory cannot be separated from God Himself, so the Father has given the Son Himself. No greater gift than this is possible.

The Father has given all things to His Son. John's Gospel frequently mentions the gifts the Father gave to Christ. These gifts included His authority to raise and judge the dead (5:25–29), the mighty works He gave Jesus to accomplish (5:36), His teaching (7:16–17) and the people whom He will save (6:37, 39; 17:6, 9). In sum, "The Father loves the Son and has given all things into His hand" (3:35).

Other passages testify to the same truth. God "has spoken to us in His Son, whom He appointed heir of all things, through whom also He made the world" (Heb. 1:2). "And Jesus came up and spoke to them, saying, 'All authority has been given to Me in heaven and on earth'" (Matt. 28:18).

All of creation is a love-gift from God the Father to His Son. The stars belong to Jesus Christ. Angels and angleworms, galaxies and guppies are His. However, the greatest gift God gave to His Son is not the material universe, the animals or even the angels. It is the people Jesus Christ came to save. They may not seem like much of a gift since Christ had to suffer so much in order to make them His own, but that is how Scripture looks at the matter. Jesus views the church as His bride, given to Him by His Father and made holy by His own death and resurrection (Eph. 5:25–33). The redeemed are a beautiful bride for an eternal Husband, and He is happy at the prospect of meeting her in glory (Heb. 12:2).

The Father gives Himself to the redeemed for Christ's sake. On the night before His crucifixion, Jesus promised to send the Holy Spirit to dwell in His disciples. The Bible calls Him the Spirit of God and the Spirit of Christ (Rom. 8:9), so when the Holy Spirit comes to indwell God's children, they have both the Father and the Son living in them. Jesus said,

> "I will ask the Father, and He will give you another Helper, that He may be with you forever; that is the Spirit of truth, whom the world cannot receive, because it does not see Him or know Him, but you know Him because He abides with you and will be in you. . . . "If anyone loves Me, he will keep My word; and My Father will love him, and We will come to him, and make Our abode with him." (John 14:16–17, 23)

There is no greater gift God can give than the gift of Himself. He does not, however, give Himself to His children for their sakes alone, but for the sake of His beloved Son. Just as the Father's delight in His eternal Son is the source of His delight in His adopted children, so His benevolence to Christ is the model and source of His benevolence toward all of His creatures. The Father grants His presence to those who listen to Christ and obey Him.

Obedience to Christ begins with faith in Him. When the Jews asked, "What shall we do, that we may work the works of God?" Jesus replied, "This is the work of God [i.e., the work that God requires], that you believe in Him whom He has sent" (John 6:28–29). All who turn from their sin and trust in Jesus have the Father and the Son living in them through the gift of the Holy Spirit. That is God's greatest gift to people, but there is much more to come.

The Father gives all things to the redeemed for Christ's sake. Parents like to leave an estate for their offspring. God is no different, except in one respect: the heavenly Father does not have to die before His children receive their inheritance:

> For all who are being led by the Spirit of God, these are sons of God. For you have not received a spirit of slavery leading to fear again, but you have received a spirit of adoption as sons by which we cry out, "Abba! Father!" The Spirit Himself testifies with our spirit that we are children of God, and if children, heirs also, heirs of God and fellow heirs with Christ, if indeed we suffer with Him so that we may also be glorified with Him. (Rom. 8:14–17)

No one will inherit the world to come simply because he is a human being or even because he is a nice person. That eternal inheritance belongs to the children of God who have received the Spirit of His Son and have been adopted into His family. God, who sent His Son, gives everything to those whom the Son redeems. "He who did not spare His own Son, but delivered

Him over for us all, how will He not also with Him freely give us all things?" (Rom. 8:32).

The consummation of God's giving lies ahead of us, but God's gifts are not all future. Throughout the present age, He answers the prayers of His children for the sake of Christ. Jesus said, "Until now you have asked for nothing in My name; ask and you will receive, so that your joy may be made full. . . . In that day you will ask in My name, and I do not say to you that I will request of the Father on your behalf; for the Father Himself loves you, because you have loved Me and have believed that I came forth from the Father" (John 16:24, 26–27).

God does not promise to listen to "nice" people. He does not promise to listen to anyone except those who love His Son. Since the Father loves His Son more than He loves anything or anybody else, He loves those who are rightly related to Christ. On the other hand, He hates those who stubbornly reject His Son (3:36). Therefore, God is pleased to give good gifts, both here and hereafter, to those who love Christ because God loves His Son first and most of all.

God's Beauty and the Purpose of Creation

God's reason for creating the world was the most morally beautiful motivation of all. This world came into being because of the Father's love.

God did not create the world just so He could have some twinkling stars or intriguing animals. He is pleased with those things, but their existence is subordinate to His grand design for the universe.[8] He made the world in order to create and redeem a people on whom He would lavish His love for Christ's sake. The world exists for the sake of the people of God. The people of God exist for the sake of Jesus Christ.

Everything God the Father does revolves around His beloved Son. Every tree, every flower and every star in the sky exist because God loves Jesus Christ. Every person you meet walking down the street is here because the Father loves Jesus Christ. You are here on earth because God loves Jesus Christ. If you are a Christian, you will enter eternal glory because God loves Jesus Christ.

Our natural human notions have to undergo a transformation of gigantic proportions in order to see the beauty of such a plan. As soon as we came from our mother's womb, we instinctively expected the world to revolve around us. Our parents existed to feed and entertain us. Our aunts, uncles and grandparents doted on us. We were the center of the universe, or so we thought.

As we grew, our understanding of our place in the world changed. We saw ourselves as part of a network of people, including family, friends and neighbors. We learned to care about them because they were related to us. Our well-being was bound up with theirs. The concern of some people stops at the boundaries of their personal relationships, but most of us feel some connection with and concern for our fellow human beings wherever they live in the world. Our hearts are saddened when we hear that several thousand people have died in a natural disaster, and we may send money to help them.

But now step outside everything you know. Imagine the time before time when there were no people, no earth, no sun, moon or stars. God did not decide to create anything for your sake—you did not exist. All that existed was the triune God. The love that bound the Trinity together was infinitely beautiful and infinitely pleasing to God, so He decided to extend the scope of that beauty by creating a family of sons and daughters to share in His eternal love. That is the big picture we need to grasp if we are to understand what God is doing in the world.

The reason, or at least one reason, why God has made this kind of mutual agreement of things beautiful and grateful [pleasing] to those intelligent beings that perceive it, probably is, that there is in it some image of the true, spiritual, original beauty, which has been spoken of; consisting in being's consent to being, or the union of spiritual beings in a mutual propensity and affection of heart. . . . And so He has constituted the external world in analogy to the spiritual world in numberless instances. . . . [He] makes an agreement of different things, in their form, manner, measure, &c. to appear beautiful, because here is some image of an higher kind of agreement and consent of spiritual beings.

—Jonathan Edwards

2   Does Science Reveal a Designer in Nature?

We live in a beautiful world. Christians and atheists, Jews and Buddhists all stop to admire a colorful sunset or the rainbow in a cascading waterfall. It is a natural human reaction to prefer roses to rubbish and gardens to garbage. Sometimes the experience of beauty is so intense that it seizes our hearts for a while, and when it lets go, it leaves behind a lovely longing for its return.

Back in the days of the phonograph, we had a recording of soprano Beverly Sills. Whenever the needle reached the track with "Italian Street Song," I would stop what I was doing, sit down and listen. The haunting strains of that aria used to pierce my heart with yearning and fill my eyes with tears.

We lived in northwestern Montana for a few years, and one of my favorite hikes took me to the razor-thin ridge at the end of Bear Creek Canyon. After a last breathless climb over loose rubble, I would stand with the wind whipping through my hair looking down several hundred feet at a vast, unspoiled wilderness. While my anxious wife was at home wondering whether she should call the search and rescue squad to pick up my mangled body, my spirit was being refreshed and renewed. Even now decades later, I find myself longing to go back, wondering if that place still has the power to capture my heart.

Why does beauty have such power over us? Is beauty only

in the eye (or ear) of the beholder, or does it point us toward something higher that is eternal, ineffable and infinitely engaging to the soul? A distinctively Christian view of beauty helps us to answer the question and gain a deeper appreciation for the world God has made.

Where Does Beauty Originate?

Although philosophers argue over the concept of beauty, Jonathan Edwards's definition seems like a sensible place to begin. Beauty, he wrote, is "a mutual consent and agreement of different things, in form, manner, quantity and visible end or design; called by the various names of regularity, order, uniformity, symmetry, proportion, harmony, &c. . . ."[1] Edwards describes beauty as "consent and agreement" because he wants to highlight the parallels between the beauty of personal relationships and other kinds of beauty we can see or hear. In all cases beauty involves both difference and unity.

For example, when a pianist plays the first, third and fifth notes of a major scale, the result is a pleasing harmony, but a toddler slamming both hands down on the keyboard is more likely to jangle our nerves than to soothe them. The first sound is beautiful; the second is not. Even more irritating to a frazzled mother would be a child's tapping the same note on a piano at one second intervals for thirty minutes. Beauty includes both diversity and unity, not just the diverse notes of a child's two-handed banging, nor the unity of a single note endlessly repeated. Similarly, the regular pattern of carefully laid parquet flooring is attractive; odd scraps of lumber attached to the floor joists with bent and rusted nails may be solid and functional, but they are not beautiful because they exhibit no unifying pattern.

Why are we attracted to beauty? In the quotation at the beginning of this chapter, Jonathan Edwards suggests that an ability to enjoy the harmonious union of diverse things was put into us by God when He created us. God enables us to delight in the beauties of nature, art and music because these things reflect the harmony of interpersonal relationships, which is a higher kind of beauty.

We have a natural longing for a well-ordered society. Such a society, which is as attractive as it is elusive, has inspired works as diverse as Plato's *Republic*, Thomas Moore's *Utopia* and James Hilton's *Lost Horizon*. As desirable as harmony in broader society may be, individual relationships are even more important to most people. Friendship, romantic love and the comfortable companionship of a forty-year marriage all involve the union of people with diverse temperaments, desires and outlooks on life. At their best these relationships are truly beautiful.

The most beautiful instance of unity and diversity, however, does not occur in nature or in human love. God Himself is the infinitely great Original of all natural and spiritual harmonies, because in the Trinity three distinct Persons share the same divine nature and together constitute one God. The importance of Trinitarian theology for understanding beauty appears when we contrast it with two different popular worldviews, pantheism and materialism.

Pantheism teaches that God is all and that all is God. In the language of Indian philosopher Shankara (AD 788–820), the universal being is *Brahman*, while the individual soul is the *atman*. The atman is Brahman within; Brahman is the atman without. Since there is in truth only one being, our perception of distinct individuals is an illusion (*maya*) based on ignorance. The entire material world is no more real than a dream. Therefore, pantheism has no place for genuine difference that is held in tension by true unity.[2]

Materialism has the opposite problem even though it, like pantheism, is a variety of monism. (Monism means there is only one substance in the world. The pantheist says this substance is spiritual. The materialist says it is physical.)[3] The materialist has no problem seeing that individual things or people are truly distinct, but there is no overarching purpose or unity that draws individuals into a unified whole. Postmodern materialism is openly hostile to *meta-narratives*—stories, ideas or principles that are universally valid. An individual's view of the world is only valid for that individual or, at best, for small communities.

Unlike pantheism and materialism, the biblical doctrine of the Trinity insists that unity and diversity are both ultimate. Both find their origin in God, because God is both one and three. The divine unity and the divine diversity shine through the real (though secondary) beauties of the created world. It is helpful to look at beauty in the realms of biology and physics—such beauty may be more difficult to appreciate than a sunset is, but it is easier to analyze.

Beauty in Biology

Much that is attractive to us impresses the eye or the ear with a spontaneous sense of wonder. Complex beauty, however, is not always immediately apparent. As Jonathan Edwards notes, "The beauty which consists in the visible fitness of a thing to its use, and unity of design, is not a distinct sort of beauty from" symmetry, proportion and harmony.[4]

To an engineer, a well-designed machine is beautiful. To a mathematician, a straightforward, simple proof of a theorem is more elegant than one that is convoluted and encumbered by needless repetitions.

These examples illustrate the fact that complex forms of beauty require training, or at least careful attention, in order to be enjoyed. A person whose musical appreciation extends only to volume and rhythm may need guidance to hear and then to love the mingled melodies of a baroque master like Handel. Similarly, the beauty of an intricate design in nature may not be immediately apparent to the eye or the ear, but we can see it with the eyes of our understanding as we consider how elegantly its form and function fit together.

Scripture frequently encourages this kind of careful thought. Psalm 104, for example, is an extended meditation on the wonders of God's world. The psalmist lists numerous examples of

God's careful ordering of nature and concludes with an enraptured exclamation: "O LORD, how many are Your works! In wisdom You have made them all; the earth is full of Your possessions" (104:24).

The beauties of nature's Designer are reflected in the following examples of harmony, fitness and order:

The monarch butterfly. For the most part, butterflies are colorful fairies dancing in air. The monarch butterfly is visually attractive, and it also has a beautiful life cycle. Every year millions of them leave the Eastern United States and Canada, and they fly up to two thousand miles to spend the winter in the high mountains of central Mexico. Since their winter retreat comprises only about sixty square miles, the weight of monarchs gathered in one place often bends down the branches of the trees on which they rest. When they take flight together, observers can hear millions of wings flapping.

During the spring and summer, each generation of monarch butterflies lives about six weeks. The final annual generation that emerges early in the fall lives for six or eight months. This generation makes the long trek south to a place they have never been before. They land on exactly the same mountains, in exactly the same forests as their great, great grandparents did. In the spring they return north to lay their eggs on milkweed plants. Then they die. After the eggs have hatched and the caterpillars have matured and metamorphosed, the fresh crop of monarchs resumes the northward migration until it arrives at their ancestral summer territory. Their descendants will make the long voyage south a few months later.

Recent research has shown that monarchs orient themselves for their migration by the light of the sun, but knowing how they head in the right general direction does not explain the butterflies' precise homing instincts, nor does it explain how this instinct was built into them in the first place. If scientists are able to figure out more details of the monarch's amazing homing instinct, each deepening layer of complexity ought to excite greater astonishment at the wisdom of God, the exquisite Designer.

Microbiology. Once upon a time, protoplasm was considered undifferentiated jelly inside living cells; blood was only seen as a red fluid with three or four kinds of cells floating around in it; bacteria were believed to be just small bugs. All that has changed. As biologists have learned to unravel the proteins of life, they have been amazed at the complexity in what once seemed like rather simple systems. Many of these systems exhibit a property that Michael Behe calls "irreducible complexity." If one component of the system is missing, the system does not just function poorly, it ceases to function at all.

Take blood, for example. I expect to lose a little blood whenever I work in my yard or shop. Perhaps a rapidly turning grindstone will gouge a trench in my knuckle, or a wild rose will poke holes in one of the large veins in my forearm. Maybe the utility knife will slip or the hammer will miss the nail. Fortunately, even moderately deep cuts only bleed for a short time. With a proper pressure bandage in place, the flow stops, and I can go back to work. By the end of the day, the injury is covered with a hard, dark clot of dried blood.

In order for blood to clot properly, over twenty different proteins must work together in a specific sequence. All those proteins are necessary. If one link in the chain is missing, the blood does not clot, and even a small cut can lead to a fatal loss of blood. If you poke a hole in the bottom of an open paint can, all the paint will run out. Something similar would happen in our bodies if the protein chain for clotting were broken.

The very efficiency of the clotting mechanism introduces a second problem. Clotting is a little bit like the chain reaction in a nuclear bomb. Once it starts it tends to keep going. However, the body also has a number of proteins that work together to stop the clotting process. If those proteins were missing, blood would continue to congeal until all the blood in the body had turned to a solid.[5]

Clotting illustrates how a complicated biochemical process

can work quickly and efficiently to produce a very desirable result. Your life is constantly being maintained by hundreds of similarly complicated interlocking chemical reactions, many of them involving highly specialized protein molecules. The result of all this complexity is a single organism that can catch a football, savor a turkey dinner or whistle a response to a bright red cardinal. From an electrical, chemical and mechanical point of view, the human body is a beautifully structured whole consisting of many complex systems. Occasionally something breaks down, but if your car contained as many vital systems as your body does, it would be in the shop three days out of five. If you were a computer, your body wouldn't even boot up on most mornings.

The beauty of the body's biochemical systems would be impossible apart from the way God has structured atomic particles and the forces that act upon them. If the fundamental constants of nature were not finely tuned, there would be no life at all in our universe.

The Fine-tuning of Physics

Mid-twentieth-century physicists identified four forces that govern the behavior of all matter: the electromagnetic force, gravity, the weak nuclear force and the strong nuclear force. In the closing years of the last century, astrophysicists discovered a mysterious fifth force called dark energy, which is causing the expansion of the universe to accelerate. How these forces are related to each other and to the multitude of presently known particles is the holy grail of theoretical physics.

Physicists have known for several decades that the relative strengths of these forces and the properties of matter's basic building blocks are all fine-tuned for life. At least a dozen fundamental constants must be fit within very tight limits for the universe as we know it to exist and for life to be possible.[6] Here are two examples that are relatively easy to understand:

The strong nuclear force. Two positive charges repel each other.

Hydrogen has a single positively charged proton in its nucleus, but other naturally occurring atoms have from two to ninety-two protons. What keeps them from flying apart? The strong nuclear force. If this force were weaker, atomic nuclei containing more than one proton would be impossible because the protons would refuse to stay together in the same nucleus. The whole universe would consist of hydrogen. If it were stronger, protons would clump together too easily, and there would be little or no hydrogen and hence no stars, which shine by fusing hydrogen into helium. In either case, life would be impossible.

The electromagnetic force. Electrons have a negative charge. They swirl around the positively charged protons in the nucleus of an atom like moths swarming around a porch light. Since positive and negative charges attract each other, the attractive electromagnetic force keeps electrons from flying out of their orbits around the nucleus. When atoms cluster together to form molecules, they share their electrons with each other. If the electromagnetic force were only a little bit stronger, the positively charged nucleus of an atom would hold on to its electrons. Like a selfish child, it would not share, and no chemical bonds could form. On the other hand, if the electromagnetic force were just a little bit weaker, electrons would escape too easily from their parent atoms. Chemical bonds would not be strong enough to last. In either case, the stable molecules necessary for life would not be able to form.

The fine-tuning of the universe for life is impressive enough to have a name in scientific and philosophical literature: the anthropic principle. In 2004 the premier magazine for amateur astronomy devoted a major article to the subject.[7] There are several versions of the anthropic principle. At the bottom of the ladder is the weak anthropic principle, the simple observation that if the universe were not fine-tuned for life, we would not be here to observe its lack of fine-tuning. Near the other end is the (perhaps) whimsical suggestion that our universe was designed in the laboratory of some advanced civilization in another universe. Over the top (and way above the clouds in my opinion) is physicist John Wheeler's proposal that our observation of the universe has created a feedback loop into the early universe, adjusting conditions in the Big Bang so that human beings would eventually evolve. Hugh Ross summarizes Wheeler's thoughts: "In other words, the universe creates man, but man through his observations of the universe brings the universe into reality."[8] Since we supposedly participate in the creation of the universe, Wheeler's proposal has been dubbed the participatory anthropic principle.

Fine-tuning is a fact, but what does it mean? Is there a way out of the obvious implication of a Designer for the universe? Two suggestions are worth noting:

Parallel universes. One theory is that our universe may be one of an infinite number of parallel universes. Current physical theories imply that empty space is a beehive of activity at the quantum level. If space is infinite, then quantum fluctuations might be continuously spawning new universes which would exist side by side like bubbles in a tub full of bubble bath. If that is the case, it might not be so surprising that at least one of these universes (namely ours) is suitable for life. Does such a theory really provide an atheistic explanation for the fine-tuning of the universe? Two problems are immediately apparent.

First, the same theories that suggest the idea of parallel universes also tell us that we will never be able to enter or examine them. It will always be physically impossible for us to know what they are like or even if they exist. Therefore, parallel universes must forever be a matter of speculation. Second, the theory assumes the existence of infinite, empty space. But it is not at all clear that space can exist without matter, for in our common experience, space is simply the distance between objects. If, however, an infinite, empty space does exist—though we can never observe it—why does it have the precise characteristics necessary for the production of a multitude of universes? In other words, the existence of all universes (including our fine-tuned one) would depend on the fine-tuning of the primordial empty space. So the hypothesis of multiple universes does not eliminate fine-tuning. It just pushes the tuning back one level.

A mathematically constrained universe. Another proposal for avoiding an intelligent Designer for our universe is that perhaps all those amazingly adjusted physical constants are part of a tightly interlocking reality that cannot be any different from what it actually is. Perhaps no matter how many universes there are—whether one or an infinite number—they must all have exactly the same basic physical characteristics as ours does. Maybe physicists will eventually discover one equation that includes all the fundamental forces and particles of nature and specifies exactly the characteristics each one must have. In this case fine-tuning of the universe for life is not eliminated. Again, it is simply pushed back from the individual particles and forces to the whole interconnected reality.

Both theists and open-minded agnostics may fairly ask, "Does not such an intricate design suggest a cosmic Designer?" Or, in the words of Sir Isaac Newton, "Whence is it that Nature does nothing in vain and whence arises all the Order and Beauty that we see in the World?"[9]

As with the biological sciences, I am not attempting to prove that the universe was fine-tuned by a Designer, although I think the evidence is quite suggestive. I am more concerned to point out that the mere existence of our world, and indeed of ourselves, depends on the precise interlocking of the fundamental forces and constants of nature. To use a medieval expression, "the music of the heavenly spheres" is a harmony that arises out of sub-atomic diversity.

An Objection: The Complexity of God

I have been arguing that the complexity of creation—its unity in the midst of diversity—is a reflection of the beauty of God. However, this complexity has also been used to challenge belief in God.

In his book *The God Delusion*, Richard Dawkins includes

a chapter entitled "Why There Almost Certainly Is No God." Dawkins eloquently explains the utter improbability of life arising by chance. He also takes note of the anthropic principle, which he interprets as an alternative to divine design. Then he argues that if life and the universe are so complex as to be improbable, any putative Creator would have to be even more complex. God is therefore more improbable than the universe He is supposed to have created. To make matters worse, says Dawkins, Christian theologians claim that God is simple. How, then, can the world's complexity arise from a simple God?[10]

This superficially clever argument suffers from a serious misunderstanding of God's simplicity. God's essence is simple because it cannot be divided, changed or have anything added to or subtracted from it. However, God's tri-personal life is inherently complex. The three Persons of the Godhead cannot be separated from each other, but they do interact with each other. In addition, His knowledge comprehends an infinite number of actual and possible situations, and the operations of His power are vastly varied. The argument against creation from divine simplicity fails. God is simple in the sense that He is indivisible and unchangeable, but He is also infinitely more complex than the world He created. As it turns out, God's simplicity and complexity are both essential for the biblical doctrine of creation.

Dawkins's charge that a God more complex than the universe must be more improbable than the universe rests on the failure to recognize another important concept: it ignores the difference between an entity that does not change and those that have a beginning and are subject to decay. The psalmist describes God this way:

> Of old You founded the earth,
> And the heavens are the work of Your hands.
> Even they will perish, but You endure;
> And all of them will wear out like a garment;
> Like clothing You will change them and they will be
> changed.

But You are the same,
And Your years will not come to an end.

(Ps. 102:25–27)

The early Greeks realized that changeable, decaying things must have a beginning, but many of them also believed the universe was eternal. In keeping with this idea, the ancient Greek philosopher Leucippus or his disciple Democritus coined the word *atoma* (indivisibles) from which we derive our word *atom*. An atom had no parts. It was indivisible and, therefore, unchangeable and eternal. Atoms could combine endlessly to form the vast variety of sensible objects in the world, but they themselves never changed.

According to Christian theology, the Greeks were right about one thing and wrong about another. Only an entity that is indivisible and unchangeable can be eternal. That is correct, but atoms and the universe possess neither of these characteristics. The best estimate for the age of the universe is about 13.7 billion years. If current theories are correct, protons formed about one thousandth of a second after the Big Bang, but even protons will eventually wear out. The average lifetime of a proton is believed to be about 10^{35} years (1 followed by 35 zeroes). That is a very long, but still finite, amount of time. Cosmologists once put their hopes for an eternal universe in a perpetual cycle of Big Bangs. Each Big Bang would be followed by a collapse (called a Big Crunch) and then by another Big Bang. That idea has now been abandoned in the light of recent research. Apart from some hitherto undiscovered principle, it appears the universe will expand until even photons are too far apart to interact with each other.

However, God's essence is simple because He is indivisible and unchangeable. Therefore, it is possible for Him to be eternal in both directions—with neither a beginning nor an end. Since He is also tri-personal and His mind is infinitely complex, He is able to be the cause of a universe that is fine-tuned for life and the source of the highly improbable complexity that scientists observe at the biochemical level.

Just one of nature's intricate designs ought to fill us with wonder and admiration for the wisdom of God who created it as a reflection of His beauty. There are multiplied thousands of interlocking systems in the physical world, in plant and animal life, and in our own bodies. Though this chapter has focused on a few of the intricate designs in nature discovered by modern science, any human being looking at his own body might well exclaim with the psalmist,

> For You formed my inward parts;
>   You wove me in my mother's womb.
> I will give thanks to You, for I am fearfully and
>   wonderfully made;
>   Wonderful are Your works,
>   And my soul knows it very well.
> My frame was not hidden from You,
>   When I was made in secret,
>   And skillfully wrought in the depths of the earth;
> Your eyes have seen my unformed substance;
>   And in Your book were all written
>   The days that were ordained for me,
>   When as yet there was not one of them.
> How precious also are Your thoughts to me, O God!
>   How vast is the sum of them!
> If I should count them, they would outnumber the sand.
>   When I awake, I am still with You.
>
> (Ps. 139:13–18)

The unity and complexity of the triune God provide a metaphysical basis for the oneness and diversity of the universe. As Jonathan Edwards points out, there is no apparent necessity for our ability to sense and value beauty. We could eat, sleep and reproduce without ever enjoying a sunset or a song. But God gave us an ability to appreciate complex beauty because the harmonies of art and nature reflect His own three-in-oneness. Our enjoyment of created beauty prepares us to adore the great Original.

Of all insects, no one is more wonderful than the spider, especially with respect to their sagacity and admirable way of working. [There follows a careful explanation of how spiders float through the air suspended by a long strand of web.]

Corollary 1. We hence see the exuberant goodness of the Creator, who hath not only provided for all the necessities, but also for the pleasure and recreation of all sorts of creatures, and even the insects and those that are most despicable [that is, spiders].

Corollary 2. Admire also the Creator in so nicely and mathematically adjusting their multiplying nature, that notwithstanding their destruction by this means and the multitudes that are eaten by birds, that they do not decrease and so, little by little, come to nothing; and in so adjusting their destruction to their multiplication that they do neither increase, but taking one year with another, there is always just an equal number of them.

—Jonathan Edwards

3 Where Is God in the Brutality and Inefficiency of Nature?

They say that beauty is in the eye of the beholder, and to a certain extent that must be true. A mother looks at her newborn child and sees the most adorable face in the world, while a somewhat less prejudiced observer silently judges that the little one is uglier than a bulldog. But does the mother see true beauty in her baby that the stranger has missed?

We see the same difference of opinion when theists and atheists look at the world around them. Believers see God's handiwork in every amazing creature, whether it swims, slithers, crawls, runs, hops or flies. Jonathan Edwards enjoyed watching spiders, and even though he shared the common notion that they were despicable creatures, he saw their tiny lives as evidence of God's care and wisdom. The committed atheist, however, is more likely to echo Tennyson's evaluation of nature:

> [Man] trusted God was love indeed
> And love Creation's final law—
> Tho' Nature, red in tooth and claw
> With ravine,[1] shriek'd against his creed.[2]

The blood lust of predators and the agony of a brutal death seem to militate against the idea of a loving God. Some also charge that nature exhibits a clear lack of intelligent design. Consider Sam Harris:

When we look at the natural world, we see extraordinary complexity, but we do not see optimal design. We see redundancy, regressions, and unnecessary complications; we see bewildering inefficiencies that result in suffering and death.[3]

He goes on to argue:

Our own bodies testify to the whimsy and incompetence of the creator. As embryos, we produce tails, gill sacs, and a full coat of apelike hair. Happily, most of us lose those charming accessories before birth. This bizarre sequence of morphology is readily interpreted in evolutionary and genetic terms; it is an utter mystery if we are the products of intelligent design.[4]

Nature seems to be careless at best. At worst it appears to be harsh and hostile. Where is the beauty of love behind "nature, red in tooth and claw"? While some see nature's beauty as the handiwork of a Creator, others point to nature's brutality as proof that God must be blind and deaf. A tiny speck of dust can fill the eye with tears, turning a delicate rose into a blur. Is there, perhaps, a mote in the eye of the atheistic beholder so he cannot see the love of God reflected in the beauty of God's creation? Consider three objections to a wise Creator's design in the universe.

First Objection: Similar Biological Structures

Atheists and agnostics frequently cite homology, embryology and molecular biology as proof that different kinds of animals have developed through blind evolution rather than being designed by a Creator.

Homologous structures arise from the same parts of the embryos in different species. They exhibit a similar configuration across those species, but they may have entirely different functions. For example, the human arm, the wing of a bird, the flipper of a porpoise and the leg of an elephant all have similar bone structures.[5] Evolutionists assume the original pattern for homologous structures evolved on one occasion in the distant past. As various kinds of animals evolved from that ancient ancestor, each subsequent group used the original pattern in a different way.

Embryology, the study of how embryos develop, provides another common example of cross-species similarity. Unsurprisingly, the embryos of creatures that look somewhat alike when they are mature tend to develop in a similar fashion. Examples include dog and cat embryos and the embryos of apes and humans.

Finally, DNA and the proteins it encodes vary more for animals that are distantly related than for species that are kissing cousins, so to speak. Although this result may be touted as fresh proof for the theory of evolution, it seems like a rather unremarkable finding. Why shouldn't look-alikes have more chemistry in common than do earthworms and elephants?

The existence of similar physical and chemical structures across widely separated species may not be as impressive as it appears at first glance because several of the standard examples have been challenged. However, rather than citing specific examples where the argument from similarity appears to break down, I propose a broader theological context for the similarities that do exist.

First, almost all Bible-believing creationists accept the idea that closely related species evolved from a common ancestral stock. For example, Chihuahuas, Great Danes and wolves have all apparently descended from a common wolf-dog ancestor. According to Genesis 1, earth's creatures reproduce after their "kinds." A biblical "kind" is almost certainly much broader than a species, so limited evolution within kinds is unproblematic. Second, the existence of similar structures in very different kinds of animals may simply indicate that God was using common design elements in a fascinating variety of ways. But if God is infinitely intelligent, why didn't He make each sort of creature from scratch so it would be entirely different from all the others? Was the Creator short on creativity?

God was creating a harmony, not a cacophony. He designed earth's creatures and earth's history to be a beautiful whole composed of many interlocking elements, and He intended human beings to be part of a community of creatures. Spiritually we are very different from animals. Physically we are not, and our likeness to the rest of earth's creatures makes us suitable to be God's stewards to care for His creation.

When God said, "Be fruitful and multiply, and fill the earth and subdue it; and rule over the fish of the sea and over the birds of the sky and over every living thing that moves on the earth" (Gen. 1:28), He was not giving mankind a license to rape the earth and wantonly slaughter its creatures. We are supposed to care for the earth as its gardeners, to guide and guard the animals as ancient shepherds lovingly watched over their sheep.

We were made from the dust of the earth in order to care for the earth. We share a likeness to the animals so they might serve us with gladness and we might rule over them with gentleness. But this primordial beauty has been broken by our sin, and our stewardship has often become a tyranny.

Second Objection: The Inefficiency of Nature

Efficiency may be considered in two very different ways. First, there is efficiency of scale. For example, businesses do not want to hold more inventory than they are likely to need in order to maintain a smooth flow of resources and finished products. A second kind of efficiency may be termed efficiency of design. To an engineer, a machine with fewer parts that works well seems more attractive than one with extra dials, gears and processes that are non-functional or redundant.

Inefficiency of scale is a reasonable concern for human beings because we have limited resources. We never have enough time, money or energy to accomplish everything we would like to do. It is not at all clear, however, that a Being with infinite resources would have the slightest interest in this kind of efficiency.

Take for example the apparent age and size of the universe. According to several independent lines of evidence, the universe exploded into existence about 13.7 billion years ago. The most distant galaxy observed to date is about 13 billion light-years away—it has taken light about 13 billion years to travel from that galaxy to our telescopes. Astronomers estimate that our Milky Way galaxy contains one hundred billion to two hundred billion stars. Beyond our galaxy lie just about as many galaxies as there are stars in the Milky Way. Why would God create all that just to have a few billion people living on one small planet orbiting a very ordinary star? Such inefficiency of scale looks like the result of pretty poor planning, doesn't it?

Isaiah 40 provides a number of word pictures to help us visualize the vast power of God: "Who has measured the waters in the hollow of His hand, and marked off the heavens by the span, and calculated the dust of the earth by the measure, and weighed the mountains in a balance and the hills in a pair of scales?" (40:12).

The Bible does not say ours is the only inhabited planet, but suppose it is. Imagine a Being so great that all the water in earth's oceans and lakes is like a few drops puddled in His palm. Imagine a hand so huge it stretches easily across the 13.7 billion light years of space. If the whole of creation is smaller in God's hand than a golf ball is in ours, the question of the efficient use of space and time simply does not arise.

In fact, there may be excellent reasons for creating such a vast universe—vast from our point of view. If current theories are correct, the universe needs to be about as old as it is, and perhaps as big as it is, for enough heavy elements to form in the explosions of dying stars. (Heavy elements constitute much of our rocky planet and are important constituents of our own bodies as well.) Of course, God could have made the whole visible universe in less than a second, but He is not a deceiver. If God was planning to make a universe that looked old, He might have thought it best for the universe to be as ancient as it appeared. The apparent inefficiency and wastefulness of nature are an effective argument only against a very small god, but not against the infinitely mighty God of the Bible.

Inefficiency of design may seem a greater challenge to the idea of the beauty of God than inefficiency of scale because it strikes more closely at our working definition of beauty as a kind of harmony. Evolutionary biologists frequently point to the existence of apparently useless organs or inefficient biological systems as evidence that a wise Creator did not design earth's creatures. The appendix, for example, has often been regarded as a useless organ left over from a time when our animal ancestors needed it to process a high cellulose diet, such as leaves. Recent research suggests, however, that the appendix provides a defense against infection, especially in the fetus and during childhood. In view of the uncertainties surrounding this and some other apparent examples of inefficiency, the following proposal attempts to deal with the problem in a general way.

The concept of concurrence suggests a perspective on apparent inefficiencies of design. It is the way God ordinarily works in the world. Concurrence means that "God cooperates with created things in every action, directing their distinctive properties to cause them to act as they do."[6] Concurrence is opposed to some common misunderstandings of God's relationship to His creation.

The first misunderstanding is that God's job is to fill in the gaps where natural law breaks down. As long as people did not understand lightning, they ascribed it to the power of God. As soon as Benjamin Franklin discovered that lightning was just a big electrical spark, the God hypothesis was no longer needed for that phenomenon. The more explanations of our world that science is able to give, the less God has to do. The doctrine of concurrence implies there are no gaps in the ordinary workings of nature because God is at work all the time in all His creation.

The second common misunderstanding of God and nature is that nature operates entirely on its own according to its own laws unless God intervenes to produce a miracle. To the contrary, according to the Bible, everything that happens as the result of natural forces is, at the same time, also the result of God's superintending will.

> The young lions roar after their prey
>> And seek their food from God.
>
> [All creatures] wait for You
>> To give them their food in due season.
>
> You give to them, they gather it up;
>> You open Your hand, they are satisfied with good.
>
> (Ps. 104:21, 27–28)

Lions have to hunt, but God feeds them; both factors are at work every time a lion eats. Even random events like the rolling of a die fall under God's direction. "The lot is cast into the lap, but its every decision is from the Lord" (Prov. 16:33). A human being casts a pair of dice, imparting a certain momentum and spin to them which determine how they will land. Even though God does not alter the physics involved, the dice land as God pleases. That is concurrence.

A third, and less common, misunderstanding of God and nature is the idea that God is the only true cause of everything that happens; all other apparent causes, such as human decisions, are a sham. To the contrary, the Bible teaches that animals and people take real actions that have real effects. Their activities are not an illusory covering for the only true worker, God. According to the New Testament, Jesus Christ "upholds all things by the word of His power" (Heb. 1:3) so that "in Him all things hold together" (Col. 1:17).

The Lord does not override, but rather sustains the unique properties He has given to each creature. "The doctrine of concurrence affirms that God *directs* and *works through* the distinctive properties of each created thing, so these things themselves bring about the results we see. In this way it is possible to affirm that in one sense events are fully (100 percent) caused by God and fully (100 percent) caused by the creature as well."[7]

We can apply the concept of concurrence to the question of inefficiency beginning at the molecular level. During the long ages that various types of creatures have existed and developed within their limited biblical kinds, God has sustained the chemical properties of the atoms and molecules essential to life. Perhaps a cosmic ray breaks loose a section of DNA, which then swaps places with another bit in such a way that it produces some level of inefficiency in an organism that still functions fairly well. If this inefficiency happens to be propagated throughout a species, it does not represent a design defect in the original creation.

How, then, do the inefficiencies of nature relate to the concept of beauty in the natural world? They cannot overthrow the vastly more numerous examples of elegant design throughout creation. Rather, functional inefficiencies illustrate beauty in another way. The machine of nature is so robust that it is able to withstand multiple deviations from the original creation without crashing. The various created kinds are able to evolve into many different species—some more efficient than others—without losing the basic characteristics imparted to them by God at their creation. God's concurring power sustains them throughout this process without any miraculous interference on God's part.

What about the human appendix? My guess, and it is only that, hinges on the fact that human beings once lived for hundreds of years (Gen. 4–5). Originally they ate only plants, but after the flood, meat became part of their diet (9:3). After the flood, the span of human life dropped precipitously (Gen. 11), presumably because of numerous deleterious physiological changes. These changes could have begun through a few genetic alterations in just one or two individuals, Noah and his wife. Perhaps a more efficient appendix was useful for the pre-flood vegetarian diet or for better protection against disease. A change in the efficiency of the appendix might have been caused by random genetic mutation, not by God's miraculous manipulation of nature, but nevertheless resulting in a divinely planned judgment on the human race. Hence, concurrence.

I label this proposal a guess. The typical evolutionary explanations of how and why animals have developed certain biological structures or patterns of behavior are also guesses. Unfortunately, they are rarely labeled as such, although neither my guess nor those of others are testable hypotheses.

Inefficiency of design may result from natural mutations in the original kinds of creation. Inefficiency of scale is meaningless to an omnipotent God. In view of God's vast power a supernova is nothing, but because of His vast love He takes note of every sparrow that falls (Matt. 10:29). God's stated care for His creatures leads us to consider the next objection to God's beautiful design in creation.

Third Objection: The Cruelty of Nature

Nature is indeed "red in tooth and claw." If God is all wise and infinitely benevolent, why are death and decay built into the fabric of our world? The argument proceeds in two stages: First, animal death was part of God's original creation. Second, God's goodness and wisdom are evident in the wonderful balance of nature.

Many Christians blame animal death on the fall of Adam and Eve. They base this conclusion on several facts. First, God gave the green plants for food to people and animals (Gen. 1:29–30). Second, death came into the world through Adam's sin (Rom. 5:12). Third, the fall brought the bondage of corruption to the whole sub-human world (8:18–22). Finally, in the future kingdom of Christ, wild carnivores will lie down peacefully with domestic herbivores (Isa. 11:6).

The easiest objection to answer is the one based on Romans 5:12 because the context makes it clear that Adam's sin brought death upon the human race. Animals are not even mentioned in the chapter. On the other hand, several scriptural considerations clearly imply animals were originally designed to die.

According to Genesis 3:22–24, Adam and Eve were driven

from the Garden of Eden to prevent their access to the tree of life. If they had eaten the tree's fruit (whether once or regularly, the text does not say) they would have lived forever. Clearly, the tree of life only existed in the Garden. Therefore, human beings were not inherently immortal; they were only able to live forever by means of that one tree. It is possible God would have granted never-ending life to animals in Eden by their eating from the same tree, but the millions of creatures scattered over the rest of the globe had no access to it. It seems exceedingly strange to suggest animals outside Eden would have lived forever without the tree of life, while humans could have continued to live only by eating its fruit.

Another reason for concluding animal death was part of God's original creation is that the Bible does not say God made some herbivores into carnivores after the Fall, nor does Scripture suggest meat-eaters fasted until after Adam sinned. Tyrannosaurus Rex and saber-toothed tigers were not well suited to consuming cabbages. The natural conclusion is that God designed some animals to eat other animals. What, then, shall we make of the provision of green plants for food for man and beast?

Genesis 1 does not specifically say all animals ate only vegetation. The passage appears to be teaching that green plants are at the bottom of the food chain. All animal life ultimately depends on plant life because carnivores eat herbivores. Although mankind may not have eaten meat until after the flood (Gen. 9:3), we should not assume the same was true of animals.

How does the Bible view the death and suffering of animals? Scripture sees the balance of nature, including animal death, as an example of God's wise ordering of the world. Psalm 104 is a poetic celebration of God's creative activity based on the general flow of events in Genesis 1. The following chart shows how each passage unfolds the creation events.

Genesis 1	Psalm 104
Light (1:3)	Light (104:2)

Firmament or expanse = heaven (1:6–8)	Heaven (104:2)
Waters above and below the firmament (1:6–8)	Upper waters (104:3)
Waters below heaven gathered and dry land appears (1:9)	Waters covering the earth flee and mountains arise (104:5–9)
Sun, moon and stars for day, night and seasons (1:14–19)	Sun and moon for day, night and seasons (104:19–23)
Vegetation, animals and man (104:10–23)	Animals, vegetation and man (1:11–13, 20–28)

The parallels with Genesis 1 make it clear that the psalmist is describing the created order of the world, not a fallen distorted order. God causes vegetation to grow as food for cattle and people (Ps. 104:14), but the lions "seek their prey from God" (104:21). The psalm does not present the hunting instincts of lions as though they were a horrible result of the Fall. The author sees them as part of the good plan of God, which includes wild donkeys, birds, grass, cultivated crops, cedar trees, goats and swarming multitudes of sea creatures. Job 38–41 contains a similar perspective on creation. Lions, ravens, deer, donkeys, wild oxen, ostriches, horses and hawks receive their instincts from God. The young ones of the eagle "suck up blood" that God gives them for food (39:30). God cares for every creature, and He has put each one in its proper niche. They live and they die at His command.

> They all wait for You
>   To give them their food in due season.
> You give to them, they gather it up;
>   You open Your hand, they are satisfied with good.
> You hide Your face, they are dismayed;
>   You take away their spirit, they expire
>   And return to their dust.
> You send forth Your Spirit, they are created;

And You renew the face of the ground.
Let the glory of the LORD endure forever;
   Let the LORD be glad in His works.

(Ps. 104:27–31)

The living and dying of earth's creatures shows the glory of God's creative wisdom, and the Lord is glad when He views what He has made.

Sixteen hundred years ago Augustine, Bishop of Hippo, used the balance of nature as a defense of the goodness of God and the beauty of creation:

> The heretics mention, for example, fire, cold, wild beasts, and things like that, without considering how wonderful such things are in themselves and in their proper place and how beautifully they fit into the total pattern of the universe mak-ing, as it were, their particular contributions to the common-weal of cosmic beauty. . . .
>
> There is a hierarchy of created realities, from earthly to heavenly, from visible to invisible, some being better than others, and . . . the very reason of their inequality is to make possible an existence for them all. For, God is the kind of art-ist whose greatness in His masterpieces is not lessened in His minor works—which, of course, are not significant by reason of any sublimity in themselves, since they have none, but only by reason of the wisdom of their Designer. Take the case of the beauty of the human form. Shave off one eyebrow and the loss to the mere mass of the body is insignificant. But what a blow to beauty! For, beauty is not a matter of bulk but of the symmetry and proportion of the members.[8]

Augustine clearly saw animal death as part of the beautiful sym-metry of nature.

The charge is that nature is cruel; therefore, God cannot be good. Yet, animal death was a part of God's original creation and the beauty of creation only appears when we consider the proper function of each creature as a part of the whole. One further point: when God finished His creative work, He pronounced it "very good" (Gen. 1:31). However, God intended to improve on His own good work. The final state of all creation will be better than very good, as we see in the Bible's description of the future kingdom of the Messiah:

> And the wolf will dwell with the lamb,
>> And the leopard will lie down with the young goat,
>> And the calf and the young lion and the fatling together;
>> And a little boy will lead them.
> Also the cow and the bear will graze,
>> Their young will lie down together,
>> And the lion will eat straw like the ox.
> The nursing child will play by the hole of the cobra,
>> And the weaned child will put his hand on the viper's den.
> They will not hurt or destroy in all My holy mountain,
>> For the earth will be full of the knowledge of the Lord
>> As the waters cover the sea.
>
> (Isa. 11:6–9)

It is a mistake to read these conditions back into the original creation narrative because God commanded Adam and Eve to "subdue" the earth (Gen. 1:28). The Hebrew word behind this expression means to subdue by force, to dominate, as when a captive is forced into slavery. Adam and Eve were placed in a beautiful garden, but the world outside the garden was wild. God told them to conquer the world and to bring its wildness under their authority so the whole world would become like the garden in Eden. Because our first parents and we have sinned, we have not fulfilled our creation mandate, but God will bring it to pass when Christ comes to set up His kingdom.

Romans 8 points us in the same direction. In this age the children of God suffer along with the rest of creation:

> For the anxious longing of the creation waits eagerly for the revealing of the sons of God. For the creation was subjected to futility, not willingly, but because of Him who subjected it, in hope that the creation itself also will be set free from its slavery to corruption into the freedom of the glory of the children

of God. For we know that the whole creation groans and suffers the pains of childbirth together until now. And not only this, but also we ourselves, having the first fruits of the Spirit, even we ourselves groan within ourselves, waiting eagerly for our adoption as sons, the redemption of our body. (8:19–23)

We have here a poetic description of the subhuman creation similar to Old Testament references to trees clapping their hands and mountains skipping like lambs. The whole created order is eagerly looking forward to the day when the sons of God will be revealed.

The world was subjected to futility because of the Fall; it was made a slave of corruption, and it suffers certain pains, probably including such things as disease and drought, tornados and the trembling of the earth. It is significant that Paul calls these things the pains of childbirth, not the throes of death. Creation is not winding down and coming to an end; it is struggling to produce new life. It pushes and strains, but it cannot give birth because at the Fall it incurred the curse of God.

Under the loving labors of Adam and Eve, the earth outside Eden should have begun to reflect the tranquility of the Garden. It should have become better than very good under their care, but that did not happen. The ground was cursed; it became unresponsive to man, and Adam's dominion over the world became severely limited. Now, instead of turning the world into a garden, mankind has turned it into a garbage dump. A day is coming, however, when the created order will be redeemed, lifted to a higher plane and made into a suitable home for the redeemed children of God. Its labor pains will end, and the old creation will give birth to the new.

The world around us is often very beautiful as it strikes our senses and as we consider its intricate design, but sin has marred us and the world under our care. There is ugliness where beauty should have reigned and we fail to see anything attractive where beauty actually exists. As the apostle Paul notes, men "suppress the truth in unrighteousness" (Rom. 1:18), and that includes the truth of beauty. Because we hide the truth from ourselves, it is not possible to prove the existence of God by an argument from design. In recent years increasingly sophisticated design arguments have been persuasive to some agnostics and atheists, but others remain more impressed by death, destruction and decay than by the beauty of the earth. Beauty is a sign pointing toward God rather than a sealed proof of His existence.

Where Does Beauty Point?

The world around us suggests things about the God who made it. The Bible mentions several divine attributes that may be inferred by listening to the testimony of our own hearts and to the voice of creation. Among these are God's eternal power and divine nature (Rom. 1:20); His wisdom and understanding (Prov. 3:19–20); His goodness (Acts 14:17); His just law (Rom. 1:32; 2:14–16); His majesty, splendor and glory (Ps. 8:1, 3; 19:1). This last set of verses gives the enraptured response of the psalmist to the starry heavens.

The striking thing about this list is that it is not particularly striking. Poets, prophets and philosophers in almost all times and places have said much the same thing. For example, in his *Tusculan Disputations* (1.13) the Roman orator Cicero (106–43 BC) concluded that the universal testimony of all races was an evidence of a God or gods:

> And this may further be brought as an irrefragable argument for us to believe that there are Gods—that there never was any nation so barbarous, nor any people in the world so savage, as to be without some notion of Gods. Many have wrong notions of the Gods, for that is the nature and ordinary consequence of bad customs, yet all allow that there is a certain divine nature and energy. Nor does this proceed from the conversation of men, or the agreement of philosophers; it is not an opinion established by institutions or by laws; but, no doubt, in every case the consent of all nations is to be looked on as a law of nature.[9]

In *Concerning the Nature of the Gods,* Cicero concluded the Deity is rational, benevolent and the source of beauty and order in the heavens and on earth.[10]

Imagine an isolated Tribe X, which has concluded that a deity exists. God provides food for man and beast, so the tribe thinks He must be good. He impresses their minds with a sense of His law and a realization of their guilt; and since they know that transgressions of the law ought to be punished, they assume God must be just. The animals are remarkably well adapted for their individual niches in nature, so Tribe X concludes that He is wise. Thunder, lightning and the wind suggest God is very powerful, while the glory and orderliness of the heavens point to His majesty and splendor.

But Tribe X also has to account for the further observation that nature is often hostile and harmful to human life and that human beings themselves are also often hostile and harmful to each other. Two possibilities are open to them. On the one hand, Tribe X might decide that their original convictions were all wrong and that there is no divine order and beauty in the world—but this entails setting aside a great mass of evidence and an inner conviction that initially seemed compelling to them. On the other hand, they might conclude something has gone dreadfully wrong with a world that was once beautifully right. The beauty remains, but it is beauty marred.

That is the conclusion many of the world's peoples appear to have reached, though often obscured by the welter of their confusing and conflicting mythologies: "The folk-tales of many peoples explain that in olden times the sky was quite near the earth; then the High God became offended with men, for some transgression which may or may not be specified, and withdrew himself to a distance at which he is no longer approachable by men."[11]

This is a reasonable conclusion that may be inferred from the evidence, but other factors are also at work. The Bible teaches that God has impressed a sense of His divinity into the hearts of mankind (John 1:9; Rom. 1:19). That sense may be ignored or squelched, but it persistently manifests itself in one way or another in all earth's people groups. In addition, we should not discount the possibility of a dim racial memory of the Garden of Eden and our expulsion from it.

What do we lose if we deny that the beauty in the world points to a powerful and beautiful Creator?

The loss of beauty. If God dies, so does beauty. If you glance out the back window of your house and see a stunning sunset, you probably call out to anyone else at home, "Come look at the sunset. It's gorgeous!"

When you exclaim over the beauty of a rose or a child or a work of art, you expect others to have a similar response. If they happen to disagree with you, they can usually give a reason for their different evaluation: "The shape of the rose is exquisite, but its color is rather dull." "The child has an attractive face, but her manners are atrocious." "The painting is well done from a technical point of view, but the brokenness and misery it portrays make me sad."

All such discussions imply there are objective standards of beauty. We may not be able to articulate what those standards are, and we may disagree about their application, but we have an intuitive awareness that some things really are more beautiful than others.

If, however, there is no transcendent standard of beauty, if no beautiful God lies behind the beauty of the world, then the exclamation, "What a beautiful sunset!" really only means, "I have beautiful feelings. The sunset is producing certain pleasurable sensations in my mind." Such a person may think he is talking about the sunset, but he is really only talking about himself.

The loss of an objective standard of beauty may not seem significant to a self-absorbed generation that only cares about its own feelings, but it undercuts the argument of the atheist who says that God cannot exist because the world is full of ugliness. According to his frame of reference, "The world is ugly" only means "I don't like it."

If yardsticks and rulers were abolished, who could correct a child who insisted he was ten feet tall? Neither inches nor feet would have meaning. If God exists, so do beauty and ugliness. If God does not exist, neither beauty nor ugliness can be defined.

The loss of moral evil. Virtuous love is the highest kind of beauty. Two simple corollaries follow: first, moral evil is the grossest kind of uglines; second, the loss of objective beauty necessarily entails the loss of moral evil.

Moral evil is a deliberate harm or offense committed by rational agents. The evil that human beings knowingly do to each other comes first to mind, but we should also include sins against God and the harm done by the devil and his legions. Natural evil, on the other hand, is the harm done by non-rational agents. The devastation caused by an earthquake is one example. Another is the economic damage a rancher suffers from predators. There is nothing morally wrong with a pack of wolves tearing into a flock of sheep. The sheep may bleat in confusion and pain, but the wolves are simply acting according to their nature.

If there is no God, the distinction between moral evil and natural evil evaporates. Everything is part of nature, so human beings are only animals who act according to their natural dispositions. Sometimes, like guppies, they eat their young. Sometimes, like robins, they care for them. If people are only animals, there was nothing morally wrong with the horrifying attacks on the World Trade Center and the Pentagon in 2001. We cannot deny that murderous hatred is a part of human nature, at least for some people, so human wolves attacked in accordance with their nature, and bleating, human sheep fled in panic from the carnage.

Our hearts instinctively rebel against such a caricature of Terrible Tuesday. We know the vicious actions of September 11 were morally wrong. Our hearts may be fearful, grieving and angry, but we also have an inalienable sense that the terrorists violated a higher standard of justice against which all human actions must be measured.

Therefore, it is foolish to conclude from horrendous injustice that God does not exist. If there is no God, then the murder of thousands was not morally evil; it was merely unpleasant to many, but not to all. After all, the attacks on that fateful September day inspired dancing in the streets in some places.

The loss of true worth. Beauty and value are connected in much the same way as beauty and goodness. We consider some things valuable because they are hard to get and useful, even if they are not particularly attractive. Crude oil is one example. In most cases, however, we see greater value in beautiful things. Diamonds cost more than coal not only because coal is easier to find, but also because diamonds are far more beautiful.

Consider the young lady who lives next door or down the street. She is fair of form and face, but her outward beauty is overshadowed by her kindness, gentleness, purity and cheerfulness. She wastes no opportunity to help the needy. She gives without any expectation of return, yet she is openly grateful for the smallest favor shown to her. Virtuous love and lovely virtue sparkle in her eyes.

What is such a girl worth? Is she valuable only in the sense that oil is valuable? She has some social utility in the neighborhood, but is that all? If a young man willingly lays down his life in order to save hers, is he a fool? After all, when he is dead, he will not enjoy even her smile in return.

Is there anything in the world with such intrinsic beauty and value that its preservation is worth our lives? From an evolutionary point of view it makes sense for me to save my own child at the cost of my life because my child carries my genes. But why, beyond herd instinct, should I care what happens to your beautiful baby? Why should I care about you? It is no accident that Sigmund Freud, the atheistic founder of analytic psychiatry, openly mocked the commandment to love our neighbors as ourselves.[12] Atheism does not always or even typically lead to such cynicism. Freud's attitude is a logical (not the necessary) result of atheism. When a man despises the God of beauty, goodness and truth, there is nothing logically worth more to the individual than the individual himself. Whenever such a person risks his life for others, he is acting contrary to his own principles.

The loss of science. In the popular mind, religion and science are often considered to be enemies, yet the scientific revolution owed much to the expectation of order and beauty in the world, and this expectation rested in turn on the unchangeableness of the God of the Bible.[13] Even when faith in a personal God began to decline in the scientific community, belief in order and beauty continued to drive the search for new truth. Classical Newtonian physics conceived of the world as a giant mechanical clock. The movements of planets were governed by immutable laws and so could be computed and predicted with great accuracy.

In the twentieth century, largely because of quantum mechanics, a massive change in attitude began to take place. Quantum mechanics says it is impossible to determine precisely both the position and the momentum of a fundamental particle such as a proton. It is also impossible to know in advance which atom of a radioactive substance will decay on a given day. Suddenly the world seems to be ruled by chance and the law of averages. Albert Einstein, who remained by temperament a classical physicist, famously objected, "God does not play dice with the world." His unhappiness with quantum mechanics resulted in a famous controversy with Danish physicist Niels Bohr.

Without going into a long and complicated story, the result has been a suspicion in some quarters that physicists do not really discover order in the universe. Rather, they impose order on nature by the kinds of instruments and theories they use in their experiments. According to this view, sometimes called instrumentalism, scientific theories do not tell us about the real world. If they are successful they make reliable predictions. They are practical; they work. Who cares if they are true?

Although this point of view is probably not an active concern for most practicing scientists, it highlights a philosophical problem for atheism. The word "science" comes from the Latin *scientia,* meaning "knowledge." Science is supposed to provide true knowledge about the real world. Instrumentalism, however, replaces the quest for truth with a search for results. Science dies and technology rises in its place.

Some might say, "Who cares? If science or technology provides us with the tools and toys we want, what does it matter how the philosophical eggheads think about the business?" The scientific worldview is supposed to offer the kind of truth that undercuts the need for religion. If science no longer cares about truth and the beauty of the world, where is its vaunted superior knowledge?

Science, as the pursuit of knowledge about reality, finds its best underpinnings not in technology but in a solid conviction that the universe is a beautiful and orderly place. Once scientists admit that premise, the existence of an intelligent Designer becomes a dangerous possibility. Furthermore, if a Designer exists, He may have a design for our lives that runs contrary to the desire for unfettered moral freedom. Could it be that a hatred of biblical morality is the mote that blinds at least some beholders so they cannot see the beauty of the Lord in the beauty of His world?

Part 2

The Beauty *of* God
the REDEEMER

There is a conjunction of such excellencies in Christ, as, in our manner of conceiving, are very diverse one from another.

—Jonathan Edwards

4 What Was Jesus' Appeal to His Contemporaries?

I like blue. A blue sky set off by a few puffy white clouds float-ing over a green forest—now that is beautiful. But if the whole world were painted one shade of blue, my favorite color would no longer be appealing. It would be boring. For this same reason Jesus is uniquely attractive, because He combines in His own person a set of qualities not found in such perfect proportion in any other figure in history.

Have we not all been drawn to certain kinds of people? I have a friend I have not seen in several years. We live in dif-ferent states now and move in different circles, but I still think of him often, and I still pray for him. He is one of the most attractive people I have ever met. At well over six feet tall, my friend's presence is commanding. People gravitate toward him when he enters a room in much the same way the members of a family gather around the carver of the Thanksgiving turkey. His voice carries well across a crowded room; at a dinner gathering of two hundred people, his table is notable for the sound of jovial laughter. He is not laughing alone; people seem happier when they are near him. Yet he is serious about the things of God and deeply compassionate toward hurting people. He also remem-bers names—hundreds of them.

He is a pastor, but unlike some clergy, he does not use guilt to manipulate his people; rather he leads by painting a bright, hopeful vision of the future. I know he is not perfect. He has made a few costly mistakes, but they were mistakes of judgment, not of the heart. The last time I saw him he had been through deep and difficult waters. On that evening he was not bright and cheerful, but neither did he seem bitter or angry. There was a chastened, humble goodness about him that lingers in my memory even several years later. I have known other attractive Christians, both men and women, but none with the largeness of personality this man has. Often I find myself wanting to see him again.

My friend, however, is as nothing beside the Master both he and I serve. No one in history has been as attractive to so many, over so many centuries, as Jesus Christ. The prophets of ancient Israel foresaw His coming and spoke in glowing terms of His beauty.

Psalm 45 is a picture of the ideal king. It may have been composed as a wedding song for Solomon or some other Israelite ruler, but several of its expressions point beyond that limited historical setting. Since Old Testament writers consciously looked forward to the coming messianic king, the New Testament appropriately applies the psalm to Jesus Christ (Heb. 1:8). The psalmist exclaims:

> My heart overflows with a good theme;
>> I address my verses to the King;
>> My tongue is the pen of a ready writer.
> You are fairer than the sons of men;
>> Grace is poured upon Your lips;
>> Therefore God has blessed You forever.
> Gird Your sword on Your thigh, O Mighty One,
>> In Your splendor and Your majesty!
>
> (45:1–3)

The ideal king is not only clothed with kingly splendor and majesty, He is fairer (literally, more beautiful) than the sons of men.

A beautiful king of David's line was the hope of all the godly people of ancient Israel. Seven hundred years before Christ, in the middle of a prophecy about the coming messianic kingdom, Isaiah promised, "Your eyes will see the King in His beauty" (Isa. 33:17). Israel waited for that king until at last Jesus was born to Mary, a virgin of David's royal line. When He grew to manhood, He began to preach and heal. Large crowds dropped their ordinary daily activities to follow Him from place to place, and they openly wondered whether He might be the promised Messiah. In the last year of His life, Jesus began deliberately to offend and drive away the shallow and superficial among His followers, but the excited crowds that greeted His arrival at His last Passover in Jerusalem were still large enough to vex the authorities.

Why were His contemporaries drawn to Him? Why does He continue to fascinate us? As Jonathan Edwards observed, the excellence of Christ comes from a unique combination of very diverse qualities. We can best understand Edwards's analysis of Christ's excellence in terms of his definition of beauty. Beauty is "a mutual consent and agreement of different things, in form, manner, quantity and visible end or design; called by the various names of regularity, order, uniformity, symmetry, proportion, harmony, &c. . . ."[1] According to this analysis, there can be no beauty without diversity.

It is sometimes helpful to examine something in terms of contrasting characteristics. Such an approach helps bring Jesus into greater focus.

The Beauty of Jesus in His Authority and Humility

The authority of Jesus. In a series of succinct summaries, the Gospel of Mark zeroes in on the tremendous impact Jesus' preaching made on those who heard Him:

> They went into Capernaum; and immediately on the Sabbath He entered the synagogue and began to teach. They were amazed at His teaching; for He was teaching them as one having authority, and not as the scribes. (1:21–22)

The chief priests and the scribes heard this, and began seeking how to destroy Him; for they were afraid of Him, for the whole crowd was astonished at His teaching. (11:18)

When Jesus saw that he had answered intelligently, He said to him, 'You are not far from the kingdom of God.' After that, no one would venture to ask Him any more questions. (12:34)

Jesus was smart. He was quick-witted enough to respond to any question or to upset any challenger. Ordinary people were captivated by His parables and His clear moral teaching, which was a distinct contrast to the convoluted arguments of the Pharisees. The people hung on His words, but when we read His sermons and sayings, it becomes clear Jesus was not like the average rabble-rouser or modern religious shyster on television. He did not labor to wring tears out of His audience with gut-wrenching stories. He did not promise them a chicken in every pot. He did not incite them to fury against the established authorities. He studiously avoided all the normal methods of crowd manipulation. He spoke the truth simply, directly and backed up by the invisible authority of God's Holy Spirit.

Jesus reinforced the authority of His words with demonstrations of supernatural power. His reputation as a miracle worker extends beyond the pages of the New Testament. The tractate *Sanhedrin* (43a) of the Babylonian Talmud, probably composed sometime in the first two centuries after Christ's death, represents a hostile Jewish assessment of Jesus: "On the eve of the Passover, Jesus of Nazareth was hung. During forty days a herald went before him crying aloud: 'He ought to be stoned because he has practiced magic, has led Israel astray and caused them to rise in rebellion. Let him who has something to say in his defence come forward and declare it.' But no one came forward, and he was hung on the eve of the Passover."[2]

The forty days given for Christ's defense is an attempt to place the Jewish trial of Jesus in a more favorable light than the hasty nighttime condemnation described in the Gospels. The tractate's charge that Jesus practiced magic parallels the Pharisees' accusation during Jesus' lifetime that He cast out "demons only by Beelzebul the ruler of the demons" (Matt. 12:24). "The same charge is found in Celsus' attack on Christianity in the second century, where it is claimed that Jesus went to Egypt and there learned the secrets of the magicians, afterward returning to Palestine and deceiving the people by his quackery."[3] The early enemies of Christ acknowledged that Jesus performed miracles. The burning question in the first two centuries was whether His power was demonic or divine.

When the local paper carries an article about a visiting healer who specializes in curing cancer, we may groan in disgust and frustration. Cancer is an ideal specialty for bogus faith healers. No one can tell instantly whether cancer has been cured, and by the time a poor, deluded sufferer has died from his "lack of faith," the charlatan is long gone. On the other hand, spontaneous remissions of cancer are not unknown, even apart from faith healers. So if a cancer disappears, the healer can claim an unqualified and unsubstantiated success.

Jesus was entirely different. "While the sun was setting, all those who had any who were sick with various diseases brought them to Him; and laying His hands on each one of them, He was healing them" (Luke 4:40). Blindness, deafness, lameness and even death itself were apparently no more difficult for Jesus than reducing a simple fever (4:38–39; 7:11–23).

In the New Testament the crowds were impressed by the multitude and magnitude of Jesus' miracles and the manner in which they were performed. The greatness of His miracles shocked even His closest followers. After He calmed the raging sea by commanding it, "Hush, be still," His disciples "became very much afraid and said to one another, 'Who then is this, that even the wind and the sea obey Him?'" (Mark 4:37–41). On another occasion Jesus gave sight to a man born blind. When the religious leaders tried to entrap the healed man into saying something against Jesus, he replied with clear-sighted candor, "Since the beginning of time it has never been heard that anyone opened the eyes of a person born blind. If this man were not from God, He could do nothing" (John 9:32–33).

Beyond the sheer power of Christ's miracles, however, people were astounded by His methods. This becomes quite clear when we compare Jesus' exorcisms with the practice of His contemporaries. The first century Jewish historian, Josephus, provides us with an illuminating contrast:

> I have seen a certain man of my own country, whose name was Eleazar, releasing people that were demoniacal in the presence of Vespasian, and his sons, and his captains, and the whole multitude of his soldiers. The manner of the cure was this: He put a ring that had a root of one of those sorts mentioned by Solomon to the nostrils of the demoniac, after which he drew out the demon through his nostrils; and when the man fell down immediately, he abjured him to return into him no more, making still mention of Solomon, and reciting the incantations which he composed. And when Eleazar would persuade and demonstrate to the spectators that he had such power, he set a little way off a cup or basin full of water, and commanded the demon, as he went out of the man, to over-turn it, and thereby to let the spectators know that he had left the man.[4]

The contrast with Jesus' methods could not be greater:

> Just then there was a man in their synagogue with an unclean spirit; and he cried out, saying, "What business do we have with each other, Jesus of Nazareth? Have You come to destroy us? I know who You are—the Holy One of God!" And Jesus rebuked him, saying, "Be quiet, and come out of him!" Throwing him into convulsions, the unclean spirit cried out with a loud voice and came out of him. They were all amazed, so that they debated among themselves, saying, "What is this? A new teaching with authority! He commands even the unclean spirits, and they obey Him." (Mark 1:23–27)

People were impressed both by the raw power of Jesus' mighty works and by the simple authority with which He performed them. There was no mumbo-jumbo, no waving of arms, no posturing, props or theatrical display. His simple command, often accompanied by a compassionate touch, held sway over all the forces of nature and over all the powers of the evil one.

One final aspect of Jesus' authority was His calm assertion that He was able to forgive sins. When four men carried a paralyzed friend to Jesus, His first response was to say, "Son, your sins are forgiven." Naturally, the religious leaders were scandalized. "Why does this man speak that way?" they fumed. "He is blaspheming; who can forgive sins but God alone?" In order to demonstrate He did indeed possess such authority, Jesus proceeded to heal the man (Mark 2:1–12). On another occasion He told a prostitute, "Your sins have been forgiven" (Luke 7:48). Perhaps most shocking of all was Jesus' claim that He will be the final judge of all mankind (John 5:22–30). Neither the Buddha nor Muhammad ever claimed such authority, nor did their immediate followers make such claims on their behalf. These apparently outlandish sayings appear in different settings throughout the four Gospels. Therefore, the suggestion that they are later additions which have been superimposed on the original simple message of Christ cannot withstand careful scrutiny. Jesus made greater claims to authority than the founder of any other major religion has ever done.

The Humility of Jesus. Great authority or even a great, but insubstantial, pretension to authority often begets overweening pride. It was not so with Jesus. Unlike modern tyrants, manipulative television preachers and extravagantly paid sports heroes, Jesus led an unpretentious life. He did not require His followers to carry Him on their shoulders above the crowds; He did not rake in cash so He could live in a magnificent palace surrounded by slaves who peeled His grapes. To the contrary, He said, "The foxes have holes and the birds of the air have nests, but the Son of Man has nowhere to lay His head" (Luke 9:58).

In much of the ancient world tyranny was feared but humility was not necessarily admired. To the contrary, Aristotle
thought the superior man should cultivate self-confident pride,
coupled with condescending magnanimity toward those who
were beneath him.[5]

The Old Testament, however, is filled with promises of blessing for the humble (for example, Ps. 37:11; Isa. 57:15). It is
against this backdrop that Jesus speaks about the exalted happiness of the poor in spirit, the mourners and the meek (Matt.
5:3–5). Perhaps the most surprising aspect of Jesus' teaching on
humility was His open invitation to those who are tired of life's
burdens: "Come to Me, all who are weary and heavy-laden, and
I will give you rest. Take My yoke upon you and learn from
Me, for I am gentle and humble in heart, and you will find rest
for your souls. For My yoke is easy and My burden is light"
(11:28–30). Not many of us could claim to be humble without
feeling proud of our humility. But these words do not seem out
of place in the mouth of Jesus. His disciple Matthew recorded
them without expressing any sense of impropriety.

The rich and powerful of this world are not overly eager to
share the burdens of people who are poor, distressed, guilty and
discouraged, but Jesus did so on a daily basis. People recognized
His humble willingness to lift their loads, and they loved Him
for it.

We see an example of the humility of Jesus in His sensitivity
toward children: "Then some children were brought to Him so
that He might lay His hands on them and pray; and the disciples
rebuked them. But Jesus said, 'Let the children alone, and do
not hinder them from coming to Me; for the kingdom of heaven
belongs to such as these.' After laying His hands on them, He
departed from there" (19:13–15).

Sometimes we see movie stars raising money for disadvan-
taged children, but they would not necessarily choose to spend
time alone with children, rather than in front of the cameras. By
way of contrast, children's show host Mr. Rogers was invited to

make the one hundred billionth crayon at the Crayola factory. All the cameramen and dignitaries were huddled together waiting for a fantastic photo op, but they could not find Mr. Rogers. He was off to one side talking with a small group of children. Mr. Rogers was an ordained Christian minister; in choosing children over publicity, he was following in his Master's footsteps.

Jesus' humility was beautifully displayed on the night before His crucifixion when He took the place of a household slave and washed the feet of His disciples. Then Christ followed His act of humble service with this exhortation: "You call Me Teacher and Lord; and you are right, for so I am. If I then, the Lord and the Teacher, washed your feet, you also ought to wash one another's feet. For I gave you an example that you also should do as I did to you. Truly, truly, I say to you, a slave is not greater than his master, nor is one who is sent greater than the one who sent him. If you know these things, you are blessed if you do them" (John 13:13–17).

Jesus was their rabbi. According to Jewish culture He was entitled to the respect and service of His disciples. In addition, He had gradually been leading them to the conclusion that He was much more than a rabbi or even a prophet, yet He had served them.

The humble service of Christ the Lord reached its climax in the cross. In the weeks preceding His crucifixion, Jesus repeatedly spoke about His impending death and resurrection. Though His disciples initially refused to accept His prophecy at face value, they realized in retrospect that Jesus deliberately went to Jerusalem to die. "But Jesus called them to Himself and said, 'You know that the rulers of the Gentiles lord it over them, and their great men exercise authority over them. It is not this way among you, but whoever wishes to become great among you shall be your servant, and whoever wishes to be first among you shall be your slave; just as the Son of Man did not come to be served, but to serve, and to give His life a ransom for many'" (Matt. 20:25–28).

Jesus was not weak. He was a mighty worker of miracles and a powerful public speaker. He claimed to be the judge of all men who would one day raise all the dead. If a beggar is humble, we think it fitting. When an ignorant man is humble, it is certainly appropriate. But when the almighty, omniscient Lord of heaven and earth is humble, it is astonishing and beautiful.

The common people who saw Jesus did not recognize His deity; they were attracted nevertheless by His evident authority, coupled with His remarkable humility.

The Beauty of Jesus in His Sternness and Compassion

The sternness of Jesus. Jesus angrily chased a horde of noisy merchants out of the temple in Jerusalem early in His ministry and again at its close. "He made a scourge of cords, and drove them all out of the temple, with the sheep and the oxen; and He poured out the coins of the money changers and overturned their tables" (John 2:15). Jesus did not politely speak in a soft, simpering voice when He requested the merchants to leave. He must have been shouting, and when they refused to go, He gave them a sound thrashing.

Most of the time we become angry because we believe we have suffered a personal offense. Even when we explode at an inanimate object, our language tends to personalize the thing: "That *stupid* computer crashed again." Jesus appears never to have lost His temper over a personal insult or injury. Even as He hung on the cross, He prayed, "Father, forgive them; for they know not what they are doing" (Luke 23:34). His explosion at the temple was not a fit of petty anger. He was zealous for the honor of God, whose house had been turned into a robbers' den, and concerned for the people who could not find a quiet place to pray (John 2:16–17; Mark 11:17).

In a perfectly just world, anger would never be warranted, but we do not live in such a world. Anger is righteous if it is directed at the right person, for the right reason, in the right measure, at the right time. Not to be angry in such a case would be a character defect. We also see the sternness of Jesus in His dire warnings regarding hell:

> If your hand causes you to stumble, cut it off; it is better for you to enter life crippled, than, having your two hands, to go into hell, into the unquenchable fire, where their worm does not die, and the fire is not quenched. If your foot causes you to stumble, cut it off; it is better for you to enter life lame, than, having your two feet, to be cast into hell, where their worm does not die, and the fire is not quenched. If your eye causes you to stumble, throw it out; it is better for you to enter the kingdom of God with one eye, than, having two eyes, to be cast into hell, where their worm does not die, and the fire is not quenched. (Mark 9:43–48)

Jesus never soft-pedaled the difficult truth of everlasting judgment. Many modern preachers erroneously teach either that God will save everybody or the wicked will be annihilated after they have suffered for an adequate time in hell. Jesus, however, said the lost will suffer "eternal punishment" in "eternal fire," while the righteous will enter into "eternal life" (Matt. 25:41, 46). The same Greek word translated "eternal" is used in all these cases, so if eternal punishment lasts for a limited time, we should conclude the same for eternal life—which, for very good reasons, these preachers are not willing to do. Jesus was not shy about threatening the unrepentant with hell, and on one occasion He told a group of grumbling Jews their father was the devil (John 8:44).

Finally, we see the sternness of Jesus in His hatred of hypocrisy:

> Woe to you, scribes and Pharisees, hypocrites! For you tithe mint and dill and cummin, and have neglected the weightier provisions of the law: justice and mercy and faithfulness; but these are the things you should have done without neglecting the others. You blind guides, who strain out a gnat and swallow a camel! Woe to you, scribes and Pharisees, hypocrites! For you clean the outside of the cup and of the dish, but inside they are full of robbery and self-indulgence. You

blind Pharisee, first clean the inside of the cup and of the dish, so that the outside of it may become clean also. Woe to you, scribes and Pharisees, hypocrites! For you are like white-washed tombs which on the outside appear beautiful, but inside they are full of dead men's bones and all uncleanness. So you, too, outwardly appear righteous to men, but inwardly you are full of hypocrisy and lawlessness. (Matt. 23:23–28)

Jesus despised leaders who used their privileged position to enrich themselves. He railed against teachers who did not practice the rigorous religion they demanded of others. He was angry when people clung to their self-made religious rules and used them as an excuse to neglect to show mercy to the poor and sick (Mark 3:1–6). They would pull a sheep out of a pit on the Sabbath, but they stubbornly refused to countenance Jesus' healing on that day (Matt. 12:9–14).

Jesus was undeniably a stern preacher of righteousness, but sternness by itself is not attractive. Most of us have met people who are judgmental, self-righteous and harsh. They think it their holy duty to point out and punish everybody else's flaws. The beauty of Jesus lies in the admirable conjunction of His sympathy and His sternness.

The compassion of Jesus. Sometimes Jesus used His miracles to illustrate spiritual truths. For example, He opened the eyes of a man born blind to back up His claim that He was the light of the world (John 9:1–7). Although His disciples sometimes missed the lessons He was teaching them, they could not fail to observe and record His compassion toward suffering people. Jesus was as drawn to the sick as they were drawn to Him.

Nowhere is this more evident than in Jesus' treatment of lepers. "And a leper came to Jesus, beseeching Him and falling on his knees before Him, and saying, 'If You are willing, You can make me clean.' Moved with compassion, Jesus stretched out His hand and touched him, and said to him, 'I am willing; be cleansed.' Immediately the leprosy left him and he was cleansed" (Mark 1:40–42).

Jesus touched the untouchable. Under the Law of Moses, lepers were not allowed to mingle with healthy people. They had to cover their faces with a cloth and cry out, "Unclean! Unclean!" Since the leper would never have dared to touch Jesus, Jesus took the initiative to reach out to him. Although Jesus sometimes healed people at a distance with a simple word, on this occasion, moved with compassion, He laid a gentle hand on the leper. He knew the man had been rejected and despised for years even by his family. With the touch of His hand, Jesus reached out to heal the man's soul as well as his body.

We also see the compassion of Jesus toward the suffering and the needy in settings unrelated to healing. When Jesus took His disciples across the Sea of Galilee for a much-needed rest, five thousand people walked around the north end of the Sea looking for Him. By the time they caught up with Jesus, they were tired and hungry. Jesus "felt compassion for them because they were like sheep without a shepherd; and He began to teach them many things" (6:34). Then, concerned that they might faint with hunger, He miraculously fed them by multiplying the loaves and fish of a little boy's lunch. On another occasion He fed four thousand people, saying, "I feel compassion for the people because they have remained with Me now three days and have nothing to eat. If I send them away hungry to their homes, they will faint on the way; and some of them have come from a great distance" (8:2–3).

Perhaps the most unexpected example of Jesus' compassion occurred after His friend Lazarus died. When Jesus met the man's weeping sisters, He was so "deeply moved in spirit" and "troubled" that He wept (John 11:33–38). Even though Jesus planned to raise Lazarus from the dead by divine power, His human emotions were overwhelmed with sympathy for the mourners and with sorrow for the suffering of Lazarus. The compassion of Jesus was never a cool and detached willingness to help. He was passionate in His compassion.

Jesus also exhibited tender compassion toward notorious

sinners. When the Pharisees criticized Him for eating with a crowd of morally undesirable people, Jesus replied, "It is not those who are healthy who need a physician, but those who are sick. But go and learn what this means: 'I desire compassion, and not sacrifice,' for I did not come to call the righteous, but sinners" (Matt. 9:12–13). His enemies called Him "a friend of tax collectors and sinners" (11:19). Even worse from the Pharisaic perspective, Jesus permitted a prostitute to wash His feet with her tears and dry them with the hair of her head, then He reassured her that her sins were forgiven (Luke 7:36–50). According to the common notions of Jesus' day, the touch of an immoral woman would defile a righteous man. On this occasion just the reverse was true: pardon and purity flowed from Jesus to overcome her pollution.

Finally, Jesus showed compassion even toward the stubbornly unrepentant Jews who were soon to put Him to death. "When He approached Jerusalem, He saw the city and wept over it, saying, 'If you had known in this day, even you, the things which make for peace! But now they have been hidden from your eyes'" (19:41–42).

Some people reduce God to a benign grandfather who would never even swat a fly; others swing to the opposite extreme. They imagine He is completely unmoved by the death of the ungodly as they fall into the pit of hell, while the Lord turns His back on them to lavish gifts on His lucky favorites. This passage shows us otherwise. Jesus pronounced a terrible doom on Jerusalem, but He wept to think of the coming devastation. The fulfillment of this prophecy in AD 70 did not bring joy in heaven.

On the night before His crucifixion, Philip asked Jesus to show him and the other apostles God the Father. Jesus replied, "Have I been so long with you, and yet you have not come to know Me, Philip? He who has seen Me has seen the Father; how can you say, 'Show us the Father'" (John 14:9)? Jesus was a true revelation of the Father; His compassion, even when judgment was necessary, reveals the heart of God. Furthermore, Jesus insisted that the Father who sent Him was the God of Abraham and Moses. Neither Jesus nor the apostles saw any difference between the God of the Old Testament and the God whom Jesus preached.

Jesus was compassionate, but He was not a sentimental push-over. He was also stern. He combined sternness and compassion at the right time, to the right people and in the right way. He spoke and acted with divine authority, yet He remained gentle and humble. The Bible says He was full of grace and truth, and it describes Him as both a lion and a lamb (John 1:14; Rev. 5:5–6). The harmonious combination of such diverse character traits explains why so many were attracted to Him two thousand years ago and why Christians, who long to be more like Him, may sing:

> Let the beauty of Jesus be seen in me,
> All His wonderful passion and purity;
> Oh, Thou Spirit divine,
> All my nature refine,
> Till the beauty of Jesus be seen in me.[6]

Men can be happy in no other but the God of Israel: He is the only fountain of happiness. Other gods cannot help in calamity; nor can any of them afford what the poor empty soul stands in need of.

—Jonathan Edwards

5   Is Christianity a Unique Religion?

The continuing appeal of Jesus Christ rests not only on His character, which surpasses all the claims made for other religious leaders, but even more on His death and His subsequent resurrection. Christianity differs from all other religions in that it alone offers a genuine Savior. This makes Christianity the most beautiful of religions.

As many of my fellow believers are lamenting the precipitous decline of our civilization, I am comforted to realize our age is increasingly coming to resemble the age in which Christianity first flourished. The beauty of our God shone brightly then, and if the church does not lose her vision of her Lord, He may yet show His glory through her in the days to come.

In the century before and after Christ's time on earth, the grand confidence of Plato (428–347 BC) and Aristotle (384–322 BC) in the power of reason was losing ground to various mystical sects, which came complete with elaborate mythologies. At the same time Rome's noblest statesmen were turning to Stoicism, which preached an ethic of discipline and self-control as a means of escaping the passions and desires that disturb the ordinary life. It was a pluralistic age in which religions of all stripes were tolerated as long as they caused no trouble and paid appropriate homage to the emperor.

The same kinds of trends are at work today. The modern

confidence in reason, which consciously looks back to Descartes (1596–1650) and Newton (1642–1727) but has deeper roots in late Medieval Christianity, has begun to deteriorate. In its place we see a growing and serious interest in the occult, a resurgence of pagan deities and a fascination with ancient Gnostic alternatives to orthodox Christianity. This would all be quite surprising if Christian thinkers had not recognized such tendencies long ago. John Wesley wrote, "If a man will not believe God, he will believe anything. Why, he may believe a man could put himself into a quart bottle."[1] At the same time, those who cannot swallow the current revival of mythology are increasingly turning to Buddhism. Like ancient Stoicism, the philosophical form of Buddhism seeks to escape the torment of unfulfilled desires by the expedient of quenching all the passions. Both Stoicism and Buddhism stand opposed to the biblical teaching that our desires need to be purified, not stifled, and when they have become pure, our desires can and will be most exquisitely satisfied in God.

Above all, our age is one of religious pluralism, like the glory days of Rome. It is tolerant of everything except truth. The early Christians could easily have escaped official persecution if they had been willing to offer a pinch of incense at the shrine of the divine emperor. No one (except the Jews) minded adding another god to the already burgeoning pantheon, and many would have been willing to worship Christ alongside the emperor and their ancestral deities. What they minded was the message that the God of the Bible is the only true God. Jewish monotheism was sometimes tolerated because the Jews kept pretty much to themselves, but Christians were evangelistic from the start and thoroughly hated as a result.

Likewise in our day, Christian pastors and chaplains are coming under increasingly vitriolic pressure to eliminate the name of Christ from their public prayers. Modern secularism assumes the only way to maintain public civility in matters religious is publicly to despise anyone with genuine religious convictions.

America's founding principle that "all men are created equal" has come to mean all *religions* are created equal. In the eyes of some, religions are equally bad; in the eyes of others, they are equally good. In the eyes of nearly everyone, they ought to be equally bland—like rice without butter and salt or some kind of sauce. To such people Christianity seems ugly precisely because it claims Jesus Christ is the only way to God.

The inescapable teaching of Scripture is that Yahweh, who has become incarnate in Jesus Christ, is the only true God, and specifically the only God who offers salvation:

> "You are My witnesses," declares the LORD [Yahweh],
> "And My servant whom I have chosen,
> So that you may know and believe Me
> And understand that I am He.
> Before Me there was no God formed,
> And there will be none after Me.
> I, even I, am the LORD,
> And there is no savior besides Me."
>
> (Isa. 43:10–11)

Similarly, the prophet Micah asks, "Who is a God like You, who pardons iniquity?" (7:18). The obvious implication is there is no one like Him because no other god forgives sin as He does.

One of the many indirect testimonies to Christ's deity in the New Testament is the assertion that He alone is able to save (Acts 4:12), so it is not surprising that the apostles sometimes specifically link Jesus' title as Savior with His identity as God. In Titus 2 Paul writes of "God our Savior" (2:10) and then reminds us to look for "the blessed hope and the appearing of the glory of our great God and Savior, Christ Jesus" (2:13). Similarly, Peter greets "those who have received a faith of the same kind as ours, by the righteousness of our God and Savior, Jesus Christ" (2 Pet. 1:1).

The beauty of the Bible's saving God appears in three ways: first, when we look for a savior among the gods of polytheism (both ancient and modern); second, when we consider what it cost God to save us; and finally, in the attributes of God that come to light through His saving activity.

No Other Savior among the Gods

The Ancient Gods. By and large, the gods of classical polytheism were an immoral, fickle and fallible lot. The pagan peoples of ancient Palestine worshiped Ashtoreth, the Canaanite goddess of fertility, whose devotees engaged in religious prostitution and ritual sexual practices. Religious prostitution has been part of polytheism throughout the centuries. In the first century men looking for pleasure frequented the temple of Artemis in Ephesus or the temple of Aphrodite in Corinth, which employed more than one thousand prostitutes. In India, where literally millions of gods are acknowledged, young girls of poor, lower caste families were regularly sold to temples to become prostitutes or sex slaves of the priests. This practice went virtually unopposed until the twentieth century. Amy Carmichael, an English missionary to southern India who did much to bring the unholy traffic to light, began rescuing temple girls in 1901. She faced kidnapping charges on several occasions for her work, which shows how deeply entrenched child prostitution in the temples had become. The cases were eventually dismissed.

Religious prostitution and ritual sexual practices were a natural outgrowth of polytheism because the gods themselves were immoral, whether Greek, Babylonian or Hindu. Zeus, the chief of the Greek gods, was always seducing some human woman while his jealous wife Hera was busy trying to catch him and punish the hapless girls who bore his bastard children.

Envy, hatred and even murder are also common to the stories of gods everywhere. In Norse mythology Loki managed, by deception, to kill Balder, the most beloved of all the gods. The gods of Greece and Rome used individual human beings and nations as pawns in their continual quarrels with each other. Most notably, the Trojan War resulted from the jealous wrangling of Hera, Athena and Aphrodite over which of them was the most beautiful goddess. Though human sacrifice was rare in Greek mythology, it was not unknown. At the outset of the Trojan War, King Agamemnon sacrificed his daughter Iphigenia in order to obtain favorable winds for his fleet. On the other hand, the ancient Canaanite god Molech regularly demanded that children be burned to death in his worship.

It is hardly surprising that none of these ancient gods was a true savior. St. Augustine made this point early in the fifth century AD. When the Visigoths sacked Rome in AD 410, the people of Rome were divided between Christians and worshipers of Rome's traditional gods. The pagans claimed Rome had fallen because the city had deserted its ancestral religion. In response Augustine wrote his massive rebuttal, *The City of God*.

The first part of the book contains an extensive comparison of the gods of the polytheists with the true God. Augustine notes that none of the pagan gods even promised to give eternal life.[2] Each of the gods and goddesses had specific areas of responsibility, but all of them promised only earthly blessings. Bacchus was the god of wine, while the Lymphae were the goddesses of water. One could not ask Bacchus for water; to provide it was not his job. One could not ask the Lymphae for fire; creating it was not their specialty. Ceres was the goddess of grain, and Venus was the goddess of love. There was no sense in a man pleading with Ceres to help him win a girl, and Venus did not care about the crops. Each god or goddess had his or her own specific duty, but none of them had the specific task of saving sinners and giving them eternal life. Looking beyond the Greco-Roman tradition, we find gods such as the Persian Mithra and the Egyptian Osiris, who are righteous judges of the dead. In every case the only people rewarded after death are those who deserve it by good deeds or those who earn it through religious rituals.

Some people claim that Mithraism embodied all the essential elements of Christianity before Christ, and that Christ is therefore only a deliberate fabrication in imitation of Mithra.

The charge is too complex to discuss in detail here, but several points can be made briefly.[3]

First, most of the cited parallels relate not to early Persian Mithraism but to Mithraism after it was imported into Rome in the century after Christ.

> There is little notice of the Persian god in the Roman world until the beginning of the 2nd century, but, from the year AD 136 onward, there are hundreds of dedicatory inscriptions to Mithra. This renewal of interest is not easily explained. The most plausible hypothesis seems to be that Roman Mithraism was practically a new creation, wrought by a religious genius who may have lived as late as ca. AD 100 and who gave the old traditional Persian ceremonies a new Platonic interpretation that enabled Mithraism to become acceptable to the Roman world.[4]

Since Roman Mithraism only became popular in the two centuries after Christ, it is ingenuous to insist that the borrowing flowed in only one direction. There is good reason to suspect that the cult of Mithra copied some ideas from the rapidly expanding church.

Second, some parallels are irrelevant. For example, Mithra's birth was celebrated on December 25, but the Bible nowhere indicates when Christ was born; Christmas was a later ecclesiastical tradition.

Third, several claims are simply not true. For example, the claim is made that Mithra shed his blood to save his followers, and he rose again on the third day. However, no text indicates Mithra ever died, so he never experienced a resurrection; and the only blood Mithra shed was the blood of a bull. He did not personally die for sinners.

Fourth, since some of the alleged parallels depend on artistic representations rather than written texts, they are tenuous deductions at best.

Finally, the clearest background for understanding Christ

remains the Old Testament. In the Old Testament sacrificial system, we find the true basis for the New Testament doctrine of atonement through the blood of Christ.

In spite of the occasional savior designation, the gods of the ancient world were not saviors. In such a world one of the attractions of Christianity, one of its beauties, was that Christ saves sinners.

Neo-Paganism and Its Evil Twin. Building on nineteenth century interest in magic and ancient religions, Neo-Paganism has experienced impressive growth since the mid-twentieth century. With no clearly defined doctrines or universal rituals, Neo-Paganism encompasses Wiccans, Neo-Druids and a generous variety of other groups and individuals. At the risk of oversimplification, the following are some general characteristics of the movement.[5] While all Neo-Pagans revere the ancient gods, there is great diversity in the way the gods are viewed. Some Neo-Pagans are devoted to the gods of specific cultures—whether Norse, Druid, Egyptian or Greco-Roman. Worship of a female-male pairing like that of Diana and the horned god Pan is fairly common. Many believe the individual gods are all manifestations of one all-pervading god (pantheism). Some Neo-Pagans believe they themselves are divine, while others treat the gods as symbols of the forces of nature.

While doctrine is quite fluid among Neo-Pagans, two ethical concerns seem almost universal: The first is to do no harm to anyone. The second is an earnest desire to preserve and protect the earth (often revered as the divine Mother). Both of these are commendable, but their love for nature and whatever is natural leads to a more problematic corollary: they view the natural state of men and women as inherently good. For many this means nudity, being natural, is liberating. Sexuality is generally celebrated, but this does not mean that Neo-Pagans are normally promiscuous. Many would see promiscuity as contrary to one of their fundamental ethical principles, since indiscriminate sex can harm others.

The problem with Neo-Paganism's view of human nature is not its celebration of sexuality. After all, the Song of Solomon is unabashedly enthusiastic about sex within marriage. The true ethical shortcoming of Neo-Paganism is its unrealistic optimism about human nature. Neo-Paganism has no satisfactory answer to the question, "What is the source of quarrels and conflicts among you?" The biblical answer is that they come from lusts waging war in our own hearts (James 4:1–2). Like Neo-Paganism, the Bible recognizes the greatness and glory of humankind because God made us in His own image. Unlike Neo-Paganism, the Bible deals honestly both with the atrocities committed by notoriously evil people and with the more common moral weaknesses that keep us from fulfilling the dictates of our nobler ideals.

Since Neo-Paganism fails to account for the debilitating effects of human depravity and our desperate need for redemption, it has no place for a savior. But the Savior is just what Christianity offers. If, in spite of their belief in human goodness, Neo-Pagans begin to sense their own deep moral weakness, perhaps the message of a Redeemer will become more attractive to them.

Although the basic ethical tenets of Neo-Paganism are laudable, there is a negative aspect to its worldview. One of the major problems with pantheism and polytheism is that evil and good stand on the same metaphysical platform; they are equally ultimate realities. Side by side with the benign gods we find paganism's evil twin: the deification of malicious, spiteful gods.

In Norse mythology the trickster Loki is a god who will lead the giants out of Hel to fight the gods of Valhalla in the last battle, during which both good and evil gods will die.

Hinduism contains such a vast, multifaceted, contradictory welter of ideas and deities that almost any statement about it is apt to be both true and false at the same time. Shiva is the supreme deity in some strains of Hinduism, but more often he is the destroyer linked with Brahma (the creator) and Vishnu (the sustainer). Destruction has a divine status equal to the creation and maintenance of the world. Or consider Kali, the black mother goddess of Hinduism. She is often pictured spattered with blood, wearing a string of skulls as a necklace and a girdle made of human hands. In one story she became so frenzied during a killing spree that she began blindly destroying everything in sight. And yet she is a mother, beloved by her devotees.[6]

The pairing of good and evil or of creation and destruction, common in polytheism and pantheism, leads some to worship evil. It is no accident that the rise of Neo-Paganism is accompanied by open devotion of a few to its evil twin, Satanism. Modern Satanism is real. It is not just an invention of tabloid journalism. I was overseeing a church booth at a community fair when a young man walked over to glance at my tract entitled, "Do You Believe in Magick?"[7] As soon as he realized it was a Christian rebuttal to the occult arts, he stomped off, shouting that I was "dissing" his religion. The back of his T-shirt read "I love Satan."

The "Eleven Satanic Rules of the Earth" posted on the church of Satan's website are diametrically opposed to the basic tenets of Neo-Paganism.[8] Consider, for example, rule number four: "If a guest in your lair annoys you, treat him cruelly and without mercy." Or rule number eleven: "When walking in open territory, bother no one. If someone bothers you, ask him to stop. If he does not stop, destroy him." Though they hold no ethical precepts in common, Satan worship and Neo-Paganism thrive or decline together because they feed off the same polytheistic worldview.

In the Bible, by contrast, Satan is not on an equal metaphysical footing with God. He is a creature who was originally good but who has become terribly twisted by his own free choice. God alone is infinite in power, eternal in existence and unchangeably good. Satan's power is not even close to God's omnipotence, and when Satan's role in God's wise plans is complete, he will be cast into the lake of fire. The God of the Bible is a saving God because the struggle between good and evil is not eternal. Time is not cyclical, as it is in some forms of Greek and Hindu thought.

It has a beginning; it has a direction; and it leads to the eternal city of God where those whom God has rescued will live with Him forever.

The Cost of Salvation to God

Although they might have looked with favor on a few individuals, most of the ancient gods had little love for the human race as a whole. There were, however, a few gods that were kindly disposed toward humanity. The interesting thing about the benevolent gods is that they often suffered terribly or were even murdered.

Among the Greeks we find the titan Prometheus. Contrary to the wishes of the other gods, he gave mankind many gifts, including various crafts, healing drugs, the alphabet and the arts. He further offended the rest of the Greek pantheon when he stole fire from the gods and gave it to people. Then he tricked Zeus into allowing them to eat the flesh of every animal sacrifice, leaving only the bones and the fat to burn on the altar for the gods. For these crimes Zeus had him shackled to the side of a crag high in the Caucasus Mountains. Each day an eagle came to shred the immortal flesh of Prometheus and to devour his liver. Each night his torn flesh was restored so the eagle could begin anew at the first touch of dawn.

Prometheus was sometimes called the savior of humanity, and clearly he paid a terrible cost for his deeds of kindness. However, Prometheus did not *willingly choose* to be punished. He was *forced to suffer* for centuries until at last Hercules broke his chains and freed him.

Aside from Prometheus, most of the benevolent dying gods of antiquity were not killed for any benefits bestowed on people but because of the jealousy of other gods. In Egypt Osiris's evil brother Set murdered him, hacked his body into pieces and then scattered and hid the pieces. Isis, the wife of Osiris, found all the dismembered parts, but after she put Osiris back together again, he was no longer allowed to rule over the land of the living. Instead, he became the righteous judge of the dead.

In Hinduism the good god Krishna, the eighth incarnation of Vishnu, was accidentally shot and killed by a hunter's arrow. His death did not atone for sins, nor did he erase bad karma for anyone. Joining Krishna in paradise is a reward for good karma (good deeds). Though he is sometimes called a savior, he saves no one. The same is true for the multitude of other gods in Hinduism. None of them save their devotees; the faithful hope to earn their way to paradise. The more philosophical kind of Hinduism does not even offer a personal salvation. The Hindu philosopher looks forward to his little drop of existence being dissolved in the great ocean of being.

When we turn to Buddhism we see a similar difference between the philosophical and polytheistic forms of the religion. In classical or Theravada Buddhism, Buddha (the enlightened one) is viewed as a human being. He taught the way to enlightenment, but each individual must seek it for himself. The Theravada Buddhist hopes for an end to the weary round of rebirth through enlightenment. The goal of enlightenment on earth is a greatly expanded consciousness and the extinction (nirvana) of the desires that cause suffering. The enlightened Buddhist hopes to achieve final nirvana at death; the little flame of his life will no longer pass from candle to candle. What happens next is unclear. Perhaps the flame will simply burn out. There is no concept of salvation.

In the somewhat later but widespread Mahayana Buddhism, nirvana becomes a state of bliss. The Buddha is regarded as a manifestation of a divine being. In addition, there are many "bodhisattvas, enlightened beings who, through compassion, delay their final passage to the transcendent state of nirvana in order to labor on behalf of universal salvation. A bodhisattva can transfer his supreme merit to others."[9] In the minds of many simple devotees, Mahayana Buddhism is essentially polytheistic since its adherents worship the various bodhisattvas as gods. Although the concept of transferring merit bears a superficial resemblance to the imputation of Christ's righteousness to believers, there is a great difference between the two. Christ saves sinners who hate Him and who have no righteousness of their own. The bodhisattvas give a hand up to those who are already doing their best. Only Christ is truly a savior, rather than a helper.

The suffering, dying gods of the old religions point toward a basic truth either recognized by observation or perhaps dimly remembered from some ancient revelation. It is this: The best men suffer most from those who are evil, but somehow goodness will triumph in the end. In Plato's *Republic* Socrates insists it is better to be just than to be unjust, even though the just man is likely to be hated for his goodness. Socrates describes the likely fate of the perfectly just man in terms that sound strangely prophetic: "They will tell you that our just man will be thrown into prison, scourged and racked, will have his eyes burnt out, and, after every kind of torment, be impaled."[10] When I taught *The Republic* to university students, some of them erroneously assumed this passage was a prophecy of Christ. It is not. Plato was simply reflecting on the hostility of the Athenians toward his master, Socrates. Socrates was not impaled, but he was required to drink hemlock poison because he so easily and so frequently poked holes in the self-righteous folly of his contemporaries.

The righteous sufferer is a constant theme throughout the Old Testament as well, but there we find an added dimension which never appears in the polytheistic myths or the philosophic musings of the ancients: The righteous sufferer of Isaiah 53 is punished *for the sins of others*. The prophet predicts the Servant of the Lord will "justify the many, as He will bear their iniquities" (53:11). Death, however, will not be the end for Him; after He bears the sins of His people, God promises to elevate Him because of His sacrifice:

> Therefore, I will allot Him a portion with the great,
>   And He will divide the booty with the strong;
>   Because He poured out Himself to death,

And was numbered with the transgressors;
Yet He Himself bore the sin of many,
And interceded for the transgressors.

(53:12)

None of the ancient gods or their modern Neo-Pagan coun-terparts willingly suffered the punishment deserved by sinners. Yet that is exactly what Jesus did, and then He rose again from the grave.

The myths of the old gods are not rooted in history; their stories take place in the distant undateable past. The death and resurrection of Jesus are locked into a specific time and place. We know when, where and how He lived and died. The myths may be expressions of the fears and longings of humanity, but Je-sus Christ is the concrete fulfillment of the dimly foreseen truths the myths embody.

The suffering of the ancient gods was incidental to their kindness to men and women. They did not choose to suffer, and suffering was not part of their mission or purpose. What a con-trast to the God of the Bible! God paid a terrible price to redeem sinners, but the cost was not forced upon Him. Because of His great love, He chose the way of a painful redemption, and He inflicted those pains on Himself.[11] Each member of the Trinity was involved in some way in the divinely self-imposed cost of salvation.

The Father gave His Son. Perhaps the best-loved verse in the Bible is John 3:16: "For God so loved the world, that He gave His only begotten Son, that whoever believes in Him shall not perish, but have eternal life." God the Father loved the Son with an infinite love. God's love for His Son is greater than His love for us. Therefore, He did not sacrifice His Son for us because He loved us more than He loved Him. Rather, God loved His Son so much that He sent Him to earth to bring more sons and daughters into the family. He loved a world of sinners not for what they were, but for what He would make of them. He loved the world so much that He was willing to put His Son through terrible suffering on our behalf. Isaiah makes it very clear that the suffering of Christ came directly from the hand of God:

> Surely our griefs He Himself bore,
>> And our sorrows He carried;
>> Yet we ourselves esteemed Him stricken,
>> Smitten of God, and afflicted.
> But He was pierced through for our transgressions,
>> He was crushed for our iniquities;
>> The chastening for our well-being fell upon Him,
>> And by His scourging we are healed.
> All of us like sheep have gone astray,
>> Each of us has turned to his own way;
>> But the Lord has caused the iniquity of us all
>> To fall on Him.
>
> (Isa. 53:4–6)

It was the *Lord*, not man, who caused our iniquity and its punishment to fall on Christ. This was the cost of our salvation to God the Father. He punished His beloved Son as though He were guilty of all our sins. Stop to meditate on how difficult this was for the Father. It was much harder than creating the stars, the mountains, the seas and all the living creatures of the earth. It was harder for the Father to punish the perfectly innocent Christ than it will be for Him to send rebellious, Christ-hating sinners to hell. Laying our sin on His beloved Son was the hardest thing the Father has ever done. It was a divinely difficult work.

The Son endured the cross. Although in some sense God the Father shared in the sufferings of Christ, we must not say the Father suffered for our sins. The Bible is clear: Jesus alone paid the price of our redemption.

Jesus did not undergo beatings, mockery, the nails and the heavy hand of God crushing His human soul simply because the Jewish leaders caught Him unaware. He voluntarily laid aside the outward trappings of glory and majesty in order to take on Himself the form of a servant and to suffer and die for our sakes

(Phil. 2:5–8). During the last year of His ministry, Jesus foretold His death and resurrection on several occasions (Mark 8:31–32; 9:30–31; 10:32–34). A few months before His death, Jesus said, "I lay down My life for the sheep. . . . No one has taken it away from Me, but I lay it down on My own initiative. I have authority to lay it down, and I have authority to take it up again. This commandment I received from My Father" (John 10:15, 18). When Jesus hung on the cross, He cried out with a loud voice, "'Father, into Your hands I commit My spirit.' Having said this, He breathed His last" (Luke 23:46).

Jesus was not a martyr to a noble cause. He was a sacrificial victim who offered Himself up to God as payment for the sins of His people. He endured the shame and suffering of the cross because He had His eyes fixed "on the joy set before Him" (Heb. 12:2). He looked forward to the joy of His Father's approval and the joy of eternal fellowship with the people whom He planned to redeem.

Because of this future joy, He was willing to be defiled by the filth of our sins— sexual immorality, murder, blasphemy, idolatry, disobedience to parents, greed and every other kind of iniquity. Then, when the stench of His innocent soul polluted by our sins rose up before the throne of God, Jesus endured the worst burden of all: The Father turned His back on the Son, and the Son cried out, "My God, My God, why have You forsaken Me?" (Matt. 27:46). Jesus, who had never known a moment's separation from His Father's loving presence, was suddenly more alone than a whole world of loneliness. Then the Father poured out the full weight of His holy wrath on the soul of His righteous Son. Jesus' spiritual torment far exceeded the physical pain of being scourged and crucified. No other religious teachers, martyrs or ancient gods have ever endured such torment in their soul. There is no one else but Jesus who is worthy to be called Savior.

At the Crucifixion, the Holy Spirit grieved over sin. Several passages teach that God's Holy Spirit grieves over human sin.

God was "grieved in His heart" at the wickedness of human-kind before the flood, and He said, "My Spirit shall not strive with man forever" (Gen. 6:3–6). Similarly, the rebellious sons of Israel "grieved His Holy Spirit" (Isa. 63:10). The apostle Paul evidently had these passages in mind when he wrote, "Do not grieve the Holy Spirit of God, by whom you were sealed for the day of redemption" (Eph. 4:30).

When the Bible says the Holy Spirit grieves, we must not imagine the Lord says to Himself, "Oops! I guess I made a mis-take. I really should not have made the human race after all." God's plans, His knowledge and His eternal attributes never change. According to Isaiah 40–48, one of the key differences between the Lord and false gods is that He alone is able to pre-dict the future, because He has planned all of its details. (See 46:9–11, for example.) God, however, has chosen to become emotionally involved with His creatures. Our emotions of love, joy, grief, anger and so on are dim reflections the Lord's holy passions, so when Holy Spirit grieves over sin, His is not a sham emotion.

The Holy Spirit was intimately involved in the crucifixion of Jesus, because Jesus "through the eternal Spirit offered Himself without blemish to God" (Heb. 9:14). Without diminishing the agony of Christ's suffering, the Spirit sustained Him throughout the whole ordeal. Since the Holy Spirit was united to the hu-man soul of Christ, He was in intimate contact with Christ's de-spair when the Father abandoned Him to bear our sin alone. If the Holy Spirit was grieved by the sins of Old Testament rebels and is now grieved by the sins of New Testament believers, how much more must He have been grieved by the sin of the world that crushed the soul of the Savior!

The moral beauty of our God appears not just in the fact that He is the only God who saves, but even more in that our salvation cost Him so much. In this respect He differs not only from the ancient gods and their modern counterparts, but also from His chief current rival, Allah. Every Surah in the Qur'an (except Surah 9) begins with the phrase, "In the name of God [Allah], the Compassionate, the Merciful." Allah offers his followers an eternal paradise of pleasure, but it does not cost him a cent. In the Muslim scheme of things, paradise must be earned: "For those who believe and work righteous deeds, there will be Gardens of Bliss" (Surah 31.8). The vaunted compassion of Allah is nothing beside the undeserved mercy of our Savior and God, Jesus Christ.

The Perfect Harmony of the Cross

Jonathan Edwards pointed out that beauty is never simple. It always involves a combination of different things, like the varied notes in a musical composition or the blended and contrasting hues in a painting. The character of Christ as He walked on earth exhibited an attractive combination of authority with humility and of sternness mixed with compassion. We see a similar harmony of divine attributes in the death of Christ:

> But God demonstrates His own love toward us, in that while we were yet sinners, Christ died for us. Much more then, having now been justified by His blood, we shall be saved from the wrath of God through Him. For if while we were enemies we were reconciled to God through the death of His Son, much more, having been reconciled, we shall be saved by His life. (Rom. 5:8–10)

In these verses the apostle Paul brings together two attributes of God which, in the minds of many, are inconsistent with each other: God's wrath and His love. Both of these divine perfections find their greatest expression in the cross.

God's holy wrath. The word "wrath" occurs six times in Romans before the verses quoted above. It is one of the major themes of the first part of the epistle. God's wrath is holy because it is the reaction of His holy nature against sin. "Your eyes are too pure to approve evil," says the prophet Habakkuk (1:13). God's hatred of sin is a result of His own purity.

It is hard for us to think of God's wrath as an aspect of His beauty because we are not normally attracted to someone who is furiously angry. Nevertheless, holy wrath is commendable because it is leveled against the right people, for the right reasons, in the right proportion, at the right time. God's character would not be beautiful if He yawned or winked at someone who enjoyed brutally killing babies. We instinctively feel God ought to lay a heavy hand on the barbaric commanders who ordered their soldiers to rape Muslim women in Bosnia, or those who issued similar orders against the Christians of southern Sudan. Similar atrocities by the strong against the weak have been practiced in all eras. God hates them. Wrath is an essential aspect of a morally beautiful character.

The cross is a revelation of how much God hates sin. Nothing but the cross provides an adequate understanding of God's attitude toward human transgressions. The greatness of Christ's suffering is the true measure of God's abhorrence of sin, because God would never have inflicted more physical and spiritual pain on His beloved Son than was absolutely necessary to provide the gift of salvation. Ponder the outpouring of God's wrath on Christ. If sin were not utterly detestable to God, Jesus would not have needed to suffer so horribly to pay its price.

God's incomprehensible love. If the cross reveals the extent of God's wrath, it even more clearly demonstrates the depth of His condescending love—the love of the Father who gave, the love of the Son who died and the love of the Spirit who grieved over the sin laid on the Son. According to Romans 5:6–8, Jesus did not die for people who already loved Him. He died for His enemies in order to make them His friends. Scripture teaches that we are born sinners, and therefore, by nature we are children of wrath (Eph. 2:3). Until God's Holy Spirit changes us, we are hostile toward God and His law (Rom. 8:6–9).

It is contrary to human nature to love our enemies; the default response of many people is to love their friends and to hate those who hate them. No other god in any religion ever loved his antagonists. Jesus taught us to love our enemies, and then He showed us how to do it.

When some modern thinkers reject Christ, they also reject the idea of loving our enemies. Sigmund Freud scathingly denounced both loving our enemies and loving our neighbors, because in his eyes they amounted to the same thing. He quoted with approval Heinrich Heine's mockery of forgiveness:

> Mine is a most peaceable disposition. My wishes are: a humble cottage with a thatched roof, but a good bed, good food, the freshest milk and butter, flowers before my window, and a few fine trees before my door; and if God wants to make my happiness complete, he will grant me the joy of seeing some six or seven of my enemies hanging from those trees. Before their death I shall, moved in my heart, forgive them all the wrong they did me in their lifetime. One must, it is true, forgive one's enemies—but not before they have been hanged.[12]

The beauty of our God appears clearly when we see how despicable and hateful we were in His holy eyes and how much He loved us while we were yet His enemies. Both characteristics appear unambiguously in one place: the cross of Christ. No other religion offers to the world such an attractive Savior.

> Beautiful Savior! Lord of the nations!
> Son of God and Son of Man!
> Glory and honor, praise, adoration
> Now and forever more be Thine.[13]

If faith be an instrument, it is more properly the instrument by which we receive Christ, than the instrument by which we receive justification.

[Justifying faith] is that by which the soul, which before was separate and alienated from Christ, unites itself to Him.

God does not give those that believe an union with or an interest in the Saviour as a reward for faith, but only because faith is the soul's active uniting with Christ, or is itself the very act of union, *on their part*.

God will neither look on Christ's merits as ours, nor adjudge His benefits to us, till we be in Christ: nor will He look upon us as being in Him, without an active unition of our hearts and souls to Him.

—Jonathan Edwards

6 What Did Jesus' Dying on the Cross Achieve?

Once upon a time a man had twin sons named Bart and Brent. Brent was sweet and simple, but his brother was dark and devious. Bart broke the cookie jar and blamed his innocent brother. Their gullible father believed Bart and spanked his obedient son. This success encouraged Black Bart so much that the break-and-blame routine became a regular facet of his weekly entertainment schedule, and his behavior grew increasingly worse.

In this story the Christian may see an ugly parody of Christ's substitutionary atonement, but to inquisitive non-Christians or the enemies of Christ, this tale may appear to be a true parable of one of Christianity's central dogmas. People who conclude this think it ridiculous that one man could justly be punished for the sins of another; and even if Jesus was, wouldn't that encourage worse offenses from those He meant to save? For this reason, non-Christians find the doctrine of the cross as offensive now as they did in the first century. Before we look at a biblical response to these charges, we need to bring these criticisms into sharper focus.

Objections to Substitutionary Atonement

The substitutionary atonement of Christ is intimately connected to the doctrine of justification by faith alone. If Christ's death does not cover the debt of sin, then sinners must earn their own way to heaven. Conversely, if sinners are unable to pay for their own ticket, then salvation must be based on the grace of God. As we shall see, salvation through faith in the death of Christ preserves both the graciousness of salvation and the justice of God. Most objections to Christ's bearing the punishment for the sins of believing sinners can be grouped under four headings:

Substitutionary atonement is immoral. A judge cannot justly punish anyone for sins he did not commit, so the argument goes, nor is it right to let criminals off scot-free. In the 1970s Ted Bundy raped and murdered at least three dozen young women in various states across the country. Shortly before his execution, Bundy made a profession of faith in Jesus Christ. If his conversion was genuine, then according to the Bible he will spend eternity with God in heaven. In addition, a number of his victims were presumably unconverted and will, therefore, end up in hell. Finally, Jesus, who took the rap for Ted Bundy's crimes, was completely innocent. To many people this whole transaction appears to be downright immoral.

Justification by faith is individualistic. If salvation comes through my personal faith in the death and resurrection of Christ, then it is just a matter between Jesus and me. I don't need the church, and I sure don't need other Christians. In fact, I can be a better Christian without them. The Lord and I can have a great time together out on the lake or by a trout stream where I won't be bothered by all those hypocrites who act like the devil on Saturday night but sound so pious on Sunday morning.

Since a number of professing believers regularly echo such sentiments, the unbelieving world may be pardoned for thinking they are organically connected to the doctrine of salvation by faith alone. Evangelical preachers do not help matters much when they persistently maintain that going to church saves no one. While the statement is true as it stands, evangelicals need to listen more carefully to the voice of the ancient church. According to Cyprian (ca. AD 200–258), "You cannot have God for your Father, unless you have the church for your Mother."[1] While many evangelicals might brush this off as the words of a proto-Catholic, they need to remember the Protestant reformers taught the same thing.[2]

The whole scheme is irresponsible. What will happen if people believe all their sins—past, present and future—are already forgiven? Why should they bother trying to keep God's commandments if it will not make any difference in their eternal destiny? Isn't it irresponsible for a preacher to offer his congregation a Get out of Jail Free card that is good for an unlimited number of uses?

This charge is as old as the Bible, for the apostle Paul had to answer those who "slanderously reported" that Christians taught "Let us do evil that good may come." His contemptuous retort was, "Their condemnation is just" (Rom. 3:8).

The salvation offered is inadequate. It is shallow and not intrinsically appealing. The evangelist tells the inquirer to "pray the sinner's prayer" so he can go to heaven. Then the traveling preacher packs up his bags and boards his big bus adorned with the slogan "Brother Billy Bob's Preaching, Healing, Musical and Prophetic Ministry." As the bus rolls out of the parking lot, the puzzled convert wonders, *What next? I'm saved and headed for heaven, right? Heaven is surely better than hell, but what is so great about sitting on a cloud and playing a harp all day long? Is there any real connection between receiving Christ now and what I can expect once I pass the pearly gates? This whole business seems rather shallow—receive Christ, be forgiven, go to heaven. Is that all there is to it?* For all but a few—perhaps professional harpists—such a depiction of heaven sounds unbelievably boring. For the (probably) larger number who cringe at church music, playing a harp forever is only marginally more appealing than roasting in eternal fire.

The Key that Solves the Puzzle—Union with Christ

The key to understanding how Christ's death saves His people is the New Testament doctrine of union with Christ. Consider four aspects of that union:

First, Christ has a *natural* union with His people. This union was produced by Jesus' supernatural conception and His natural human birth. God became a man to save lost men and women:

> Therefore, since the children share in flesh and blood, He Himself likewise also partook of the same, that through death He might render powerless him who had the power of death, that is, the devil, and might free those who through fear of death were subject to slavery all their lives. For assuredly He does not give help to angels, but He gives help to the descendant of Abraham. Therefore He had to be made like His brethren in all things. (Heb. 2:14–17)

Jesus Christ took on a human nature in such a way that He became a blood relative of every man, woman and child who has ever been born. Although in the Old Testament the preincarnate Son of God occasionally appeared as the angel of the Lord, it is not at all clear that He could have died for even one of the fallen angels.[3] The reason is that each angel is apparently a separate creation of God. Angels were present when God made our world (Job 38:4–7), so they are not people who have died and gone to heaven as popular movies sometimes suggest. Jesus said the angels in heaven do not marry (Matt. 22:30), so there are no angelic families with papa angels, mamma angels and little baby angels. Therefore, Jesus could not have entered into the same kind of union with the angels as He did with the human family. It was appropriate for Him to die for His human relatives because He was able to suffer a human penalty to pay for human sins.

Second, Christ has a *representative* union with His people. We elect men and women to represent us in Congress or on a local school board, but some representatives are not elected. For example, a governor may appoint someone to fill the unexpired term of a congressman who has died or resigned. Jesus Christ is the representative for His people before the judgment seat of God, but He was not elected by a popular vote of humanity; He was chosen and appointed by God to be our high priest.

> Christ did not glorify Himself so as to become a high priest, but He who said to Him, "You are My Son, today I have begotten You". . . says also in another passage, "You are a priest forever according to the order of Melchizedek." (Heb. 5:5–6)

According to the Bible, the primary tasks of a priest were to offer sacrifices and to pray for the people he represented. The old covenant priests did not offer sacrifices and pray on behalf of the Aborigines in Australia or the Aleuts of Alaska. They only represented the nation of Israel, so it is natural to ask, "When God appointed Christ to be a priest, whom was He supposed to represent?"

Several times in the Gospel of John, Jesus refers to certain people whom God the Father has given Him. They alone will come to Him, believe in Him and receive eternal life (John 6:37–44). As the good Shepherd, Jesus says that He will lay down His life for the sheep God has given Him, but that some of those listening to Him are not His sheep (John 10:11–18, 24–30). These texts help us to understand the priestly imagery in the book of Hebrews. Jesus Christ is both the priest and the sacrificial offering (Heb. 9:11–12), and He offered His blood specifically for the people God gave Him.

John's Gospel also shows us the Lord Jesus praying for this same group. On the night before His crucifixion, He poured out His heart to God for the preservation of His people. "I ask on their behalf; I do not ask on behalf of the world, but of those whom You have given Me; for they are Yours. . . . I do not ask on behalf of these alone [the eleven apostles], but for those also who believe in Me through their word" (John 17:9, 20).

Jesus' prayer in John 17 was not a one-time event; it is a sample of what He is doing now in heaven. "The former priests, on the one hand, existed in greater numbers because they were prevented by death from continuing, but Jesus, on the other hand, because He continues forever, holds His priesthood permanently. Therefore He is able also to save forever those who draw near to God through Him, since He always lives to make intercession for them" (Heb. 7:23–25). Jesus only prays for "those who draw near to God through Him."

Christ's representative union with the people He saves is much closer than His natural union with all human beings. As a high priest appointed by God, Christ offered Himself as a sacrifice for a specific group of people and He continues to pray for the people God gave to Him.

Third, Christ has a *voluntary* union with His people. Jesus and His people have willingly entered into a loving union of marriage. First, consider Christ's voluntary union with His bride. He is the heavenly husband who "gave Himself up for her, so that . . . He might present to Himself the church in all her glory, having no spot or wrinkle or any such thing" (Eph. 5:25–27). Jesus did not have to be forced to die for us. People in love willingly bear any burden for each other. Jacob left his home to seek a wife. When he found her, "Jacob served seven years for Rachel and they seemed to him but a few days because of his love for her" (Gen. 29:20). In the same way, Jesus left the glory of His heavenly home and took on the form of a servant in order to win a bride for Himself. When He faced the suffering of the cross, He was sustained by "the joy set before Him" (Heb. 12:2), not only the joy of pleasing His Father but also the joy of an eternal love relationship with His bride, His redeemed people.

Although Jesus initiated the voluntary union with His bride—as in traditional circles a man takes the initiative to woo the young lady whom he wishes to marry—the individual members of Christ's bride must say their "I dos" and "I wills" in order for the marriage to be finalized. This is the function of faith, which the Bible identifies as coming to Christ and receiving Him (John 1:12; 6:35). Individual faith in Christ thus completes our voluntary union with Christ.

Before the days of prenuptial agreements, most husbands and wives rightly assumed they would share all their property and all their debts. Therefore, one of the traditional vows while exchanging rings includes the phrase "and with all my earthly goods I thee endow." In a similar fashion Christ assumed the spiritual debts of His people on the cross. When we receive Him as our heavenly Husband and Savior, He shares with us the riches of His righteous standing before God's law.

Fourth, Christ has a *spiritual* union with His people. Just as the wedding vows of a couple lead to the one-flesh union of marriage, so the Christian's voluntary union with Christ leads to a deeper spiritual oneness with Him: "He who loves his own wife loves himself; for no one ever hated his own flesh, but nourishes and cherishes it, just as Christ also does the church, because we are members of His body" (Eph. 5:28–30).

A person becomes a member of the body of Christ when he receives the Holy Spirit at conversion. "For by one Spirit we were all baptized into one body, whether Jews or Greeks, whether slaves or free, and we were all made to drink of one Spirit" (1 Cor. 12:13).[4]

How does a person receive the Spirit of God? According to Galatians 3:1–14, faith is both the means by which one is justified (counted righteous) and the means by which one receives the Holy Spirit. So a believer's voluntary union with Christ through faith leads both to righteousness and to the gift of the Spirit.

The spiritual union of believers with Christ through His Spirit is closer than the relationship between brothers or even between a man and his wife. A living union between two members of the same body makes it possible for one member to suffer for the faults of another. As the Puritan preacher John Owen quaintly notes, "The back may answer for what the hand takes away."[5] If a young child grabs another child's toy, his mother may spank his hand. A year or two later his backside may feel the paddle for a similar offense because it is capable of enduring a harsher punishment than the hand. A child's bottom will not cry out, "I never touched that toy! The hand did it!" In the same way, Jesus is so closely united to His own people He was able justly to bear the penalty they could never pay.

But now a further question arises. Since believers do not receive the Spirit of Christ and become members of the body of Christ until they come to Christ, how can their spiritual union with Christ form any part of the rationale for Christ's dying for their sins? God was looking forward to this union when He laid the sins of His elect on Christ. It was fitting in God's sight to punish the Head for the sins of the body that Christ was going to join to Himself.

The Beauty of Substitutionary Atonement

Union with Christ protects both the justice and mercy of God. The substitutionary death of Christ and justification by faith alone are incredibly gracious, perfectly just, morally empowering and spiritually satisfying. Jonathan Edwards defines beauty as an agreement of different things that together produce symmetry, proportion and harmony. The Bible's scheme of salvation is all that, and therefore, it truly deserves to be called beautiful.

If you have watched either the older westerns or a recent newscast about some country in crisis, you know that when the bad guys rule the roost, a society becomes unstable, unhappy, unjust and downright ugly. Justice is as needful for a beautiful commonwealth as harmony and rhythm are for a Mozart concerto. But justice by itself can be a hard, cold affair. Therefore, although justice is necessary, it is not sufficient for beauty in the kingdom of God; mercy is also needed. Is it possible to have one without diminishing the other? Can God truly be "just and the justifier of the one who has faith in Jesus" (Rom. 3:26)? Can He forgive sins and yet maintain the justice of His kingdom?

The New Testament teaches that no one is "justified by the works of the Law but through faith in Christ Jesus" (Gal. 2:16) and "a man is justified by faith apart from works of the Law" (Rom. 3:28). As the Protestant Reformers strenuously insisted, the verb "to justify" means "to declare righteous." God does not make us righteous in character through faith; He counts or considers us righteous because of the righteousness of Christ (Phil. 3:8–9).

How can Christ's righteousness be reckoned to the sinner's account? The answer comes in two parts. First, in view of their four-fold union with Christ detailed above, God laid the sins of Christ's people on Jesus. "He Himself bore our sins in His body on the cross" (1 Pet. 2:24); and God "made Him who knew no sin to be sin on our behalf" (2 Cor. 5:21). However, that union is not complete until sinners believe in Christ. Therefore, God waits and does not impute Christ's righteousness to individuals or declare them righteous until faith is present. For that reason, believers are "justified by faith" (Rom. 5:1). Since those the Father gave to His Son were already engaged to Christ, He paid their debt of sin but they cannot draw on the bank account of His righteousness until by faith they say, "I do," and their marriage to Him is complete.

This is the answer to the charge that salvation by faith is immoral on God's part. God is not unjust when He shows mercy to the most wicked sinner who savingly trusts in Christ because that sinner has entered into a deep, living and eternal union with the Son of God. Such a union makes it both just and merciful for Christ to bear the believing sinner's punishment.

Union with Christ promotes the unity of the church. When God saves sinners through faith in Christ, He has no intention of creating a loose conglomeration of isolated individuals. The whole New Testament stands opposed to the "Lone Ranger" mentality.

> [Be] diligent to preserve the unity of the Spirit in the bond of peace. There is one body and one Spirit, just as also you were called in one hope of your calling; one Lord, one faith, one baptism, one God and Father of all who is over all and through all and in all. (Eph. 4:3–6)

It is fashionable today to lament the fragmentation of the

church and to seek organizational union based on the lowest common doctrinal denominator. What believers ought to be doing instead is celebrating the true spiritual union God has already created. I do not need to set aside my Baptist distinctives in order to have stimulating, soul-strengthening fellowship with Bible-believing Presbyterians, Methodists and Lutherans. By placing His Holy Spirit in them, God has created a spiritual unity between all believers and His Son. This unity exists right now; believers do not create it. All they can do is to maintain it by loving and serving their brothers and sisters in Christ no matter what denomination or style of worship they may prefer. This kind of oneness can withstand vigorous debate over doctrinal differences which do not touch the core of faith as expressed in the ancient ecumenical creeds of the first five centuries.

When sinners are justified by God, they may come into the body of Christ with a very individualistic outlook on life. They may want to be isolated from other people and even from other believers. God, however, will not leave them alone. His Holy Spirit, who indwells them, nudges and prods them. He woos and draws God's people into fellowship with other believers. When people come to Christ, they bring with them their touchiness, self-centeredness, pride and an insistence that others meet their needs, but the Holy Spirit will not let them alone. He continues to fight against those harmful attitudes and to give believers a hunger for life together in the family of God.

This is the answer to the charge that salvation by faith in Christ is too individualistic. The very union with Christ that makes it possible for God to justify sinners also brings them into a spiritual union with the whole church of God. Those who have enjoyed loving fellowship and joyous worship in the church of Christ know it is a beautiful thing. Although some believers shy away from other Christians because of past hurts, God graciously and gently draws them back toward the fellowship of the church. If they continue to stay away, they do so in spite of their justification by faith, not because of it.

Union with Christ ensures the pursuit of holiness. A Christian is someone whose direction in life has been changed by the new birth. Because the Holy Spirit has caused him to be born again, he desires to obey God, and his heart is wretched when he disobeys his heavenly Father.

The Protestant reformers rightly insisted that we are justified by faith alone, but justifying faith is never alone. Some movement toward holiness of life always accompanies saving faith. However, the reason for the connection between faith and holiness is not always clear. We often hear, for example, that repentance is part of saving faith and that the truly repentant person will want to be holy. If nothing more is said, we are left with the mistaken impression that the quality of one's repentance is what ensures the pursuit of holiness. The missing element in this explanation is the work of the Holy Spirit.

Jesus told Nicodemus, "You must be born again," that is, "born of the Spirit" (John 3:5–7). Jesus did not command him to get himself reborn, because the new birth is not "of blood nor of the will of the flesh nor of the will of man, but of God" (1:13). There was nothing Nicodemus could do to produce the new birth in himself. Jesus was not giving instructions on how to be born again; He was providing Nicodemus with a diagnosis of his problem. Nicodemus did not "understand these things" (3:10); he did not "accept [Christ's] testimony" (3:11); he did not "believe" (3:12). He had never been born again, and until that happened he would never understand, accept and believe Christ. Consequently, the new birth is not God's *response* to our faith. Instead, our faith is a result of being born of the Spirit. God commands us to believe in Christ, and that is an entirely reasonable command; but we will never do it until God transforms our stony hearts by the secret working of His Spirit.

An impulse toward holiness flows from a twofold work of the Holy Spirit. First, the secret regenerating work of the Holy Spirit prompts a believer's acts of repentance and faith so that his repentance contains within it the seeds of the Spirit's holiness.

What He creates in believers bears some likeness to Himself.

Second, through faith believers receive the Holy Spirit as the Spirit of adoption into God's family (Gal. 3:14; 4:4–7). When the Spirit enters into the hearts of God's children, He begins to lead and energize them in their life-long struggle against sin in their own lives. "If you are living according to the flesh, you are going to die; but if by the Spirit you are putting to death the deeds of the body, you will live. For all who are being led by the Spirit of God, these are sons of God. For you have not received a spirit of slavery leading to fear again, but you have received the Spirit of adoption as sons by which we cry out, 'Abba! Father!'" (Rom. 8:13–15, marg.). Since the impulse toward holiness is an ongoing process, it is no surprise that Christians often exhibit symptoms of worldliness. Still, believers can take heart from the fact that "He who began a good work in you will perfect it until the day of Jesus Christ" (Phil. 1:6).

This is the answer to the charge that salvation by faith alone is irresponsible. Free forgiveness through Christ does not lead to a wild, sensual, careless life, so those who abuse the grace of God in this way give clear evidence that they have never been born again. Their faith is a fleshly convenience, not a supernatural conviction. The Spirit of Christ leads the people of Christ, not simply by hounding them with guilt—which even the unconverted experience—but by giving them a love for Christ and a consequent desire to be like their blessed Redeemer.

Love for Christ is a far more beautiful and effective motivation for holiness than guilt or a self-sacrificing sense of duty can ever be. If you are a child of God and you are concerned about your sins, the best thing you can do is to stop beating yourself up with guilt and to start looking at Jesus. Read the Gospels. Meditate on the cross and the resurrection. Ask the Father to deepen your love for the Savior, and greater holiness will inevitably follow.

Union with Christ stimulates a hope of future glory. On the night before His death, Jesus prayed for all His disciples throughout all time:

> The glory which You have given Me I have given to them, that they may be one, just as We are one; I in them and You in Me, that they may be perfected in unity, so that the world may know that You sent Me, and loved them, even as You have loved Me. Father, I desire that they also, whom You have given Me, be with Me where I am, so that they may see My glory which You have given Me, for You loved Me before the foundation of the world. (John 17:22–24)

These few words give us our most intimate insight into the future destiny of the saved. Beyond the gardens and the golden streets, beyond the crowns and thrones, beyond reunion with loved ones, there will be a glorious union with the triune God. He will somehow take us up into His own life. This is the goal God had in mind when He sent His Son to die for sinners.

Union with God will not mean the loss of one's individuality and personality. Philosophical Hinduism may speak about one's little drop of water being dissolved in the great ocean of Being, but that is not a biblical ideal. Neither does union with God entail the extinction of all desires, as philosophical Buddhism seeks to attain. The Buddhist says that unfulfilled desire makes people unhappy, so his goal is to extinguish desire. He hopes in this way to produce a calm, unruffled response to the disappointments of life. But more than that, the Buddhist looks forward to the extinction of all desire after death.

The Bible paints a far different picture. As long as a believer lives in a mortal body he will need to deny himself in order to follow Christ, but in heaven the believer's desires will not wither. They will explode with unimaginable intensity, and along with the surge of one's desires will come their unbelievably intense satisfaction. God Himself will be the believer's desire, and God Himself will be the satisfaction of believers' desires. One of the biblical images of eternal glory is the one-flesh experience of marriage. Sex at its best will pale beside the thrill of union with God.

This is the answer to the charge that salvation by faith in Christ is inadequate, shallow and superficial. Union with Christ is the beginning, middle and end of faith. Believers have been drawn by the beauty of Christ to trust in Him, so they have entered into a voluntary union with the Savior. The Holy Spirit has united Himself to believers' souls and entices them day by day to imitate the beautiful life of their Savior. Believers look forward to the ultimate consummation of union with Christ when they shall see, share and be filled with delight in His beauty forever.

From my childhood up, my mind had been full of objections against the doctrine of God's sovereignty, in choosing whom He would to eternal life; and rejecting whom He pleased; leaving them eternally to perish, and be everlastingly tormented in hell. It used to appear like a horrible doctrine to me. But I remember the time very well when I seemed to be convinced, and fully satisfied, as to this sovereignty of God, and His justice in thus eternally disposing of men, according to His sovereign pleasure. But never could give an account how, or by what means, I was thus convinced, not in the least imagining at the time, nor a long time after, that there was any extraordinary influence of God's Spirit in it; but only that now I saw further, and my reason apprehended the justice and reasonableness of it. However, my mind rested in it; and it put an end to all those cavils and objections. And there has been a wonderful alteration in my mind, with respect to the doctrine of God's sovereignty, from that day to this; so that I scarce ever have found so much as the rising of an objection against it, in the most absolute sense, in God showing mercy to whom He will show mercy, and hardening whom He will. God's absolute sovereignty and justice, with respect to salvation and damnation, is what my mind seems to rest assured of, as much as of any thing that I see with my eyes; at least it is so at times. But I have often, since that first conviction, had quite another kind of sense of God's sovereignty than I had then. I have often since had not only a conviction, but a delightful conviction. The doctrine has often appeared exceedingly pleasant, bright, and sweet. Absolute sovereignty is what I love to ascribe to God. But my first conviction was not so.

—Jonathan Edwards

7 How Can Predestination Be Fair?

Seeing the beauty of predestination depends on having a clear sense of the desperate and helpless condition into which we all were born. Those who lack such a sense put their trust in human goodness, or at least in human ability to repent. Belief in human goodness makes predestination seem unnecessary, because it assumes we can all come to God on our own. It makes predestination seem unfair, because it believes that all good creatures have an equal claim on their Creator's generosity. But predestination only shines with true brilliance and beauty in the light of the utter darkness of human rebellion.

Like Jonathan Edwards, I initially rebelled against several implications of predestination—the doctrine that God chose before the foundation of the world whom He would save and who would be allowed to perish in their sins. Predestination probably runs neck and neck with the doctrine of hell in the minds of those who find Christianity unattractive. Perhaps it is the most despised doctrine in the world, because many Christians who firmly believe in the unending torment of the lost also loathe predestination with a vigor equal to that of the atheist and agnostic.

At one time my wife and I were looking for a church to attend. One of the places we visited had no pastor at the time, so I asked to speak to an elder. When I questioned him regarding the church's position on predestination, he replied vehemently,

"Oh, we don't believe in *that!*" At the time I thought it a rather ignorant statement from a church leader who professed to believe the Bible. The word "predestined" occurs several times in the New Testament; though Christians may have differing opinions on what the word means, they ought never to deny the doctrine outright. Nevertheless, there is great antipathy, even in Christian circles, to the absolute sovereignty of God in salvation.

It is impossible to see the attractiveness of predestination apart from a thoroughly biblical view of the condition of humanity. One cannot appreciate the remedy without understanding the disease. Human depravity is not a very popular doctrine. If man's inhumanity to man in North Korea, Myanmar, Sudan, Rwanda and a dozen only slightly less infamous places has not convinced you something beyond poor education and poverty is amiss, I probably will not be able to do so either. However, if our situation is as desperate as the Bible says it is, predestination is not unfair, but rather is truly beautiful. If God's sovereignty in salvation seems like a difficult doctrine, I encourage you to set aside your disbelief for a while in order to look at the Bible's answer in terms of its own analysis of our universal problem.

The Depth of Our Depravity

When theologians speak about the total depravity of the human race, they do not mean we are all as bad as we could be. After all, we could easily become worse than we currently are. Nor do they mean everything human is sordid and contemptible. A godlike strength and beauty still cling to us even in our fallen condition, for God has made us in His own image. Our problem is that every part of our being is fatally flawed.

Think of a fatal flaw this way: If you saw a car with four bald tires, two broken headlights and a sloppy steering linkage traveling ninety miles an hour in the dark on a curvy, icy road, you could be fairly sure it was headed for trouble. However, suppose a man has a shiny new car with just a little leak in the fuel line and a little electrical short causing a little spark near the escaping gasoline. The driver might not notice such small problems, but together they constitute a fatal flaw.

In the same way, it is clear a drug-addicted robber and murderer is in bad trouble now and probably headed for something worse after death. But many people are not aware of the fatal flaws in their lives, the problems hidden under the hood that can cause a deadly crash. The doctrine of total depravity teaches that every system in the car of our lives has a fatal flaw. Our electrical systems, our brakes, our fuel systems, our steering systems—there is a fatal flaw in each of them. Our mind, emotion, will and body are all affected. What are these fatal flaws?

We are born without spiritual life. We all have natural life. Most of us can walk and talk. We can all breathe. We think, feel and make decisions. According to the Bible, our bodies will die, but they will be raised again and be reunited with our immortal souls to experience either a resurrection of life or a resurrection of judgment (John 5:24–29). The life of the body and soul which all human beings possess is our natural life. This life is created and sustained by the Spirit of God (Job 33:4; Ps. 104:27–30).

There is another kind of life that involves a more intimate connection of our souls with the Holy Spirit. The letter of the law kills, says the apostle Paul, "but the Spirit gives life" (2 Cor. 3:6). The life he then describes is one of moral transformation by the Spirit, a life thrilled by the glory of Christ and a life of triumph in the midst of weakness. According to the Bible, we do not have that kind of life when we are born: "And you were dead in your trespasses and sins, in which you formerly walked according to the course of this world, according to the prince of the power of the air, of the spirit that is now working in the sons of disobedience. Among them we too all formerly lived in the lusts of our flesh, indulging the desires of the flesh and of the mind, and were by nature children of wrath, even as the rest" (Eph. 2:1–3).

Our natural life is a gift of God, but when we are born, we are spiritually dead, and the wrath of God hangs over our heads like the sword suspended by a single horsehair over the head of Damocles.

We live in spiritual darkness. The Bible teaches that in our natural state we are like blind fish that live in the darkness of deep underground caverns. However, unlike those fish, we are engulfed in a divine radiance, a spiritual light we are unable to see. "And even if our gospel is veiled, it is veiled to those who are perishing, in whose case the god of this world has blinded the minds of the unbelieving so that they might not see the light of the gospel of the glory of Christ, who is the image of God" (2 Cor. 4:3–4).

This blindness darkens the mind and emotions. Those who are spiritually blind yet well-instructed may be able to explain the gospel, but it does not make sense to them. It does not grip them, nor are they attracted by it. The gospel is neither emotionally nor intellectually compelling.

Such people can see other kinds of truth with the eyes of their minds. They can see that honesty is the best policy and that criminals ought to be punished. Mathematics, music or the musings of their favorite sports commentator may be fascinating to them, but they are spiritually blind. Children who are raised in Christian homes may be able to spout off the gospel as easily as they can sing along with their favorite TV commercial—but even those children are blind until God shines the light into their hearts. "For God, who said, 'Light shall shine out of darkness,' is the One who has shone in our hearts to give the Light of the knowledge of the glory of God in the face of Christ" (4:6).

We cannot do spiritual good. The Bible clearly teaches that no one is able to do anything to please God apart from the gracious work of God in his heart because we are by nature hostile to God:

> "There is none righteous, not even one; there is none who understands, there is none who seeks for God; all have turned aside, together they have become useless; there is none who does good, there is not even one." (Rom. 3:10–12)

For the mind set on the flesh is death, but the mind set on the Spirit is life and peace, because the mind set on the flesh is hostile toward God; for it does not subject itself to the law of God, for it is not even able to do so, and those who are in the flesh cannot please God. (8:6–8)

People in various religions or with no religious convictions at all can be good parents, good neighbors and good workers. They can be active in alleviating human suffering in Africa, Pakistan or Indonesia. This natural human goodness does not count as true spiritual goodness because natural goodness, even at its best, has a fatal limitation.[1]

Jesus commanded His followers to love their enemies. Then He added, "For if you love those who love you, what reward do you have? Do not even the tax collectors do the same? If you greet only your brothers, what more are you doing than others? Do not even the Gentiles do the same?" (Matt. 5:46–47). Limited benevolence is not virtuous. For example, if a woman loves her own children but despises all the other children in the neighborhood, her love toward her own children is not virtuous. Universal benevolence must include people who are mean and nasty, as well as friends and family.

In addition, universal benevolence must include God as well as people. Since God is the greatest Being, no one can claim to be good who loves everyone except Him. For that reason Jesus said loving God with all our heart, soul and mind is the greatest commandment; loving our neighbors is the second (22:35–40). Kind actions that spring from love for our neighbors are not spiritually virtuous unless they also spring from whole-hearted love for God. Benevolence and delight are both included in love for God. Virtuous benevolence toward God desires that God be glorified and His will be done (Ps. 96:7–10). Virtuous delight in God desires the nearness of God more than it desires any earthly good (73:25–28). By this measure the motivation behind our best good deeds is woefully limited and fatally flawed.

We are incapable of spiritually seeking God. Many non-Christian people are very religious. When the apostle Paul visited Athens, he said to the Athenians, "I observe that you are very religious in all respects" (Acts 17:22). In another place he describes his Jewish brethren as people who have "a zeal for God, but not in accordance with knowledge" (Rom. 10:2). However, in spite of the obvious passion with which many pursue their religion, Scripture declares, "There is none who understands, there is none who seeks for God" (3:11). The reason people refuse to seek God is that they do not like Him, for "the mind set on the flesh is hostile toward God" (8:7). The natural man may acknowledge that the Ten Commandments are good, but for himself he would like one or two of them to be set aside. When he seems to be seeking the true God, he is actually seeking a false god more congenial to his own inclinations.

The cumulative effect of these fatal flaws of the natural man leads to his inability to accept the cure God offers for his sinful condition.

We are unable to come to Christ in a spiritual fashion. The Bible is filled with gracious invitations to come to the Lord and be saved:

> Ho! Every one who thirsts, come to the waters;
>   And you who have no money come, buy and eat.
>   Come, buy wine and milk
>   Without money and without cost.
>
> (Isa. 55:1)

> Come to Me, all who are weary and heavy-laden, and I will give you rest. (Matt. 11:28)

> The Spirit and the bride say, "Come." And let the one who hears say, "Come." And let the one who is thirsty come; let the one who wishes take the water of life without cost. (Rev. 22:17)

The assumption most people make when they read these exhortations is that if God commands us to do something, we must be able to do it. However, Jesus said, "No one can come to Me unless the Father who sent Me draws him; and I will raise Him up at the last day" (John 6:44).

The natural man or woman may ask, "Does God command me to come to Christ and then tell me I cannot do it? It's as if He commanded me to fly like a bird but didn't give me wings."

Quite the contrary is true. The unconverted person is like a rebellious son who refuses to come into the house when his mother calls. He is so stubborn and antagonistic that he has made a general rule for himself: *Whenever my mother calls, that is exactly when I will not go inside. I may go before she calls, or I may wait until after she is exhausted and has given up. I will go in when it pleases me, but I will not give her the satisfaction of my obedience.* This boy has ears and he has legs. He has a natural ability to respond when his mother calls, but he has hardened himself to such an extent that he has a moral inability to hear and obey.

So it is with all of us when we come into this world from our mothers' wombs. Unless God Himself softens our hearts, we will not respond to His gracious invitation to come to Christ for rest and salvation. The prophet Jeremiah described it this way: "Can the Ethiopian change his skin or the leopard his spots? Then you also can do good who are accustomed to do evil" (Jer. 13:23).

This is how the Bible describes the human condition. We are stubborn, rebellious and morally helpless to change ourselves. Against such a background, the doctrine of predestination begins to appear in a favorable light. If we have no natural desire to choose Christ, the only way we can be saved is for God to choose us. If God supernaturally softens our stubborn hearts, we will come to Christ, but not otherwise. In order to see the true beauty of predestination, it is necessary to understand more clearly the doctrine of unconditional election.

The Meaning of Unconditional Election

All the common English translations of the Bible, except for the free paraphrase versions, use the words "elect" or "election" several times to translate the Greek words *eklegō*, *eklektos* and *eklogē*. In some cases the translators have preferred "chosen" and "choice" to "elect" and "election" because that is what the Greek words mean.

The elect were chosen out of a larger number. Election in the New Testament is not like elections in some clubs and churches. Frequently only one candidate is running for an office, so there is hardly any choice—except to cast a negative ballot, which no one ever does. The Greek words translated "elect" or "chosen" contain a preposition meaning "out of," and the words clearly carry that sense. For example, consider the following statements of Christ:

> Many are called, but few are chosen. (Matt. 22:14)

> If you were of the world, the world would love its own; but because you are not of the world, but I chose you out of the world, because of this the world hates you. (John 15:19)

In both cases the ones chosen, or elected, were chosen *out of* a larger group of people.

The elect were not chosen on the basis of foreseen faith or goodness. One common mistake is to say that before the foundation of the world, God looked down through the ages of time, and when He saw someone who was going to believe in Jesus, He chose to save that one.[2] The error may arise from a superficial reading of two New Testament texts. Peter addresses his first epistle to people who were "chosen according to the foreknowledge of God" (1 Pet. 1:1–2). Paul says those whom God "foreknew, He also predestined to become conformed to the image of His Son" (Rom. 8:29). It is possible to expose the error of foreseen faith in several ways.

First, Scripture does not leave us in any doubt of what God actually foresaw when He looked down at the whole of human history. "The Lord has looked down from heaven upon the sons of men to see if there are any who understand, who seek after

God. They have all turned aside, together they have become corrupt; there is no one who does good, not even one" (Ps. 14:2–3). The Lord did not see any sincere seekers who would freely choose to trust in His Son. He saw only a mass of rebels who deserved condemnation. God's foresight of universal rebellion led Him to choose to save some, rather than to allow all to perish.

Second, it would be foolish to say that God saw only what *we* would do and not what *He* would do when He looked down through history. Did God have plans of His own, or was He utterly dependent upon watching us to see how His creation would turn out? The Bible clearly teaches that God knows what will come to pass because He has already planned what He will do in the future:

> Remember the former things long past,
>   For I am God, and there is no other;
>   I am God, and there is no one like Me,
> Declaring the end from the beginning,
>   And from ancient times things which have not
>   been done,
>   Saying, "My purpose will be established,
>   And I will accomplish all My good pleasure;"
> Calling a bird of prey from the east,
>   The man of My purpose from a far country.
>   Truly I have spoken; truly I will bring it to pass.
>   I have planned it, surely I will do it.
>
> (Isa. 46:9–11)

Third, we should not say God based His election on foreseen faith because the biblical term "foreknowledge" does not mean a bare observation of future events. After addressing those who were "chosen according to the foreknowledge of God the Father," Peter writes that Christ was "foreknown before the foundation of the world" (1 Pet. 1:1–2, 19–20). In the first instance he uses a noun, in the second a verb, but the Greek root is the same.[3] God did not simply foresee that His Son would die at the hands of wicked men. One of the first public prayers in the early church acknowledged that "Herod and Pontius Pilate, along with the Gentiles and the peoples of Israel [were gathered together] to do whatever Your hand and Your purpose predestined to occur" (Acts 4:27–28). God foreknew Christ; He determined in advance to send His Son to the cross. So Peter's phrase "chosen according to the foreknowledge of God" means that we are chosen according to the loving predetermination of God.

Finally, the apostle Paul uses the example of Jacob and Esau to illustrate the fact that God did not choose people on the basis of foreseen faith or good works. "And not only this, but there was Rebekah also, when she had conceived twins by one man, our father Isaac; for though the twins were not yet born and had not done anything good or bad, so that God's purpose according to His choice would stand, not because of works but because of Him who calls, it was said to her, "The older will serve the younger." Just as it is written, "Jacob I loved, but Esau I hated" (Rom. 9:10–13).

God did not choose Jacob because he would prove to be a better man than his brother Esau. He chose Jacob because He is the sovereign God who does what He pleases to do. This is the meaning of unconditional election: God did not foresee any conditions—whether faith or good works—in His elect people that caused Him to choose them.

God chose His elect individually, not just as members of a group. Some have argued that in Romans 9 Jacob and Esau represent nations—specifically the Israelites and Edomites. They say God elects groups, not individuals. According to this view, when God "chose us in [Christ] before the foundation of the world" (Eph. 1:4), He did not have any individuals specifically in mind. He simply chose for salvation all who would subsequently come into union with Christ through faith. There are several problems with the idea of corporate election.

First, although Jacob and Esau do represent, respectively, a favored and a rejected nation, they were also individuals. In their case individual election and corporate election are combined. Moreover, the apostle Paul's next example in Romans 9 clearly involves an individual—Pharaoh:

> For the Scripture says to Pharaoh, "For this very purpose I raised you up, to demonstrate My power in you, and that My name might be proclaimed throughout the whole earth." So then He has mercy on whom He desires, and He hardens whom He desires. (9:17–18)

Second, if God did not elect individuals, He chose a null set, an empty category. However the Scripture says, "He chose us in [Christ] before the foundation of the world" (Eph. 1:4). He did not choose Christ alone as the empty vessel of salvation; He chose certain individuals to be placed in Him.

Third, other passages confirm the individual nature of election. The preaching of Paul and Barnabas in Pisidian Antioch angered many Jews, but "When the Gentiles heard this, they began rejoicing and glorifying the word of the Lord; and as many as had been appointed to eternal life believed" (Acts 13:48). The only ones who responded to the gospel with faith were those whom God had appointed to eternal life.

Or consider Second Thessalonians 2:13–14: "But we should always give thanks to God for you, brethren beloved by the Lord, because God has chosen you from the beginning for salvation through sanctification by the Spirit and faith in the truth. It was for this He called you through our gospel, that you may gain the glory of our Lord Jesus Christ."

God chose certain individuals for salvation "from the beginning." Then He secured their faith in the gospel by the sanctifying work of the Holy Spirit.

Challenges to Unconditional Election

Was it unfair for God to predestine some to heaven? The Bible teaches that God is always fair; He is never unjust. However, in a world where people are constantly shouting about their rights

and fair treatment, we need a biblical context in order to understand God's fairness:

> But because of your stubbornness and unrepentant heart you
> are storing up wrath for yourself in the day of wrath and rev-
> elation of the righteous judgment of God, who will render to
> each person according to his deeds. . . . There will be tribula-
> tion and distress for every soul of man who does evil . . . but
> glory and honor and peace to everyone who does good. . . .
> For there is no partiality with God. (Rom. 2:5–6, 9–11)

Whenever the Bible speaks about God's impartiality, the
context is always referring to judgment. In Bible times judges
often took bribes. They tended to favor the rich and the wealthy.
Moses and the prophets warned judges to be fair and impartial
because that is the way God judges. He never lets people off the
hook just because they are rich, Jewish or because they make
grand pledges of good behavior. God cannot be bribed. That is
what His impartiality means.

It is not unfair for anyone to be generous to some people
as long as others are not harmed by the generosity.[4] When I attended Moody Bible Institute in Chicago, I often encountered
homeless men who were seeking a handout. If a man was hungry, I usually offered to buy him a hotdog at the local greasy
spoon. Some bums accepted my offer; others swore at me. The
meal I provided one man did no harm to the others I did not
feed, so my choosing to help one poor fellow was not an act of
injustice toward the rest. None of them could charge me with
unfairness.

Men and women lost in sin are not like children in a family
who have a claim to equal treatment by their parents. We are like
the tenant farmers in Jesus' parable who killed the owner's son
so they could claim the vineyard for themselves (Luke 20:9–18).
Though the parable was originally aimed at a Jewish audience,
it applies to the whole human race. In a sense, all of us sinners
have participated in the murder of Christ. If God chooses to be

merciful to some of those who killed His Son, those who receive the just reward for their crime have no reason to complain.

Was it unfair to predestine some to hell? First, it is important to see that Scripture supports the predestination of some to damnation. This appears from several texts:

> The LORD has made everything for its own purpose,
>   Even the wicked for the day of evil.
>
> (Prov. 16:4)

> What if God, although willing to demonstrate His wrath and to make His power known, endured with much patience vessels of wrath prepared for destruction? (Rom. 9:22)

> Christ is "a stone of stumbling and a rock of offense;" for they stumble because they are disobedient to the word, and to this doom they were also appointed. (1 Pet. 2:8)

Predestination to damnation is different in one important respect from predestination to life: God predestined individuals for salvation who did not deserve mercy. However, He predestines people for damnation who fully deserve wrath. When He planned the course of human history, He decided first to pour out His love on people whom He would create. Then He decided to permit Adam and Eve and all their children to sin. Finally, He elected some to salvation but passed by others, leaving them in the sinful state they would choose for themselves.[5] To predestine means to determine a destiny in advance. To elect means to choose out of a larger number. Thus, predestination can be distinguished from election. The damned were predestined to their fate, but they were not elected to it, because they were not deliberately chosen to be damned irrespective of any guilt on their part. The saved were both elected (chosen) and then predestined to be conformed to the image of Christ (Rom. 8:29).

By way of illustration let us take two ordinary, sinful people—call them Joe and Moe. Suppose God were not in the electing business. What would happen to Joe and Moe if they heard the gospel? They would reject it out of hand because of their

hatred for God, and both of them would be damned. Now suppose God, who is in the electing business, foresees the natural
result of leaving Joe and Moe to their own sinful choices, and He
decides to elect Joe to salvation. What is Moe's condition? It is
exactly the same as if God had never elected anybody. It has not
changed at all. God has not been unfair to Moe in predestining
him to condemnation because He has already taken Moe's sin
into account.

When Scripture says that God "has mercy on whom He desires, and He hardens whom He desires" (Rom. 9:18), it does
not mean that God hardens and refuses to accept sweet, innocent people who really want to come to Christ. The chief biblical
example of hardening is Pharaoh of Egypt. God sent Moses to
demand His people be released from bondage. In spite of a series of miraculous judgments on Egypt, Pharaoh refused. A few
times the Bible says Pharaoh hardened his heart (Exod. 8:15, 32;
9:34), but the overwhelming number of verses say God hardened his heart (4:21; 7:3; 9:12; 10:1, 27; 11:10; 14:4,8). Martin
Luther explained Pharaoh's hardening very well:

> Thus God hardens Pharaoh: He presents to the ungodly, evil
> will of Pharaoh His own word and work, which Pharaoh's
> will hates, by reason of its own inbred fault and natural cor-
> ruption. God does not alter that will within by His Spirit,
> but goes on presenting and bringing pressure to bear; and
> Pharaoh, having in mind his own strength, wealth and power,
> trusts to them by this same fault of his nature. So it comes to
> pass that, being inflated and uplifted by the idea of his own
> greatness, and growing vaingloriously scornful of lowly Moses
> and of the unostentatious word of God, he becomes hard-
> ened; and then grows more and more irked and annoyed, the
> more Moses presses and threatens him. . . . So God's harden-
> ing of Pharaoh is wrought thus: God presents from without to
> his villainous heart that which by nature he hates. . . . Pharaoh,
> by reason of the villainy of his will, cannot but hate what
> opposes him, and trust to his own strength; and he grows so

obstinate that he will not listen or reflect, but is swept along in the grip of Satan like a raging madman.[6]

So it is with every sinner God passes by and leaves in his own sin. He grows harder and harder every time he is confronted by God's word, which his soul hates.

Did God do evil in order to bring about good? The Bible is very clear: "God cannot be tempted by evil, and He Himself does not tempt anyone" (James 1:13). It is "impossible for God to lie" (Heb. 6:18). "The God who inflicts wrath is not unrighteous, is He? (I am speaking in human terms.) May it never be! For otherwise, how will God judge the world?" (Rom. 3:5–6). The key truth is that God did not do evil when He planned to *permit* evil in order that a greater good would come about.

Suppose there has been a series of jewel heists in New York City. Clever crooks break into upscale stores and steal the most expensive diamonds, rubies and emeralds. Police investigators realize the actual thieves are the small fry in the operation. The big player who plans the thefts and fences the jewels never actually breaks into any stores. One day the New York Police Department receives an advance tip that a particular store is going to be the target on the following night. They post their top-notch officers around the building with orders not to catch the thieves, but only to follow them. Their goal is to find and nail the mastermind of the operation. They permit the evil of the theft in order to bring about the greater good of catching the big boss.

Normally, we must not permit evil to occur when we have the power to prevent it, because we do not know enough to see when it would be better to stand aside and let evil run its course. God has infinite knowledge and wisdom. When He allows even great evil, we can be certain He has outsmarted the crooks. God elects some sinners and predestines them to become conformed to the image of Christ. He permits other sinners to continue in rebellion, but He restrains every evil act that does not fit into His plan for the world. In so doing He works no evil, only good.

The Beauty of Unconditional Election

It is a big step, even for many Christians, to move from a grudging acceptance of the necessity of election to an appreciation of its beauty. Several considerations may make that transition easier.

Unconditional election is beautiful because it flows from the love of God. Election does not flow from God's hatred for sinners, but from His love for Christ and His love for sinners. His love for Christ is clear in the opening verses of Paul's letter to the Ephesians: "He chose us in [Christ] before the foundation of the world, that we would be holy and blameless before Him. In love He predestined us to adoption as sons through Jesus Christ to Himself, according to the kind intention of His will, to the praise of the glory of His grace, which He freely bestowed on us in the Beloved" (Eph. 1:4–6).

God chose certain human beings because He already eternally loved Jesus Christ. God desired to have adopted sons and daughters who would become, by His grace, as much like "the Beloved" as a creature could be. With that end in view, He poured out His love on sinners when they were yet unlovable. Although we were "by nature children of wrath, . . . God, being rich in mercy, because of His great love with which He loved us, even when we were dead in our transgressions, made us alive together with Christ (by grace you have been saved)" (2:3–5).

Unconditional election is beautiful because it offers sinners their only hope. When we consider the helpless condition of all people, it is clear that no one has any hope of salvation apart from God's merciful election. The Christian's hope is not a mere wish but a confident expectation of eternal good, and this hope comes through the sovereign grace of God. "God has chosen you from the beginning for salvation through sanctification by the Spirit and faith in the truth. . . . Now may our Lord Jesus Christ Himself and God our Father, who has loved us and given us eternal comfort and good hope by grace, comfort and strengthen your hearts in every good work and word" (2 Thess. 2:13, 16–17).

God's unconditional election is the only hope anyone has of spending eternity in heaven. If God were not in the choosing business, none of us would ever be saved. How can someone who is presently unconverted discover if he is one of God's elect? There are two sure-fire ways of finding out right now. The first is to commit suicide—not the recommended procedure because the knowledge thereby acquired might not be what one desired. The second way of certainly determining one's status *today* is to repent of sin and trust Christ as Savior. "And working together with Him, we also urge you not to receive the grace of God in vain—for He says, 'At the acceptable time I listened to you, and on the day of salvation I helped you.' Behold, now is 'the acceptable time,' behold, now is 'the day of salvation'" (2 Cor. 6:1–2).

Whoever comes to Christ has the assurance from the Savior's own lips that he is one of God's elect, for only those whom the Father has given to the Son will come to Him. No one who comes in faith will be cast out (John 6:37, 44). A person not yet willing to come to Christ must remain for some time in doubt about his election. But if you respond to Christ's gracious invitation, "Come to Me, all who are weary and heavy-laden," then you shall surely find rest for your sin-weary soul. So do not delay; cast yourself now on the mercy of the Savior.

Perhaps, however, you find yourself unable to believe in Christ. I would do you no favor if I were to tell you (as some evangelists do) that faith is a very easy thing. They say we all exercise faith when we sit down in a chair. We believe it will hold us up, and when we make the trial, we find it to be so. Therefore, (they say) all you need to do is to exercise the same kind of faith and rest in Christ. *Saving faith is much more difficult than that.* If the walls of your room are painted white, no amount of effort will enable you to believe they are green with purple polka dots. You cannot believe in something you cannot see. If you find you cannot come to Christ because you do not see the truth of the gospel, the problem is not that you have superior sight but that you are blind. Your hard heart would rather hold on to your sins than humble itself before the mighty hand of God. The best thing to do in such a case is to cry out to God, tell Him about your blindness and helplessness, and plead with Him to give you a fresh new sense of the glory and beauty of Christ and the gospel. He is your only hope.

Unconditional election is beautiful because it encourages evangelism and prayer. One common objection to the biblical doctrine of election is that it removes any incentive for actively trying to bring lost people into the kingdom of Christ. Sometimes an objector will quote the pastor who tried to discourage William Carey from going as a missionary to India: "When God pleases to convert the heathen, he'll do it without consulting you or me."[7] Such a conclusion is a perversion of the biblical doctrine of God's sovereignty.

George Whitfield and Charles Haddon Spurgeon, two of the most energetic evangelists of former centuries, both reveled in God's sovereign election of sinners. John Calvin, though often maligned by the ignorant for his teaching on predestination, actively promoted the evangelization of France, trained preachers for other European countries and sent missionaries to Brazil. The Brazilian mission failed because of political betrayal, but Calvin took the only overseas missionary opportunity he had in an era during which Roman Catholic nations ruled the seas.

Contrary to the mistaken opinion of some, a whole-hearted acceptance of unconditional election encourages both evangelism and prayer for the lost.[8] Shortly after the apostle Paul began preaching in Corinth, opposition increased to the point that he considered leaving the city. He was encouraged to stay by a vision from God. "And the Lord said to Paul in the night by a vision, 'Do not be afraid any longer, but go on speaking and do not be silent; for I am with you, and no man will attack you in order to harm you, for I have many people in this city.' And he settled there a year and six months, teaching the word of God among them" (Acts 18:9–11).

The certainty that God had appointed some in that city

to salvation enabled the apostle to persevere in his evangelistic ministry. In the same way, Scripture declares that the saved will constitute a great multitude "from every nation and all tribes and peoples and tongues" (Rev. 7:9). This is an encouragement to missions and evangelism. Since we know God will save some wherever the gospel is preached, believers can go with boldness into the most difficult and unresponsive places, confident that His Word will not return to Him empty but will accomplish what He desires and produce the results He intends (Isa. 55:11).

The sovereignty of God also encourages prayer for the salvation of the lost. Romans 9 contains the strongest statements in Scripture regarding God's supreme authority to have mercy on some and to harden others. However, the apostle Paul begins the chapter by saying, "I am telling the truth in Christ, I am not lying, my conscience testifies with me in the Holy Spirit, that I have great sorrow and unceasing grief in my heart. For I could wish that I myself were accursed, separated from Christ for the sake of my brethren, my kinsmen according to the flesh" (Rom. 9:1–3). The burden on his heart and his confidence in divine election cause him to cry out, "Brethren, my heart's desire and my prayer to God for them is for their salvation" (Rom. 10:1).

Why does Paul bother to pray if God has already chosen to save whom He will? First, God commands us to pray for the things we need and want. Second, since Paul knows God will save some Israelites, he also knows he is praying within the revealed will of God. Third, when God has decided to save someone, He often stirs up one of His children to plead for that very blessing. Thus, God receives double honor both as the instigator of prayer and as the One who answers. Finally, though we may not understand how prayer works, the Lord tells us our prayers do make a difference. God holds gifts in His hands which He is longing to give us, but He will not release them if we fail to ask (James 4:2).

There is a mystery here to be sure, but it is one that admirers of divine sovereignty gladly embrace. If I thought God could not or would not overcome the stubborn free will of sinners who hate Him, I would not bother to pray. However, since I know God has the power to change any hostile heart (Prov. 21:1), and since I know He will draw some people to Christ, I am bold to beg for the salvation of the people He lays on my heart. I thank God that He has revealed in Scripture the beauty of His electing love because it stimulates me to persevere in the gospel ministry He has committed to me.

The Redeemed Are Irresistibly Drawn to Christ

Predestination is one of the hardest doctrines for many to accept. They think God must be unfair to choose some while He bypasses others. They wonder how God can choose people without taking away their free will and turning them into puppets. How can God choose some without being unjust to others? Consider the following parable.

Fred has decided he wants a wife. He is a gentle, yet strong man with a steady job, so he has a lot to offer a prospective bride. In his circle of acquaintants, there are ten suitable young ladies. Through common friends Fred makes it known he is interested in pursuing a deeper relationship with a view to possible marriage. Although the young ladies can see he has many good qualities, they all reject his suit. One doesn't like his hair; another thinks he is too smart; a third is looking for a good dancer, which he is not.

After all ten have turned him down, Fred selects Wanda from the group and focuses his attention on her. He pursues her with steady persistence and gradually overcomes her initial reluctance. Wanda begins to see him in a new light. She appreciates his kindness, thoughtfulness, integrity and good sense of humor. In short, she falls in love with him. She finds him irresistibly attractive, so when he asks for her hand in marriage, she gladly says yes.

Similarly, God has revealed His power, glory, wisdom and kindness in creation (Ps. 19:1; 104:24; Acts 14:17). He has revealed His righteousness in the consciences of people (Rom. 1:32; 2:14–16). He has given preachers of the gospel who extol the beauty of Christ's death and resurrection for sinners. Nevertheless, in spite of the fact that God has displayed many of His good qualities before the world, the whole human race has refused the Lord's gracious invitation to a deeper relationship.

Though many claim to be seeking God, in fact no one does so: "There is none righteous, not even one; there is none who understands, there is none who seeks for God; all have turned aside, together they have become useless; there is none who does good, there is not even one" (3:10–12).

In view of mankind's universal rejection of Him, God reveals more of His glory to the hearts of chosen sinners. He pursues them as Fred pursued Wanda until, by the secret work of the Spirit in their hearts, they see the purity of God's holiness, the justice of His judgment and the wonder of His grace in the cross of Christ. When God thus shines His beautiful light into their hearts, they find Him irresistibly attractive. He speaks to their hearts saying, "Come, my beloved," and they gladly answer yes.

God is not unfair; when people reject Him, He is under no obligation to reveal more of Himself to them. God does not turn people into puppets, forcing them to believe against their wills. He makes them willing by showing them His irresistible attractiveness. They see, and they believe.[9]

Part 3

The Beauty *of* God

the JUDGE

If the torments of hell are to last ages of ages, then it must be because sinners in hell all this while are obstinate; and though they are free agents as to this matter, yet they willfully and perversely refuse, even under such great means, to repent, forsake their sins, and turn to God.

—Jonathan Edwards

8   Why Would a Good God Allow Suffering?

I t was the best of times; it was the worst of times." So begins the Dickens classic, *A Tale of Two Cities*. Not many today would echo the first of those sentiments.

As this book goes to press, suicide bombers wreak daily havoc in Iraq. A ruthless, lascivious megalomaniac, whose people starve while he immerses himself in his vast library of movies, rules North Korea. Somalia is a training ground for terrorists and a haven for pirates. The names and places may change, but there is no reason to expect an explosion of global peace before Christ returns.

If a loving, all-powerful God created our world, why is it such a mess? Why does He allow an unwed teenage mother to stuff her baby into a garbage bag and throw it into a dumpster? If God is really in charge, why did He allow a tsunami to snuff out the lives of over a hundred thousand people in Southeast Asia on December 26, 2004? Why did over two hundred thousand perish in the January 12, 2010, earthquake in Haiti? Such numbers defy our comprehension.

Thomas Hobbes (1588–1679) described the natural life of man as "solitary, poor, nasty, brutish, and short."[1] To many of the world's people, that would seem a more apt description than "It was the best of times." So, assuming God had decided to make some world, why did He create *this* one filled with pain and evil?

There is also the question of how we square a loving God with the concept of eternal hell. After a life of unimaginable suffering, millions will enter a destiny that makes the pains of earth look like a garden of flowers, and those torments will never end. Jesus described hell as the place of "unquenchable fire" where "their worm does not die, and the fire is not quenched" (Mark 9:43, 48). He said it is the place of "eternal fire" and "eternal punishment," where "there will be weeping and gnashing of teeth" (Matt. 25:41, 46, 30). In hell those who worship anti-Christ "will be tormented with eternal fire and brimstone in the presence of the holy angels and in the presence of the Lamb. And the smoke of their torment goes up forever and ever; they have no rest day and night" (Rev. 14:10–11). In the game of Monopoly, a player can leave jail either by paying a fine or by using a Get out of Jail Free card, if he is lucky enough to have one. Once a person has been cast into hell, however, he has no opportunity for parole, no money to pay for his freedom and no chance for escape.

Although human suffering has come from the sinful exercise of free will and although God employs suffering for various beneficial purposes in the lives of His children, those considerations by themselves do not adequately explain God's reasons for permitting and punishing sin. God's delight in His Son and the inter-Trinitarian harmony form the backdrop for His hatred of sin. God's desire to express His benevolence as fully as possible to adopted sons and daughters helps us understand the reason for permitting sin in the first place.

Four Incomplete Answers

If God is good, why is the world He made so bad? If God is beautiful, why is there so much ugliness? If God is merciful, why is hell unending?[2] Four common responses to the problem of suffering have some validity, but by themselves they seem inadequate.

Free will. Probably the most common response to the problem of suffering is that it is the result of the sinful exercise of our free wills. Those who subscribe to this thesis say God wanted people who could freely love Him, not puppets that saluted whenever He pulled the proper strings. Unfortunately, freedom to love God necessarily entails freedom to hate Him, so if God wanted our free love, He had to permit open rebellion against His laws. Sinful human rebellion produces untold suffering now and merits eternal punishment, but free will is supposed to be such a great gift that it was worth all the pain of earth and hell in order to secure it.

There are at least three problems with the free will response to suffering. First, the power of free will is vastly overrated. It is true sinners freely reject God, but no one freely loves Him. After Adam sinned, all human beings have been born slaves to sin. By nature we are dominated by sinful desires and led about by the devil (John 8:34; Eph. 2:1–3). How can sin's slaves ever freely come to Christ? They cannot—not because God prevents them from coming, but because they do not want to come. It is impossible for people addicted to sin to ever develop a taste for the goodness of the Lord. Before the Holy Spirit changes a person's heart, he does not desire to serve God, "because the mind set on the flesh is hostile toward God; for it does not subject itself to the law of God, for it is not even able to do so, and those who are in the flesh cannot please God" (Rom. 8:7–8).

Jesus said, "No one can come to Me unless the Father who sent Me draws him" (John 6:44). Happy obedience to God never comes from a human heart until it has been set free from its chains. As Jesus said, "If the Son makes you free, you will be free indeed" (John 8:36). Jesus sets people free by His death and resurrection, and by giving them His Spirit (Rom. 6:1–23; 2 Cor. 3:17). Only after we receive the Holy Spirit are we able to begin loving God, for love is the fruit of the Spirit (Gal. 5:22). It is the Holy Spirit who enables us to love God, not our unaided free will.

A second problem with the free will defense of suffering is

that when we get to heaven, we will be perfectly free and our love for God will be perfect, but we will not be free to sin. If we will love God perfectly in heaven without being able to sin, why is the ability to sin necessary in order to love Him in this life?

The existence of elect angels (1 Tim. 5:21) suggests a third response to the free will proposal. Presumably they are elect or chosen because God preserved them from falling into sin when Satan and his angels rebelled. Angels are not puppets. They are rational creatures capable of initiating actions. For example, Daniel prayed for three weeks before an answer arrived by an angelic messenger. The angel explained he had been delayed by "the prince of the kingdom of Persia"—apparently a fallen angel— until Michael the archangel came to help him (Dan. 10:12–13). The angels are also called holy (Mark 8:38), and there is no true holiness apart from free, loving obedience to God. If God kept some angels from sinning without destroying their freedom and love, why didn't He do the same for human beings?

Training. Another possibility is that God created the present world as a training ground for the world to come and that therefore, suffering is a necessary part of God's discipline for those who will inherit that world. It is true God uses pain and difficulty to train us. God "disciplines us for our good, so that we may share His holiness. All discipline for the moment seems not to be joyful, but sorrowful; yet to those who have been trained by it, afterwards it yields the peaceful fruit of righteousness" (Heb. 12:10–11). However, using suffering for this purpose is different from deliberately designing the world to be a training ground for saints.

There are at least four problems with disciplinary training as God's primary rationale for creating a world of suffering: First, those who are ultimately lost are not improved by their suffering, so disciplinary training plays no part in the reason for their creation. Second, if the saved need to be tested by malicious human beings, it seems they might be adequately scourged without damning so large a percentage of the human race. Once Stalin,

Pol Pot and their ilk had achieved their purifying purpose, God might have brought even them to repentance and salvation, thus eliminating the necessity of damning anybody. Third, there appears to be far more suffering in the world than is required for disciplinary training. Who benefits from the slaughter of dozens of infants when an entire village is wiped out in one of Africa's never-ending tribal wars? Fourth and finally, consider nice, happy young children who die suddenly shortly after their conversion. They do not experience any appreciable discipline through suffering, but God allows them into the kingdom of heaven anyway. If a certain amount of suffering is not necessary for them, why do others need it?

Glory and joy. Another proposal is that God uses the suffering of His children to manifest His glory and to increase their joy. This is a scriptural perspective:

> Make sure that none of you suffers as a murderer, or thief, or evildoer, or a troublesome meddler; but if anyone suffers as a Christian, he is not to be ashamed, but is to glorify God in this name. (1 Pet. 4:15–16)

> Blessed are you when people insult you and persecute you, and falsely say all kinds of evil against you because of Me. Rejoice and be glad, for your reward in heaven is great; for in the same way they persecuted the prophets who were before you. . . . Let your light shine before men in such a way that they may see your good works, and glorify your Father who is in heaven. (Matt. 5:11–12, 16)

When Christians suffer cheerfully for Christ's sake, they show that He is more valuable to them than any of the things they have lost. Since Christ is the Christian's greatest treasure, many believers have discovered that suffering deepens the springs of their joy, because they are cast back on Christ alone, and they find Him to be more than adequate for all their needs. Although God makes use of suffering to show His worth and to increase His children's joy in Christ, it is hard to justify the existence of our present suffering on that basis alone.

Appreciation for heaven. According to Scripture, in the new heavens and the new earth, all mankind will worship the Lord:

> And it shall be from new moon to new moon
>> And from sabbath to sabbath,
>> All mankind will come to bow down before Me," says
>>> the LORD.
> Then they will go forth and look
>> On the corpses of the men
>> Who have transgressed against Me.
>> For their worm will not die
>> And their fire will not be quenched;
>> And they will be an abhorrence to all mankind.
>
> (Isa. 66:23–24)

Just as we prize our own health more when we see others who are sick, so beholding the sufferings of the lost will give the saved a greater appreciation of God's grace toward them. "The view of the misery of the damned will double the ardour of the love and gratitude of the saints in heaven."[3]

This is a use God makes of the wicked, but we need something more if we are going to answer an obvious question: Why doesn't the doom of the damned decrease the joy of the saints? If they are filled with genuine benevolence for all creatures, shouldn't the saints be eternally pained by the thought of hell? Certainly the saints are not sadists who can only be happy if they are busy torturing someone else. The brink of hell's abyss will not become an annual vacation spot where the saved can sip ice-cold sodas while they contemplate with pleasure the dancing of the damned on coals of fire.

These four perspectives on suffering are very helpful, but by themselves they are incomplete. What they have in common is their focus on human beings: *their* freedom, *their* training, *their* present joy in Christ and *their* future appreciation for heaven. The great common omission is an analysis of the nature of God.

What is there in God Himself that might help to explain the existence of suffering?

The Bible clearly teaches that human suffering—both in this life and in hell—is the result of sin, so it is necessary to ask why God punishes sin so severely and why He permitted it in the first place. If God is Love and if God is the Lord of history, is the painful story of humanity somehow the outworking of love?

Punishment for Sin Is an Expression of God's Love

One form of love is delight or pleasure. You may say, "I love chocolate," or "I love dogs," because chocolate or dogs give you pleasure. You delight in them. In order to understand God's punishment for sin, we must see what gives God pleasure. God hates sin because sin is utterly opposed to all God loves.

God delights in His own eternal Son. God loves His Son supremely. Therefore, He hates those who despise and reject Jesus. "The Father loves the Son and has given all things into His hand. He who believes in the Son has eternal life; but he who does not obey the Son will not see life, but the wrath of God abides on him" (John 3:35–36).

Jesus is God incarnate. "He is the image of the invisible God" and "the radiance of His glory and the exact representation of His nature" (Col. 1:15; Heb. 1:3). When Philip the disciple asked Jesus, "Lord, show us the Father," Jesus replied, "Have I been so long with you, and yet you have not come to know Me, Philip? He who has seen me has seen the Father" (John 14:8–9).

There is no clearer revelation of God's goodness, truth and beauty than God's revelation of Himself in Christ. To despise Christ or even ignore Him is to oppose all God is. We cannot sit on the fence. "He who is not with Me is against Me," said Jesus (Luke 11:23). We may be attracted to the secondary beauties of this world, but if we do not bow in joyful worship before the primary beauty of God in Christ, we are rebels against ultimate goodness and truth.

This is abundantly clear in Psalm 2. Even though it may have been composed to celebrate the coronation of an Israelite king, the breadth of its vision extends far beyond any historical ruler. The idealized king of Zion in this psalm is a prophetic picture of Christ, which is how the New Testament views the passage (Acts 4:24–28; 13:33; Heb. 1:5; 5:5):

> Why are the nations in an uproar
>   And the peoples devising a vain thing?
> The kings of the earth take their stand
>   And the rulers take counsel together
>   Against the LORD and against His Anointed, saying,
> "Let us tear their fetters apart
>   And cast away their cords from us!"
>
> He who sits in the heavens laughs,
>   The Lord scoffs at them.
> Then He will speak to them in His anger
>   And terrify them in His fury, saying,
> "But as for Me, I have installed My King
>   Upon Zion, My holy mountain."
>
> "I will surely tell of the decree of the LORD:
>   He said to Me, 'You are My Son,
>   Today I have begotten You.[4]
> 'Ask of Me, and I will surely give the nations as Your
>   inheritance,
>   And the very ends of the earth as Your possession.
> 'You shall break them with a rod of iron,
>   You shall shatter them like earthenware.'"
>
> Now therefore, O kings, show discernment;
>   Take warning, O judges of the earth.
> Worship the LORD with reverence
>   And rejoice with trembling.
> Do homage to the Son, that He not become angry, and you
>   perish in the way,
>   For His wrath may soon be kindled.
>   How blessed are all who take refuge in Him!

The first section indicates that rejecting the authority of God's Anointed One (Christ) is the same as rejecting the authority of God the Father. The second section shows how God responds to those who reject His beloved Son. He mocks the foolish impotence of their rebellion and rebukes them with anger and terrifying fury. In the third section the Son describes the fierce judgment the Lord has instructed Him to execute on the nations of the earth. Jesus expresses the same truth when He says, "For not even the Father judges anyone, but He has given all judgment to the Son, so that all will honor the Son even as they honor the Father. He who does not honor the Son does not honor the Father who sent Him" (John 5:22–23). In the final section the psalmist exhorts all people to joyfully worship the Lord, which is equivalent to paying homage to the Son. Failure to do so brings swift judgment.

God the Father passionately delights in His Son. Consequently, His wrath is aroused against all who despise Him.

God delights in His own internal harmony. All beauty involves a harmonious union of things that differ. This is exactly what we see in the Trinity. The harmony of love among the Persons of the Trinity is the source of all beauty and harmony in creation. Every beautiful flower shares in a small way in the beauty of God. Every beautiful friendship is a dim reflection of the love binding the Trinity together.

God designed the moral law to reflect and secure a measure of His beauty in human society.[5] His hatred of sin is not based on a petty insistence that people obey arbitrary rules that make no sense. God hates sin because it strikes at the very core of His being. Sin is rebellion against the eternal harmony that holds the world together. The first four of the Ten Commandments place the one true God at the center of our lives (Exod. 20:3–17). When people choose a different center, they distort reality and live a lie; they value something of lesser worth over the living God.

The next six commandments protect our relationships with

our parents, neighbors and members of the opposite sex. God designed these relationships to mirror the eternal submission of the Son to the Father and the loving bond of the Holy Spirit between them. Within the family, for example, the husband is to exercise loving headship over his wife (1 Cor. 11:3; Eph. 5:22–33).[6] When we overturn God's pattern for marriage or mock our parents or lie or steal, we bend and twist the mirror. Our relationships reflect a distorted image of God, just as a mirror in a fun house can make us look fat, thin or wavy. God hates to be misrepresented because He delights in His own internal harmony. He also knows that maintaining His harmony in the world is necessary for our happiness. Therefore, sin must be punished, and those who hold on to their sin and refuse to repent must be excluded from God's presence.

In a massive understatement the Lord declares that evil doers "chose that in which I did not delight" (Isa. 65:12). Scripture calls us "ungodly," "enemies" of God, "hostile toward God" and "by nature children of wrath" (Rom. 5:6, 10; 8:7; Eph. 2:3). God regards even our best actions as unclean. In His sight "all our righteous deeds are like a filthy garment," or more literally, "like a garment of menstruation," which was unclean according to Old Testament ceremonial law (Isa. 64:6).

On the Day of Judgment, the redeemed will properly praise God for revealing the true nature of sin and righteously judging sinners. Then at last it will be abundantly clear that breaking the law of God is a high-handed blow against the harmony of love that holds the world together. Now, however, it is very difficult for us to see the seriousness of sin.

Suffering in this life and suffering in hell are both consequences of sin, but in different ways. Those who suffer the agonies of hell strictly deserve what they receive, but much of the pain we endure now has no direct relationship to our individual sins. When people reported a local tragedy to Jesus, He replied, "Do you suppose that these Galileans were greater sinners than all other Galileans because they suffered this fate? I tell you, no, but unless you repent, you will all likewise perish. Or do you suppose that those eighteen on whom the tower in Siloam fell and killed them were worse culprits than all the men who live in Jerusalem? I tell you, no, but unless you repent, you will all likewise perish" (Luke 13:2–5). Sin in general—rather than specific sins—lay behind these events.

Modern people tend to think that we are all basically good and that therefore God ought to give us nice things. The prophets of the Bible insist we are not good, so any good thing we receive is a gracious, undeserved gift from God.

Jeremiah wrote Lamentations after the Babylonians had destroyed Jerusalem. The holy temple had been desecrated and demolished. The majority of the people were either slaughtered or carried into captivity. Pregnant women had been ripped open with the sword. So Jeremiah wept. For five painful chapters he opened up the raw wounds of his soul. He saw clearly that God had brought this terrible desolation, but he did not blame God or say He was unjust. And then in the midst of his tears, Jeremiah somehow rose to one of the most eloquent expressions of trust in all literature:

> The LORD's lovingkindnesses indeed never cease,
>   For His compassions never fail.
> They are new every morning;
>   Great is Your faithfulness.
> "The LORD is my portion," says my soul,
>   "Therefore I have hope in Him."
> The LORD is good to those who wait for Him,
>   To the person who seeks Him.
>
> (Lam. 3:22–24)

Why is there such suffering now, and why will there be more hereafter? The biblical answer is that our sin is a terrible affront to everything God values. We delight in the things that disgust Him, and we have despised the eternal goodness, truth and beauty embodied in Jesus Christ and in God's holy law.

In late medieval Europe many people lived in fear of God. They were acutely aware of their sin and the righteous wrath of God. That is one reason tens of thousands were overcome with joy at the love, grace and mercy of God when Martin Luther recovered the biblical doctrine of justification by faith. In our modern psycho-therapeutic age, people are taught to think well of themselves, so they cannot imagine why God would ever be angry with them. And if some poor soul should think ill of himself, isn't it God's job to make him feel better?

If we could see ourselves as God sees us, if we could see our corrupt hearts crawling with the maggots of sin, we would not be surprised at suffering in this life or hereafter. We would bow in thankful wonder at every good gift that comes from God's hand and we would exclaim with the psalmist, "He has not dealt with us according to our sins, nor rewarded us according to our iniquities" (Ps. 103:10).

God does not delight in tormenting the lost. "'As I live!' declares the Lord God, 'I take no pleasure in the death of the wicked, but rather that the wicked turn from his way and live. Turn back, turn back from your evil ways! Why then will you die, O house of Israel?'" (Ezek. 33:11). If God takes no pleasure in damning sinners, why will their torment last forever, and why will the angels and the redeemed praise God for their eternal judgment? (Rev. 19:1–6).

For an answer we must consider how the lost will respond to their punishment. If a person in hell truly repented of his sins and begged God to forgive him because of Christ's death, it is unthinkable that God would kick him in the teeth, and say, "Tough luck, sinner! You are stuck in the flames forever." The fact that hell lasts forever provides clear evidence the people who end up there will not repent.[7]

Some children become sorry and tearful at the mildest forms of discipline. Others rage and fume when they are punished. Such childish tantrums afford us a small glimpse into the way the lost will respond to their damnation. Those who reject the

Lord on earth will not become lovers of God in hell. They will react with ever-increasing hatred of Him, just as ungodly rebels will do during the Tribulation at the end of this age:

> The fourth angel poured out his bowl upon the sun, and it was given to it to scorch men with fire. Men were scorched with fierce heat; and they blasphemed the name of God who has the power over these plagues, and they did not repent so as to give Him glory. Then the fifth angel poured out his bowl on the throne of the beast, and his kingdom became darkened; and they gnawed their tongues because of pain, and they blasphemed the God of heaven because of their pains and their sores; and they did not repent of their deeds. (Rev. 16:8–11)

We should not imagine God imposes eternal punishment on nice, respectable sinners for small infractions of His law they committed in this life. Their opposition to God is not temporary; it goes on forever. Every moment the wicked rage and fume against God merits further punishment. Since their hatred has no end, neither does their punishment.

An episode from *Star Trek: The Next Generation* aptly illustrates the condition of the lost in hell. Aliens had invaded the bodies of high-ranking members of Starfleet Command. These victims still looked and acted much the same as they had before, but now they were controlled by alien minds. Near the end of the episode, Commander Riker turned his blaster against a man whom he had formerly respected and loved. As the blaster burned away the human shell, it revealed a creature underneath that resembled a giant cockroach.

In the same way, the fires of hell will burn away the fair exteriors of the lost to reveal a God-hating monster underneath. When the saved look into the pits of hell they will not see kind Aunt Matilda who used to make sweaters for orphans and feed cookies to all the children in the neighborhood. They will see a giant cockroach hissing, spitting and filled with hatred for their beloved Savior.[8] That is one reason the saved will not endure perpetual distress at the suffering of the lost. Another reason is that nothing good or beautiful will ever cease to exist. Aunt Matilda's attractiveness came from God's common grace and the image of God stamped on her soul. Her rejection of God separates her from these gifts, but they can never be lost from God who gave them. Those who loved Aunt Matilda in this life will see what they loved in her in the face of their Savior.

A conception of hell from the ancient church may offer additional help in dispelling the myth of God as malicious tyrant. It depends on important distinctions in the ways God may be present. The Bible teaches that all of God is present everywhere. "'Am I a God who is near,' declares the Lord, 'And not a God far off? Can a man hide himself in hiding places so I do not see him?' declares the LORD. 'Do I not fill the heavens and the earth?' declares the LORD" (Jer. 23:23–24).

We ought not to think of God's presence as if He were a gas diffused throughout the universe. Nor should we imagine part of God (perhaps an eyelid) is in Beijing and another part (perhaps a toenail) is in New York City. God is not bound by our space and time. All of God is everywhere. He, not a portion of Him, is in every place.

If that is so, what does the Scripture mean when it says those "who do not obey the gospel of our Lord Jesus Christ . . . will pay the penalty of eternal destruction, away from the presence of the Lord and from the glory of His power" (2 Thess. 1:8–9)? Is hell truly a place where God is not?

The answer lies in recognizing that the Bible normally connects God's presence with His presence to bless. In the Old Testament priestly benediction, God's blessing is identified with His gracious presence as expressed by His shining face. "The LORD bless you, and keep you; the LORD make His face shine on you, and be gracious to you; the LORD lift up His countenance on you, and give you peace" (Num. 6:24–26).

On the other hand, when God removes the manifest blessings of His favor and sends painful discipline, He is said to be absent or far away. "Why do You stand afar off, O Lord? Why do You hide Yourself in times of trouble?" (Ps. 10:1). In such cases God has not ceased to be omnipresent, but He is *present to judge* rather than *present to bless*. Thus, when Jesus cried out "My God, My God, why have You forsaken Me?" (Matt. 27:46), He was experiencing both the absence of God's loving fellowship and the presence of God's wrath against sin.

Some teachers in the ancient church suggested that the fire of hell is the blazing manifestation of God's glory and power without an ability to see and enjoy God's beauty.[9] Sinners whose hatred of God is perfected find nothing so painful as exposure to the glory of God's holiness. Perhaps a word picture will help.

Imagine two men, one saved and the other lost. Together they spiral down to opposite sides of the sun. One man is dancing with joyous abandon on the surface of the sun, basking in its warmth and reveling in its glorious brightness. The other's eyeballs experience continual scorching; his retinas are being constantly burned away and constantly renewed. He sees, and yet he knows only outer darkness. His flesh is continually being consumed, and yet it continues to exist in the unquenchable fire. While he lived on earth, he rejected the beauty of God revealed in Christ and in the gospel, and now exposure to the glory of God fills him with loathing and excruciating pain.

If this ancient suggestion about hell is correct, it helps us understand how God's glory in grace and His glory in judgment are one. God does not have two separate glories, but His glory has very different effects on the saved and the lost. God's judgment rests not on malice but on His nature, for He dwells in "unapproachable light" (1 Tim. 6:16). The sufferings of the lost are a direct result of their hatred of the beauty and glory of God, whose presence is painful to them.

In this present age Christians do well to imitate God and to plead with their friends and family to repent. The possibility that their loved ones may spend eternity in hell weighs very heavily on their hearts, just as the future doom of the lost weighs heavily on the heart of God. But on the Day of Judgment all things will be different. The attractive coverings of sin will be stripped away, and God will no longer restrain His wrath.

God does not delight in the death of the wicked. He "delights in unchanging love" (Mic. 7:18), but given the holiness of God and obduracy of sinners, judgment is a praiseworthy necessity. The redeemed will properly praise God for revealing the true nature of sin and for righteously judging sinners.

Permission of Sin Is Also an Expression of God's Love

We return to the foundational thesis of this book: God is love. We have been looking at the chief objects of God's delight; in the paragraphs that follow, we turn to the objects of His benevolence.

The primary object of the Father's benevolence is Christ. "The Father loves the Son and has given all things into His hand" (John 3:35). The chief secondary objects of His overflowing generosity are His adopted sons and daughters, but the rest of God's creatures are also recipients of His benevolence. "The Lord is good to all, and His mercies are over all His works" (Ps. 145:9).

God is benevolent even to the lost. Since they will not accept eternal life on His terms, natural gifts such as food, family and a measure of health are all they are willing to receive (Matt. 5:45; Acts 14:17). Those who rebel against God do not even deserve these limited blessings, so no one has a right to complain if his life or his goods are cut short. When the state is planning to execute a prisoner, it customarily offers him whatever he wants for dinner before his death. Likewise, God sometimes allows those who hate Him to fill their bellies with the goods of this world before they leave it forever.

When God decided to express His self-giving love outside the Trinity, His plan was to adopt certain men and women as His children. As a Being with an infinite capacity for love, God desired to express His love toward His sons and daughters in the fullest way possible. Any lesser exhibition of His love would not have been as satisfying to Him. It was God's will to bring into existence a world in which His love would be most fully expressed.

The Bible speaks of God's will in two very different ways. First, His will is the kind of human behavior that pleases Him: "The Lord is not slow about His promise, as some count slowness, but is patient toward you, not wishing [*willing*, KJV] for any to perish but for all to come to repentance" (2 Pet. 3:9). Second, God's will is His eternal decree of what shall come to pass: God "works all things after the counsel of His will" (Eph. 1:11; see also Isa. 46:10). God's decree includes everything He does and everything He permits others to do.

When God created Adam and Eve, they were innocent; they had an inclination toward holiness, and they experienced joyful fellowship with God. Their perpetual obedience was pleasing to God. That was His will for them. On the other hand, God had already decreed to permit them to sin, so even though God did not compel them to sin, their disobedience was certain. God could have decreed a world in which He would not have permitted them to sin, but He did not. In that sense His will included their sin. God's decree enabled Him to express His love in ways and to a degree that would not have been possible otherwise.

The plan God set in motion to achieve this end involved rescuing undeserving sinners from the greatest possible disaster at the greatest personal cost for the greatest eternal blessing.

The greatest possible disaster. If God wanted to express the magnitude of His infinite love by saving undeserving sinners, the peril from which He rescued them needed to be as awful as possible. God's greatest gift is fellowship with Himself, so the greatest possible disaster is the absence of God's loving presence. Those who do not know God will "pay the penalty of eternal destruction, away from the presence of the Lord and from the glory of His power" (2 Thess. 1:8–9). Exhibiting the fullness of God's redeeming love also required that the ultimate disaster be real. Some sinners had to experience a real hell if other sinners were going to experience true redemption.

God cannot lie or pretend something is true when it is not. First year philosophy students like to imagine they came into existence five minutes ago with their minds stocked full of memories of a fictitious past. Their present is also imaginary, and the world apparently outside of them exists only in their heads. Common sense generally prevails, and such fantasies soon end up in the dustbin of worn-out intellectual games. The Christian, however, has more than common sense. He rests on the biblical statement that the Lord is "the God of truth" (Isa. 65:16). Therefore, infinite, redeeming love can only exist in the face of a real and infinite doom. It is no intellectual game.

The greatest personal cost. God's self-giving love cost Him heaven's greatest treasure. "By this the love of God was manifested in us, that God has sent His only begotten Son into the world so that we might live through Him. In this is love, not that we loved God, but that He loved us and sent His Son to be the propitiation for our sins" (1 John 4:9–10).

I recall a story (perhaps apocryphal) about a father who saw his two-year-old son playing on the track in front of a speeding passenger train. The father had only seconds to decide whether to allow the train to continue or to pull a lever to send the train along an old, unused siding and over the edge of a cliff. I cannot imagine what I would do in such a case, but God's decision was clear. Jesus stood manfully in front of the train and nodded to His Father to let it proceed.

Only the Son of God suffered to pay the penalty for our sins, but there is another kind of cost God bears in conjunction with redemption. It is very hard for Him to stand back and watch the sin and suffering in His world. "What if God, although willing to demonstrate His wrath and to make His power known, *endured* with much patience vessels of wrath prepared for destruction? And He did so to make known the riches of His glory upon vessels of mercy, which He prepared beforehand for glory" (Rom. 9:22–23).

The Greek word translated "endured" refers to carrying a

burden. A wilderness camper *endures* as he carries a forty-pound pack on his back all day. In the same way, sinners and their sin lie like a heavy burden on the heart of God. Sin is ugly, disgusting and hateful to God. His anger is at the boiling point, but He holds in His wrath. He is patient. He is long-suffering. He puts up with non-elect sinners for the sake of those whom He has chosen to save.

God must also bear His own sorrow about the necessity of judgment. Jesus wept over the impending destruction of Jerusalem (Luke 19:41). Similarly, in the midst of a passage of doom regarding Moab, Isaiah, speaking with the heart of God, cried out in sorrow over some of Moab's principal cities: "Therefore I will weep bitterly for Jazer, for the vine of Sibmah; I will drench you with my tears, O Heshbon and Elealeh. . . . Therefore my heart intones like a harp for Moab and my inward feelings for Kir-hareseth" (Isa. 16:9, 11).

We get another glimpse of how God feels about sinners and their sins in a pair of remarkable statements in the book of Isaiah. To rebellious Israelites the Lord says, "Rather you have burdened Me with your sins, you have wearied Me with your iniquities" (43:24). Sin wearies God, but lifting the fallen and fatigued who trust in Him does not:

> Do you not know? Have you not heard?
>   The Everlasting God, the LORD, the Creator
>   of the ends of the earth
>   Does not become weary or tired.
>   His understanding is inscrutable.
> He gives strength to the weary,
>   And to him who lacks might He increases power.
>
>   (40:28–29)

Why was God willing to put His Son through hell and to bear the twin burdens of putting up with sinners for a time and grieving over their judgment? Because He desired to express His infinite benevolence by paying the greatest possible cost to redeem the people on whom He had set His love.

Although God *chose* to save sinners through the death of His Son, I do not mean He could have provided salvation in some less costly way. He need not have saved anyone. After He permitted sin to enter our race and then decided to save some, there was no other way to bring us out from under His wrath than for Him to enter the human race and bear the curse in our stead. We must not say God could have saved us some easier way and that He chose the way of the cross in order to impress us with His love. Timothy Keller makes this point vividly with the following illustration:

> Imagine that you are walking along a river with a friend, and your friend suddenly says to you, "I want to show you how much I love you!" and with that he throws himself into the river and drowns. Would you say in response, "How He loved me!" No, of course not. You'd wonder about your friend's mental state. But what if you were walking along a river with a friend and you fell into the river by accident, and you can't swim. What if he dived in after you and pushed you to safety, but was himself drawn under the current and drowned. Then you would respond, "Behold, how he loved me!" The example of Jesus is a bad example if it is only an example. If there was no peril to save us from—if we were not lost apart from the ransom of his death—then the model of his sacrificial love is not moving and life-changing; it is crazy. Unless Jesus died as our substitute, he can't die as a moving example of sacrificial love.[10]

The greatest eternal blessing. God wanted to make creatures capable of receiving the greatest blessing He could give—fellowship with Himself as His children. Angels are wonderful and glorious creatures, but they do not fulfill all God's desire. He wanted to make something better than the angels, and He succeeded, for angels are simply "ministering spirits, sent out to render service for the sake of those who will inherit salvation" (Heb. 1:14).

When God created Adam and Eve, they were lower than

the angels; by uniting His children to Christ, He will lift them higher than the angels (2:5–10). Why didn't He just create them higher than the angels in the first place? God was not able to show His love to sinless angels in as great a way as He has demonstrated it to redeemed sinners.

> Holy, holy, is what the angels sing,
> And I expect to help them make the courts of heaven ring;
> But when I sing redemption's story, they will fold their wings,
> For angels never felt the joys that our salvation brings.[11]

When God finished creating earth and its inhabitants, He pronounced it all "very good" (Gen. 1:31), but the new heavens and new earth will be better than very good. By permitting sin to spoil His creation and then planning for its redemption, God will communicate a far higher degree of His goodness to it and to His people than would have been possible in any other way:

> I consider that the sufferings of this present time are not worthy to be compared with the glory that is to be revealed to us. . . . For the creation was subjected to futility, not willingly, but because of Him who subjected it, in hope that the creation itself also will be set free from its slavery to corruption into the freedom of the glory of the children of God. (Rom. 8:18, 20–21)

God's Grand Plan

God did not need to think through His plan of creation one step at a time, but we are unable to see everything at once as He does. We sometimes need to list things sequentially in order to understand God's work. The thesis of this chapter can more easily be grasped by comparing the following two possible scenarios:

Scenario One (inadequate):

- God decided to create a world containing people with free will who might potentially choose to love Him.

- God foresaw the Fall and the reign of sin over the human race.
- God decided to save some sinners and permit other sinners to continue in their self-chosen sin, thus incurring divine judgment.

Scenario Two (better):

- God desired to pour out His love in the greatest possible way by the divinely difficult work of sacrificing Himself for the sake of others.
- God decided to create a world and to permit human beings freely to rebel against His law and His love. This rebellion was a grievous burden to God but essential for the fulfillment of His original desire.
- God chose to save some people, but not all, in order that His self-sacrifice might result in a real redemption from a real doom.

The second scenario is better because it recognizes that all the things God permits are things He might have chosen to forestall. He is not a passive observer, and the cross was not a rescue operation cobbled together after He realized His original plan was going to be washed down the drain by Adam's sin. As the apostle Peter said in his first sermon after the resurrection of Christ, "This Man [Jesus], delivered over *by the predetermined plan and foreknowledge of God*, you nailed to a cross by the hands of godless men and put Him to death" (Acts 2:23). The actions of the Jewish leaders and the Roman governor fulfilled God's predetermined plan to the letter. God knew what they would do because He had planned it before the foundation of the world. "For truly in this city there were gathered together against Your holy servant Jesus, whom You anointed, both Herod and Pontius Pilate, along with the Gentiles and the peoples of Israel, to do whatever Your hand and Your purpose predestined to occur" (4:27–28). Evil men acted freely when they sent Christ to the cross, but God had already decreed they would be allowed to follow the sinful impulses of their own hearts in order to fulfill His larger plan.

We could say the Lord did a cost-benefit analysis before He created the world. After looking at all the options available to Him, He might have decided to create nothing and continue enjoying the eternal love and harmony of the Trinity. Alternatively, He might have decided to make the holy angels and stop creating. Or He might have made a world inhabited by men and women who never chose to sin. But in any of these scenarios, God would never have been able to express His love fully. Part of His love—His grace and mercy toward guilty, miserable sinners—would have remained a hidden, unused potential. God decided it was worth the cost to Himself to express His infinite love in full.

It is difficult to look at these issues from God's perspective, but we must make the effort if we want to understand. We did not exist before the world began, so our feelings and desires could not possibly have been the motivation behind our creation. God did not consult us when He decided to create us. The Lord based His creative decisions on a wise analysis of His own desires and the cost to Himself of our redemption or damnation. The beauty of God's plan lies in the fact that what God wanted was not a creation to enjoy by Himself alone. He wanted to pour out His love and His own eternal happiness on a multitude of adopted children. For this end He was willing to impose great suffering on Himself.

Now it is possible to add one final perspective on suffering in this life. A world that was not evil and cruel would never have crucified the Son of God. Furthermore, a world that was not evil and cruel would not have needed redemption. God permitted what His soul abhors (Ps. 5:6) in order to gain that in which His soul delights. How much evil and cruelty did God need to permit to achieve His final end? Only as much as there actually is.

The sufferings of this world and the horrors of hell are very great, and it is not possible from our limited point of view to understand why there is so much pain. The Bible calls us to trust God's wisdom, love and justice in this matter. It helps when we recognize some suffering—only God knows how much—is necessary to the overall beauty of God's plan. It is like a dark blotch in the painting of a great master. Viewed from a distance of three inches, the blotch may appear ugly; step back a dozen feet, and it becomes a well-formed, integral part of a gloriously beautiful landscape. Step back if you can; try to see the big picture. Remember, the largest, darkest blotch is not your suffering or your neighbor's, but the suffering of the beautiful, self-sacrificing God.

As you contemplate God's grand plan, what is your response? After a lengthy explanation of predestination, judgment and grace, the apostle Paul exclaimed, "Oh, the depth of the riches both of the wisdom and knowledge of God! How unsearchable are His judgments and unfathomable His ways! For who has known the mind of the Lord, or who became His counselor? Or who has first given to Him that it might be paid back to him again? For from Him and through Him and to Him are all things. To Him be the glory forever. Amen" (Rom. 11:33–36).

And then it was needful that there should be a particular nation separated from the rest of the world, to receive the types and prophecies that were to be given of Christ, to prepare the way for His coming; that to them might be committed the oracles of God; that by them the history of God's great works of creation and providence might be preserved; that Christ might be born of this nation; and that from hence the light of the gospel might shine forth to the rest of the world. These ends could not well be obtained, if God's people, through all these two thousand years, had lived intermixed with the heathen world.

—Jonathan Edwards

9 How Could a Good God Command Ethnic Cleansing?

The Lord did not give Israel an unoccupied land. The original inhabitants had to be slaughtered, enslaved or driven away, and God left no doubt about which of those options He wanted Israel to pursue. When Israel went to war outside the Promised Land, they were to place cities that surrendered under tribute. If a city refused to make peace, the Israelites were to kill all the men, reserving "the women and the children and the animals" for themselves as the spoils of war (Deut. 20:10–15). Cities in the land of Canaan, however, received a harsher treatment: "Only in the cities of these peoples that the LORD your God is giving you as an inheritance, you shall not leave alive anything that breathes" (20:16).

The ethnic cleansing of Palestine raises a number of troubling questions for anyone who believes the God of the Bible is morally beautiful:

- Why did God command the extermination of the Canaanites?
- How does ethnic cleansing square with the ideal of a just war that seeks to protect the lives of innocent noncombatants?
- Did the Old Testament conquest of Canaan provide a sound biblical basis for the Crusades? If not, why not?
- How can Christians condemn the concept of a holy war

or jihad, as taught by some Muslim leaders, without at the same time casting doubt on their own Old Testament?

- Why did God command the killing of Canaanite infants, and how can that have been morally right?

This chapter sets forth four biblical principles that shed light on these questions.

The Principle of Temporal Judgment

God sometimes appoints individuals or nations to execute a portion of His wrath against sin. One common example is the authority God gives to the state. The apostle Paul reminded the Roman Christians that vengeance is the sole prerogative of the Lord (Rom. 12:19). However, he went on to say that God ordains the authority of the state, "for it is a minister of God to you for good. But if you do what is evil, be afraid; for it does not bear the sword for nothing; for it is a minister of God, an avenger who brings wrath on the one who practices evil" (13:4). Swords are not used for paddling miscreants; they are for cutting off heads. Therefore, when the state puts a criminal to death for a capital offense (from the Latin *capitalis*, meaning "of the head"), it is executing a temporal portion of God's just wrath. The eternal portion of God's justice is, of course, a far more serious matter and one God handles by Himself.

Once the fact of the universal sinfulness of mankind is admitted, it follows that God may call for judgment on a specific sinner whenever it pleases Him. If the Lord delays His judgment for a time, which He normally does, He is patiently waiting to give that sinner an opportunity to repent (2:4).

Several passages in the Old Testament indicate that God used one nation to judge another for its sins. God called Assyria "the rod of My anger" (Isa. 10:5) because He sent it to punish His people Israel. In this case, however, the Assyrians had no intention of obeying God. They were not aware of God's secret purposes. All they wanted to do was to plunder and dominate their neighbors (10:7). For that reason God announced that after He had used the Assyrians to punish Israel, He would bring judgment on them for their evil motives and actions.

There is only one example in the Bible of God openly commanding a nation to judge another group of people for its sins, and it occurred when God led Israel into the land of Canaan. Several hundred years before Joshua took Israel across the Jordan River into Palestine, the Lord promised to give that land to Abraham's distant descendants. Why the wait? Abraham did not receive the land immediately because, as God said to him, "The iniquity of the Amorite is not yet complete" (Gen. 15:16). The sinful behavior of the Amorites (and the other inhabitants of Canaan) included incest, homosexuality, bestiality and sacrificing children to the god Molech (Lev. 18:1–23). After listing these sins the Lord commanded, "Do not defile yourselves by any of these things; for by all these the nations which I am casting out before you have become defiled. For the land has become defiled, therefore I have brought its punishment upon it, so the land has spewed out its inhabitants" (18:24–25).

How does Israel's invasion of Canaan stack up against the classical concept of a just war? The answer is that just war theory does not apply in this case. A nation following just war principles seeks to spare the lives of innocent non-combatants. By definition the innocent are those who have not engaged in hostile acts against that nation. But the Bible says we are all "enemies" of God (Rom. 5:10) and "hostile" toward Him (8:7). The whole human race is at war with God, so when the Lord sent the armies of Israel into Canaan, there were no innocent bystanders who deserved to be spared. Although the Canaanites had done nothing to Israel, they were enemies of the God who was, at that point, commanding the armies of Israel.

Other nations have been guilty of the same or worse offenses than the Canaanites. Some of those nations lie buried in the dust of history; others (perhaps including our own) are still trying the patience of God. In none of these cases has God openly commanded one nation to execute a portion of His wrath against another. This is one fact that sets biblical religion apart from Islam. While the Old Testament envisioned a day when all nations would worship the true God, the Lord never commanded Israel to bear the sword to all nations in order to convert them to the one true faith. Ancient Israel was linked by the promise of God to the land of Canaan. Unlike Islam, it never claimed a mandate to enforce its laws on all the peoples of the world whether they wished it or not.

The Principle of Salvation History

The principle of salvation history enables us to see the extermination of the Canaanites as an essential part of God's plan to provide a Savior for the world. His judgment of the Canaanites was an act of justice toward them but an act of mercy toward the rest of the nations.

The modern fantasy about religion insists that if there is a true religion, it ought to be equally accessible to all people at all times and in all places. Therefore, either all religions are true, or none of them are. The postmodern twist to this fairy tale is that all religions are true for the people who believe them, but there is no comprehensive religious metanarrative true for all peoples. One stubborn fact stands against the foolish notion that all religions are valid: the major religions of the world are mutually exclusive. They cannot all be true in any meaningful sense of the word.

Christianity is set off from all other religions in the world by certain events that happened about two thousand years ago in a tiny Middle Eastern country—the incarnation, sinless life, substitutionary death and physical resurrection of Jesus Christ. No other religion has ever made such a cluster of claims for its founder. Therefore, if Christianity is true, all other religions are false in their major premises.

Christianity is starkly historical. It is so wedded to times, places and events that it cannot survive a divorce from them. Christianity has no isolated salvation principles, only a salvation history. The whole Old Testament is nothing more than a preparation for the coming of Christ. Even the Bible's lengthy genealogies, which twenty-first century readers find so boring, are a necessary part of the story. They trace the line of the Savior from Adam to Abraham, from Abraham to David and from David to Jesus Christ. God was determined to impress this crucial fact upon us: Jesus was a real human being with real ancestors who had a direct lineage back to Adam, the first man.

Buddhism, Hinduism and ancient Greek philosophy are not rooted in history. They purport to be discoveries of timeless truths that are, in principle, accessible to all people. Although Islam greatly reveres Muhammad as the final prophet of Allah, Muhammad did not claim to be teaching any new doctrine but only to be restoring lost truths that all the former prophets had taught. For that reason there is a certain timelessness to the precepts of Islam.

God's plan required that the teaching, death and resurrection of Christ take place in a certain historical context. As the Bible says, "But when the fullness of the time came God sent forth His Son, born of a woman, born under the Law" (Gal. 4:4). The incarnation of Christ had to take place among a people who recognized there is only one true God. In any other nation except Israel, Christ might have been accepted as one of many "divine beings," and His claim to be one with the Father would have fallen on uncomprehending ears. In order for Christ's sacrifice to be understood, He had to die among a people that possessed a strong sense of God's holiness and a well-developed understanding of substitutionary atonement. In other words, He had to be born under the Law.

God accomplished these goals by separating Israel from the idolatrous polytheists who surrounded them. He brought them out of Egypt by means of a stunning sequence of miracles. Then He led them into Canaan and commanded them to exterminate the former inhabitants, "so that they may not teach you to do according to all their detestable things which they have done for their gods, so that you would sin against the Lord your God" (Deut. 20:18). After the conquest of Canaan, the law of God further served to keep the pagans at bay. Circumcision, dietary laws and numerous oddities such as "you shall not boil a young goat in its mother's milk" (14:21) made Israel decidedly distinct from its neighbors.

The result of God's special protection of Israel was that when Jesus came and preached to the Jews, they understood He was either equal to God the Father (John 5:18), or He was the greatest threat to true religion that had ever arisen. His disciples accepted the former conclusion. His enemies chose the latter, and therefore, they put Him to death. In so doing, they unwittingly fulfilled the predictions of the Law and the Prophets that the Messiah would suffer for the sins of God's people.

Actually, even some Canaanites received the gift of salvation as a result of the ethnic cleansing of Canaan to make a Jewish homeland. Most notably, Rahab the Canaanite harlot adopted the Jewish faith and became an ancestress of Jesus Christ (Matt. 1:5).

The Principle of Covenantal Change

The Bible teaches that God is unchanging in His essential nature and purposes. His attributes remain eternally the same, and His plans were formed in perfect faithfulness before the foundation of the world (Num. 23:19; Ps. 102:25–27; Isa. 25:1; 46:9–10; Mal. 3:6). However, God has dealt with the human race in different ways during the major periods of human history. Biblical religion is a historical religion; it does not consist of timeless principles anyone can discover for himself. Biblical history consists of a series of definite stages by which God works out His plans. Each of these stages is marked by a new covenantal arrangement.

Although the Bible mentions several covenants, we only

need to consider two: the Old Covenant, which came before Christ, and the New Covenant, which was instituted by Christ.[1] Beyond that distinction I only need to make three general observations:

- The biblical covenants are not agreements negotiated by God and human beings working together. God alone sets the terms and conditions of His covenants with mankind.
- The individual covenants should never be seen in isolation. They are outworkings of the eternal plan the triune God formed before the world began.
- Differences between the covenants do not represent changes in God's moral demands on the human race. As the deposit of divine revelation increased, God gradually enlarged the scope and depth of His instruction without altering the basic foundation He had already laid.

The principle of covenantal change applies to religious warfare in the following way: The extermination of the Canaanites was necessary under the Old Covenant because God was preparing a people for the birth of His Son, and that nation needed to be isolated from the practices of the pagan nations around them. Now that Christ has been born and has fulfilled His earthly mission, the people of God are living under a different covenant. In this covenant the servants of Christ do not fight with fleshly weapons to defend the King or to expand His kingdom. As He stood on trial before Pilate, "Jesus answered, 'My kingdom is not of this world. If My kingdom were of this world, then My servants would be fighting so that I would not be handed over to the Jews; but as it is, My kingdom is not of this realm'" (John 18:36).

Under the New Covenant God intends for Christ's kingdom to spread by the preaching of the gospel, as the apostle Paul clearly explained. "How then will they call on Him in whom they have not believed? How will they believe in Him whom they have not heard: And how will they hear without a preacher? And how will they preach unless they are sent?" (Rom. 10:14–15).

The church has no mandate to conquer nonbelievers except by the sword of the Spirit, which is the Word of God (Eph. 6:17). As Jesus said, "This gospel of the kingdom shall be preached in the whole world as a testimony to all the nations, and then the end will come" (Matt. 24:14).

Since God intends the gospel to spread by preaching, the New Testament church has no mandate to put heretics to death. That was a necessary provision for the preservation of the Old Covenant people living in the Promised Land (Deut. 13). Now the people of God are to be protected from wolves by the faithful preaching of their pastors (Acts 20:28–32).

Unfortunately, from the early Middle Ages through the post-Reformation period, this principle was poorly understood. Roman Catholics, and later some Protestants, put heretics to the sword or fire. They tended to see an Old Covenant kind of relationship between the church and the state. Doctrinal error in the church not only endangered the eternal salvation of men, it also undermined the unity and security of the State. For that reason heresy was frequently a capital crime.

When we turn our attention to Islam we see a religious-political unity similar to the Old Testament ideal of a theocratic state. From that perspective the death penalty for Muslims who apostatize makes perfect sense. In addition to the Qur'an, Muslims regard the traditions of Muhammad (the Hadith) as authoritative. One of these traditions reads: "Narrated Ikrima: The statement of Allah's Apostle, 'Whoever changed his Islamic religion, then kill him.'"[2] This precept is still sometimes carried out in predominately Muslim countries either with government sanction or by individual initiative. Saudi Arabian law prescribes the death penalty for apostasy. (International pressure has sometimes caused that sentence to be set aside in recent years.) In the spring of 2007, normally moderate Turkey witnessed the brutal slaughter of a German missionary and two Turkish converts to

Christianity. Although many Turks were outraged at the murders, people I know personally in Turkey reported that they had encountered considerable support for the murderers, not from Muslim radicals but from ordinarily peaceable friends and co-workers.

Even though death for apostates is common to the Old Covenant and to Islam, one great difference between Israel and Islam is that the ideal Islamic theocracy is not tied to one small piece of real estate. It encompasses the whole world. Here is a sampling of commands from the Qur'an:

> Fight against them until idolatry is no more and God's religion reigns supreme. But if they desist, fight none except the evil doers. (2.193)[3]

> When the sacred months are over slay the idolaters wherever you find them. Arrest them, besiege them, and lie in ambush everywhere for them. If they repent and take to prayer and render the alms levy, allow them to go their way. God is forgiving and merciful. (9.5)

There is no apparent limitation on where idolaters may be killed or forced to convert. In general, the Qur'an is much more lenient toward people of the Book, that is, toward Jews and Christians who possess sacred Scriptures. However, Surah 9.29 commands, "Fight against such of those to whom the Scriptures were given as believe neither in God nor the Last Day, who do not forbid what God and His apostle have forbidden, and do not embrace the true Faith, until they pay tribute out of hand and are utterly subdued."

The Qur'an also justifies war if people in a nation desire to become Muslim but are in some way hindered by their government.

> Let those who would exchange the life of this world for the hereafter, fight for the cause of God; whoever fights for the cause of God, whether he dies or triumphs, on him We shall bestow a rich recompense.

And how should you not fight for the cause of God, and for the helpless old men, women, and children who say: "Deliver us, Lord, from this city of wrongdoers; send forth to us a guardian from Your presence; send to us from Your presence one that will help us?" (4.74–75)

The city in the foregoing quotation is Mecca, but the principle came to be more widely applied. According to non-Muslim scholar John Kelsay (as summarized by George W. Braswell Jr.),

> for force to be used in extending the territory of Islam and thus to achieve peace, Sunni theorists set down certain rules:
> - There must be a just cause (the refusal of a non-Islamic political entity to acknowledge the sovereignty of Islam).
> - There must be a declaration of Muslim intentions (the Muslim ruler must invite the adversary to accept Islam or to pay tribute and acknowledge the Muslim authority).
> - There must be right authority (the proper Muslim head of state or ruler).
> - The war must be conducted based on Islamic values (right intent for the cause and in the path of God).[4]

Although modern Muslim apologists often portray Islam as a peaceful religion, it is not at all difficult to see how Muslim fundamentalists can justify their attacks on the West from the teachings of the Qur'an and the example of Muhammad, who led armed raids against Meccan caravans.[5] Islam in general believes it has a divine mandate to extend an Old Covenant style of theocracy over the whole world. Jesus Christ taught that His kingdom is not of this world. Christians are to spread it by the proclamation of the gospel, unaided by the force of arms.

The Principle of Union with Adam

The slaughter of the Canaanite infants is one of the most difficult biblical events for many people to square with the love of God. Before we probe some of the weightier theological issues involved, consider two preliminary observations:

First, the fate of these infants was not necessarily different from the eternal destiny of other infants who die. Evangelical Christians fall into three distinct camps on the question of infant salvation: 1) All who die in infancy are saved by the blood of Christ (the majority view); 2) none who die in infancy are saved by the blood of Christ; 3) some who die in infancy (namely, elect infants) are saved by the blood of Christ. As we shall see, it is not necessary to give a definitive answer to that question in order to defend the justice of God. However, if God saves all who die in infancy, then the beauty of His grace shines brightly in the fate of the Canaanite children because by calling for their physical death, He preserved them from the moral degradation and condemnation of their parents.

Second, since God is the One who determines how long any individual lives, He is ultimately responsible for the death of all infants, whether they die one at a time because of illness or by the hundreds in a tsunami. When someone murders an infant, God holds him guilty because he took a human life without divine warrant. The Israelite soldiers were not guilty since they had an express command to cut short the lives of all the inhabitants of Canaan.

The questions that need to be addressed are these: Why do infants die? Why did God cut short the lives of these particular infants, and what is their eternal destiny? For the answers we need to look at our relationship to our father Adam.

"In Adam's fall, we sinned all." Thus begins the famous New England Primer. The first sin of our first father is the source of our guilt and death. The apostle Paul summarized the situation: "Therefore, just as through one man sin entered into the world, and death through sin, and so death spread to all men, because all sinned—for until the Law sin was in the world, but sin is not imputed when there is no law. Nevertheless death reigned from Adam until Moses, even over those who had not sinned in the likeness of the offense of Adam, who is a type of Him [Christ] who was to come" (Rom. 5:12–14).

A striking feature of the genealogy in Genesis 5 is, with only one exception, the description of each man's life ends with "and he died." Death reigned. Since death is the punishment for sin (6:23) and since "sin is not imputed when there is no law," the implication is that Adam's immediate descendants were involved in lawbreaking. However, between the creation of Adam and the time of Moses, God only pronounced the death penalty for two specific offences: eating from the tree of the knowledge of good and evil (Gen. 3:17) and murder (9:5–6). Since many people died who were not guilty of murder, God must have held them accountable for Adam's first sin. Why?

All Adam's descendants are so closely united to him that his guilt can be accounted to them. The relationship of all human beings to Adam is parallel to the way saved people are united to Christ. Christ has a natural, representative, voluntary and spiritual union with His people. (See chapter 6 for a fuller discussion.) All but the fourth of these are reflected in our union with Adam: All human beings have a *natural union* with Adam because we are his descendants. We have a *representative union* with him because God appointed him to that position—the proof of our representative union with Adam comes from Romans 5 and from First Corinthians 15:22, which says, "For as in Adam all die, so also in Christ all will be made alive." When people become mature enough in their mental and volitional ability to make rational choices, then all enter into a *voluntary union* with Adam—their disobedience confirms his defiance of God's law.

The penalty of physical death does not depend on individual disobedience. It comes from Adam's representative headship of the human race.[6] As Romans 5 makes clear, God did not count all Adam's sins against us, only the first one. Verse 16 declares: "the judgment arose from one transgression resulting in condemnation." If condemnation had come because of Adam's natural union with us, we would be held accountable for all his sins. If death were the penalty only for personal, voluntary sins, then no infant would die. Therefore, infants die because God appointed Adam to be the representative of all his descendants, and the sentence of physical death—whether it comes early or late—falls on us all.

There is, however, a secondary reason for saying God is just when He takes the life of an infant. Children are born sinners by nature. This is another part of the penalty of Adam's first rebellion. David said, "I was brought forth in iniquity, and in sin my mother conceived me" (Ps. 51:5). He does not mean that his mother was an adulteress but that from the moment of conception, he was a sinner. Likewise the psalmist testifies, "The wicked are estranged from the womb; those who speak lies go astray from birth. They have venom like the venom of a serpent" (58:3–4).

Since we act with finite knowledge on the presumption of innocence, our courts cannot judge a person's nature, only his actions. God, however, can justly judge us for what we are, as well as for what we do.

Let me illustrate. When I grew up in Southern California, rattlesnakes were a hated enemy. We did not wait for a snake to strike someone before we killed it. Now I live in a state where it is apparently against the law to kill copperheads even after one of them has bitten and nearly killed a young woman. After all, it was only doing what snakes do; she should have been more careful.

When God takes the life of an infant, it seems like a great injustice to us. Relative to our daily increasing mountain of guilt, the child is wonderfully innocent. In relation to God, however, the prettiest baby is still a poisonous serpent. If God saved none who die in infancy, He would be just. If He saves any, we see the glory of His mercy in turning serpents into sons.

Why were the Canaanite infants killed? According to Scripture, our union with Adam is the most far-reaching, but it is not the only example of a father's union with his offspring. The second of the Ten Commandments includes the warning, "I, the Lord your God am a jealous God, visiting the iniquity of the fathers on the children, on the third and the fourth generations of those who hate Me" (Exod. 20:5). Sometimes this dreadful visitation occurs through natural causes. The children of drug-addicted, fornicating thieves do not normally turn out very well. Yet God loves to reach down by His grace to transform some of those who are the least likely candidates for salvation.

In the later years of David's reign, we find a particularly chilling example of God's visiting a parent's sin on his offspring. When Israel entered the land of Canaan, they did not actually kill all its inhabitants as God had commanded them to do. One particular group—the Gibeonites—tricked Israel into making a solemn covenant of peace (Josh. 9). The covenant was against God's will, but once made in His name, it had to be kept. Saul, Israel's first king, broke the covenant and attempted to exterminate the whole Gibeonite clan. Years after Saul was dead, the Lord sent a three-year famine on the land "for Saul and his bloody house, because he put the Gibeonites to death" (2 Sam. 21:1). David consulted with the Gibeonites, who requested, "Let seven men from his sons be given to us, and we will hang them up before the Lord in Gibeah of Saul" (21:6). After seven of Saul's grandsons had been duly hanged, exposed for shame and finally buried, "God was moved by prayer for the land" (21:14). In other words, God accepted the death of Saul's descendants as an adequate recompense to the Gibeonites for Saul's crime.

If you are a normal product of Western Civilization, the revenge of the Gibeonites may turn your stomach sour. The Bible itself forbids human kings and judges to put children to death for their parent's crimes (Deut. 24:16). To understand the revenge of the Gibeonites in terms of the Bible's worldview requires a huge leap of the imagination.

In the beginning God revealed very little about what happens to us after death. He gave Israel some glimmerings of hope for a future resurrection, but for the nations surrounding Israel, the land of the dead was a vague, fearful place filled with shadows and uncertainty. Many Israelites must have felt the same way, as evidenced in the confused mental meanderings of Ecclesiastes.[7] Men and women expected to live on through their offspring.

On one hand, God blessed those who feared Him by being kind to their children (Ps. 103:15–17). On the other hand, an appropriate curse on a wicked man was to wish for his fatherless children to become homeless beggars (109:9–10). Children were supposed to respect their ancestors. In ancient Egypt the care of children for their parents' tombs was thought to promote the welfare of the parents in the afterlife. Generations were much more tightly bound together than they are for most Westerners.

Most peoples of the ancient biblical world also had a strong sense of belonging to a clan. Loyalty to one's clan was a defensive necessity when central governments were inadequate to punish serious crimes against individuals. Today we can see clan loyalty gone to seed in the violent tribal rivalries of Iraq and Afghanistan. By way of contrast, a far more positive aspect of family unity appears in the priorities of many recent immigrants to America. The fortunate newcomer often foregoes a comfortable lifestyle for himself in order to support a large extended family in India, Central America or elsewhere, and he expects to care for his aged parents in his own home.

Compare this strong sense of family with the rising devaluation of family in our highly individualized society. Increasing numbers of couples are deciding not to have children—either because they feel inadequate to raise them or because they don't want to be bothered. As for the treatment of ancestors, consider the many elderly nursing home residents who never receive a visit from their families.

Western individualists assume that they alone understand what it is to be human, but true humanity entails deep connections with our immediate families, our ancestors and even our first parents. The Bible holds both insights into our humanity—our individual rights and our social solidarity—in a productive tension. Each man and woman must repent and come to Christ individually, for "no man can by any means redeem his brother, or give to God a ransom for him" (Ps. 49:7). On the other hand, the Bible teaches that God has created a representative unity between Adam and all human beings, and a lesser unity is often the basis for God either blessing the offspring of the righteous or visiting the iniquity of the fathers on the children. It is a lesser unity because union with Adam involves *all* human beings in the *guilt* of Adam's sin. In contrast to that, union with parents causes *many* (not all) children to reap the *effects* (not the guilt) of their parents' actions, good or bad.

The Canaanite infants posed no special threat to Israel's political security or national worship, so why did God command them to be killed? The answer is twofold: First, they were probably regarded as defiled by the sin of their parents.[8] Second, they were put to death as a portion of God's punishment of their parents. The Canaanites fell under the same striking curses David pronounced against the unrepentant, wicked people of his time:

> Let there be none to extend lovingkindness to him,
>   Nor any to be gracious to his fatherless children.
> Let his posterity be cut off;
>   In a following generation let their name be blotted out.
> Let the iniquity of his fathers be remembered before
>   the LORD,
>   And do not let the sin of his mother be blotted out.
>   (Ps. 109:12–14)

Virtually all parents would respond with dismay if they knew their children would be killed along with them. For ancient peoples who placed such a high value on family solidarity, the thought would be even more devastating. The command to kill everything that breathed, as an act of God's judgment on an accursed race, would have made sense to Israelite soldiers.

What is the eternal destiny of infants who die? If all human beings have a representative union with Adam, it will not do to say some people (adults) are held accountable for all of Adam's guilt, while other people (infants) are held accountable for just a part of it. If the sentence of death passed down from Adam includes physical, spiritual and eternal death, all those who are united to Adam must bear the full weight of his sin unless that sin is covered by the atoning blood of Christ.

Of the various arguments for infant salvation, two seem weightier: First, Romans 5 exalts the effect of Christ's death as being more powerful and far-reaching than the effect of Adam's sin: "Where sin increased, grace abounded all the more" (5:20). From this statement and indeed the whole passage, Charles Hodge draws the following conclusions:

> The benefits of redemption far exceed the evils of the fall; . . . the number of the saved far exceeds the number of the lost. . . . It is more congenial with the nature of God to bless than to curse, to save than to destroy. If the race fell in Adam, much more shall it be restored in Christ. If death reigned by one, much more shall grace reign by one. This "much more" is repeated over and over. The Bible everywhere teaches that God delighteth not in the death of the wicked; that judgment is his strange work. It is, therefore, contrary not only to the argument of the Apostle, but to the whole spirit of the passage (Romans v.12–21), to exclude infants from "the all" who are made alive in Christ.[9]

The second argument of weight is that whenever Scripture speaks of eternal damnation, the basis of judgment is always an individual's own sins:

> Do not marvel at this; for an hour is coming, in which all who are in the tombs will hear His voice, and will come forth; those who did the good deeds to a resurrection of life, those who committed the evil deeds to a resurrection of judgment. (John 5:28–29)

> And I saw the dead, the great and the small, standing before the throne, and books were opened; and another book was opened, which is the book of life; and the dead were judged from the things which were written in the books, according to

their deeds. . . . And if anyone's name was not found written in the book of life, he was thrown into the lake of fire. (Rev. 20:12, 15)[10]

If damnation only follows an individual's personal, voluntary deeds of disobedience, then those who die in infancy will not be condemned. If they are not condemned, the reason is not that they are innocent. As already noted, they are little vipers only waiting for strength in order to strike. Therefore, they must be forgiven on the basis of Christ's shed blood.

The Beauty of God

Things that are practical are not always pretty. How is it possible to see the attractiveness of God in the judgment of the Canaanites? There are two fruitful approaches to that question: We must see the beauty of justice, and also the beauty of our representative union with Adam.

Jonathan Edwards reminds us that justice is attractive even when it calls for harsh punishments on the guilty:

There is a beauty in the virtue called *justice*, which consists in the agreement of different things, that have relation to one another, in nature, manner, and measure; and therefore is the very same sort of beauty with that uniformity and proportion, which is observable in those external and material things that are esteemed beautiful. There is a natural agreement and adaptedness of things that have relation one to another, and a harmonious corresponding of one thing with another. He who from his will *does* evil to others, should *receive* evil from the will of him or them whose business it is to take care of the injured, and to act in their behalf, in *proportion* to the evil of his doings. Things are in natural regularity and mutual agreement, in a literal sense, when he whose heart opposes the general system, should have the hearts of that system, or the heart of the ruler of the system, against him; and, in consequence should receive evil, in proportion to the evil tendency of the opposition of his heart. So there is an agreement in nature and measure, when he that loves has the proper returns of love; when he that from his heart promotes the good of another has his good promoted by the other; for there is a kind of justice in becoming gratitude.[11]

The beauty of justice, like beauty in nature, consists in harmony, fitness or proper proportion between an act and its consequences. No one finds the absence of this harmony attractive. Who thinks it beautiful when a teacher awards the highest grades to the students who bring her the nicest gifts? Or when a convicted rapist and murderer is accidentally released while officials are attempting to ease prison overcrowding? What about when teenage hoodlums terrorize a neighborhood with impunity, breaking windows, stealing cars and roughing up younger children on their way to school?

In order to see the beauty of divine justice, it is only necessary to admit the depth of human depravity. Complaints about the treatment of the Canaanites disappear when we are willing to admit that, apart from the mercy of Christ, we are all corrupt in our nature, defiled in our conscience, despisers of the divine beauty and rebels against divine authority. Until we come to that point, our complaints about the Canaanites are simply a cover for our own protestations of innocence. Our unspoken argument may run something like this: *Since the Canaanites were worse than I am, and God was unjust in judging them, surely I would have a clear right to complain if God rejected me.* But if we, who are generally upright, moral citizens, deserve divine wrath, then God could justly do whatever He pleased to the Canaanites. In short, the ethnic cleansing of the Canaanites was beautiful from God's perspective because it was just.

It is very difficult for us to look at things the way God does, but when we begin to see ourselves in the light of God's holiness, all our objections to God's justice melt away and we say with the prophet Isaiah, "Woe is me, for I am ruined! Because I am a man of unclean lips, and I live among a people of unclean lips; for my eyes have seen the King, the LORD of hosts" (Isa. 6:5).

Seeing the goodness of God in the death of the Canaanites also requires a deep appreciation for our union with Adam. That we should suffer because of Adam's sin seems grossly unfair and unattractive to many people, but it is a shining example of God's wisdom and mercy. The common assumption is that if we had been in Adam's shoes (or bare feet), we might have resisted the temptation to which he fell. However, a good argument can be made that *every* human being in Adam's circumstances would eventually have become corrupt. Only God is eternal and unchangeable. His nature alone cannot become worse. Although Adam was created innocent with an inclination toward God and goodness, no creature is capable of sustaining his own goodness—unless he is supernaturally preserved by God's Holy Spirit. The fall of Adam was inevitable not because he was poorly designed by God, but because God did not choose supernaturally to preserve him from sinning.

Although it is not given to us to see all the possible scenarios consistent with God's holy nature, it is given to us to see the consistency of the plan God chose to institute. Making us one with Adam was the divine foundation for making believers one with Christ. Instead of condemning us all as discrete, individual sinners, God chose to gather believing sinners into the body of Christ, thus making one out of many so that the sinless One might die for the many. Adam was our first representative; Christ is the last Adam who represents all who come to God through Him (1 Cor. 15:45).

There is a beautiful harmony and consistency in the work of God. One part agrees with another so our union with Adam, far from being an unmitigated disaster, was a loving provision for the salvation of untold multitudes of his descendants. If our first parents were saved, as Genesis 3 seems to suggest, then Adam's representative union with his posterity provided the foundation for Christ's representative union with Adam.[12] He was saved because his sin was counted against the whole human race, including Christ. Therefore, Christ was able to die for His ancestor's sin. Without a clear understanding of union with Christ, union with Adam makes no sense at all. Once the two concepts are linked, the amazing harmony of God's just judgment and His merciful salvation begins to shine with new and glorious brilliance.

Part 4

The Beauty *of* the TRIUNE God

There has been much cry of late against saying one word, particularly about the Trinity, but what the Scripture has said, judging . . . that, if we did, we should err in a question so much above us. But if they call that which rises and results from the joining of reason and Scripture, though it has not been said in Scripture in express words, I say, if they call this what is not said in Scripture, I am not afraid to say twenty things about the Trinity which the Scripture never said. There are deductions of reason from what has been said of the most mysterious matters, besides what has been said, and safe and certain from 'em too, as well as about the most obvious and easy matters.

—Jonathan Edwards

10   Is the Trinity Nonsense?

In the preceding chapters I have frequently referred to the love of God the Father for God the Son, constantly presupposing the classical doctrine of the Trinity without exploring the eternal Three-in-One. Although skeptics frequently mock the doctrine of the Trinity as illogical nonsense, it is the brightest jewel of Christian theology, because the sparkling light from this many-faceted truth illuminates every aspect of our relationship to God.

Defining the Doctrine of the Trinity

Many problems people have with the doctrine of the Trinity arise from an inadequate definition of the doctrine. The word "Trinity" does not occur in the Bible. It was coined in the third century after Christ. Even though Trinity is not a scriptural term, the doctrine the word describes is entirely faithful to Scripture. Finite minds cannot comprehend the infinite majesty of the Lord, yet God expects us to learn what He has revealed about Himself in the Bible. Thus, the triune God is incomprehensible as He is in Himself, but the basic doctrine of the Trinity may be stated rather simply:

There is only one God.

The one God includes three Persons.

These three Persons are distinct.

Scripture has a great deal more to teach about the Trinity, but the fundamentals come first. Each of these three statements has strong and abundant Scriptural support. Here is a sampling.

There is only one God. Modern pagans, polytheistic Hindus and Mormons deny this basic fact of biblical revelation. The Church of Jesus Christ of Latter Day Saints teaches that there are many gods, each in charge of his own world, and also that we may progress to become gods and creators. Scripture, however, is quite clear that there is only one true God. All others are false gods—either impotent nothings (Ps. 115:3–7) or demons (Deut. 32:17; 1 Cor. 10:19–20).

> "You are My witnesses," declares the LORD,
>   "And My servant whom I have chosen,
>   So that you may know and believe Me
>   And understand that I am He.
>   Before Me there was no God formed,
>   And there will be none after Me.
> I, even I, am the LORD,
>   And there is no savior besides Me."
>
>   (Isa. 43:10–11)

> Thus says the LORD, the King of Israel and his Redeemer,
>   the LORD of hosts:
> "I am the first and I am the last,
>   And there is no God besides Me."
>
>   (44:6)

> "Do not tremble and do not be afraid;
>   Have I not long since announced it to you and declared it?
>   And you are My witnesses.
>   Is there any God besides Me,
>   Or is there any other Rock?
>   I know of none."
>
>   (44:8)

> "I am the LORD, and there is no other;
>   Besides Me there is no God.
>   I will gird you, though you have not known Me."
>
>   (45:5)

The Mormon claim that the Lord is the only God with whom we have any dealings (even though other gods exist) simply does not do justice to these verses.

The one God includes three Persons. Several passages mention the three Persons of the Trinity together in such a way as to imply they are equals. For example, Jesus commanded the church to baptize "in the name of the Father and the Son and the Holy Spirit" (Matt. 28:19). We baptize in *the name*, not in the *names*. The three Persons share one divine Name, the name of God or Yahweh. It would be the gravest blasphemy to join any other person to the Father in such a fashion. No one would think of baptizing in the name of the Father, Cephas (Peter) and Paul (1 Cor. 1:12–17). Even an archangel would be too low a creature to include in the baptismal formula beside the Father.

John 1:1 says, "In the beginning was the Word, and the Word was with God, and the Word was God." In order that no one might be confused about the identity of the Word, John adds, "And the Word became flesh, and dwelt among us, and we saw His glory, glory as of the only begotten from the Father, full of grace and truth" (1:14). Unfortunately, this clear, direct assertion of the deity of Christ is deliberately altered by the Jehovah's Witness's *New World Translation* which says, "The word was *a god*." This false translation is easily refuted by anyone with a good grasp of New Testament Greek (which most people do not possess). However, even a person who does not know Greek can see a problem with this false translation. If Jesus is *a god*, but not the one true God, then He is a false god who is not worthy of our worship. Yet the Scriptures accord Him glory, honor and worship equal to the Father's.

Yahweh says, "For My own sake, for My own sake, I will act; for how can My name be profaned? And My glory I will not give to another" (Isa. 48:11). Jesus insisted during His conflict with the devil that no one may lawfully worship anyone except the Lord God (Matt. 4:10). When the apostle John fell down to worship at the feet of an angel, the angel rebuked him and commanded him instead to worship God (Rev. 19:10; 22:8–9). Yet God Himself commanded the angels to worship the Son (Heb. 1:6), and we see them doing exactly that in the book of Revelation:

> Then I looked, and I heard the voice of many angels around the throne and the living creatures and the elders; and the number of them was myriads of myriads, and thousands of thousands, saying with a loud voice, "Worthy is the Lamb that was slain to receive power and riches and wisdom and might and honor and glory and blessing." (Rev. 5:11–12)

There is no degree of honor accorded to the Father, who sits on the throne, which the angels do not also ascribe to the Lamb (the Lord Jesus Christ). Since God will not share His glory with anything less than Himself, we must recognize the full deity of Christ (Col. 2:9) or be counted heretics and enemies of God.

At the end of John's Gospel, we find a further confirmation of Christ's deity in the confession of Thomas, the doubting apostle. When he saw the risen Lord, he said to Jesus, "My Lord and my God!" (John 20:28). In the next verse Jesus commended his faith and the faith of all who will believe without seeing His resurrection body. A Jehovah's Witness once told me that Thomas was not calling Jesus God. He was just uttering an expression of surprise. However, when someone bursts out with "Oh, my God," he is taking God's name in vain, thus breaking the third commandment. When did God begin to praise people for blasphemy?

Those who acknowledge the deity of Christ normally have no problem recognizing that the Spirit is also God. Here are three brief Scriptural testimonies to His deity:

- The Spirit of God is omnipresent, and His presence is equivalent to the presence of God (Ps. 139:7–12). To have the indwelling Holy Spirit is to be a dwelling place of God. Christians, both collectively and individually, are temples of God because the Holy Spirit dwells in them (1 Cor. 3:16; 6:19; 2 Cor. 6:16; Eph. 2:19–22).

- Only an infinite Person could know all the secrets of God, as the Holy Spirit does (1 Cor. 2:11).
- Lying to the Holy Spirit is equivalent to lying to God (Acts 5:3–4).

Some suggest that the Holy Spirit is not a distinct Person in His own right. They say that since God is Spirit (John 4:24), "the Spirit of God" is simply another way of saying God. For a response, consider the third defining statement in the doctrine of the Trinity.

These three Persons are distinct. After John baptized Jesus, "and while He was praying, heaven was opened, and the Holy Spirit descended upon Him in bodily form like a dove, and a voice came out of heaven, 'You are My beloved Son, in You I am well-pleased'" (Luke 3:21–22). Here we see all three Members of the Trinity present at one time and doing different things. Other passages reinforce the distinction of the Persons from each other. Jesus regularly prayed to His Father and obeyed His Father. Furthermore, Jesus promised to send the Spirit from the Father to His disciples (John 15:26), and obviously the Sender is distinct from the One sent.

The three Persons are distinct; they are not separate. They are distinct because Scripture distinguishes between the activities of the Father, Son and Holy Spirit. They are not separate Persons because it is impossible to have one without the others. They cannot be separated or pulled apart, as would be possible if they were three different gods.

It is crucial to keep the three defining statements of the doctrine of the Trinity firmly in mind. Doing so enables us to avoid making contradictory statements about God. Although the Trinity is a mystery, the doctrine itself is not contradictory. A mystery is a truth beyond our comprehension. (Einstein's general theories of relativity and quantum mechanics are mysteries to most people.) A contradiction consists of two or more statements that cannot all be true at the same time. It is a contradiction to say that in the Trinity there are three Gods, and yet one God. It is also a contradiction to say God is one Person and also three Persons.[1] It is not contradictory to say the Trinity is one God who eternally exists as three Persons.

The Trinitarian triangle drawn below is a common visual summary of the three defining statements.

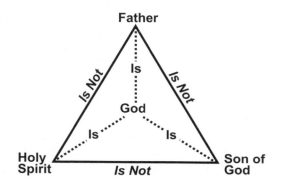

Read the triangle this way:

- There is only one God.
- The Father is God; the Son is God; the Holy Spirit is God.
- The Son is not the Father; the Father is not the Holy Spirit; the Holy Spirit is not the Son.

Illustrating the Doctrine of the Trinity

Although the Trinity is an infinite mystery, our minds naturally search for an image or picture to aid our comprehension. There are no perfect illustrations of the Trinity because the God who made the world is too great to be represented completely by anything in the world. Some common illustrations are so inadequate they should not be used at all because they actually illustrate ancient heresies regarding the Trinity. These heresies fall into two groups:

The Arian heresy (named for Arius, ca. AD 250–336). This heresy denies that the Father and Son have exactly the same divine nature. Arianism (represented today by Jehovah's Witnesses) teaches that the Father and Son are entirely separate beings. The egg is a popular Trinitarian symbol that actually illustrates Arianism. An egg is one object with three parts—the eggshell, egg white and egg yolk. The egg illustration obscures the fact that there is only one divine nature, one God. The shell, the white and the yolk do not have the same nature—just try eating the shell.

The Sabellian heresy (named for Sabellius, in Rome ca. AD 198–220). This heresy acknowledges that the Father, Son and Holy Spirit are all God, but it denies they are distinct Persons. A popular Trinitarian illustration (actually Sabellian) compares God to a man who has three different roles. He may be a father of several children; he is also a son and a husband. But the father is not a distinct person from the son or the husband, whereas God the Father, God the Son and God the Holy Spirit are distinct Persons. The three states of water (solid, liquid, gas) also illustrate Sabellianism, because a given quantity of water cannot exist in all three states at the same time.

The illustration on the next page, though imperfect, has some advantages over those already mentioned. Certain kinds of trees can produce more than one treetop out of the same root or from an old stump.

In this diagram the root represents the one divine nature; the three treetops stand for the three Persons who share that nature. Like all illustrations of the Trinity, this one has flaws. We could cut down one treetop without affecting the others, but the three Persons of the Trinity cannot be cut off from one another. Also, the treetops do not interact with each other as the Persons of the Godhead do. Nevertheless, this picture does have the advantage of illustrating two major aspects of the doctrine of the Trinity: the three divine Persons and the one divine Nature.

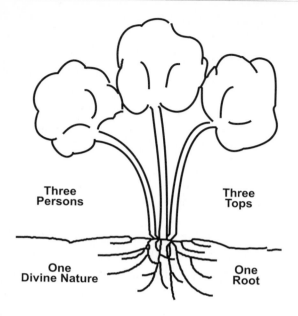

Three Persons

Three Tops

One Divine Nature

One Root

Personal Relationships within the Trinity

According to the common usage, a person is a self-conscious individual who is able to reason, feel and act. There are difficulties in applying this understanding to the Trinity because each human person has a separate mind, a separate emotional make-up and makes separate choices. God the Father does not have a separate reason, emotion and will from that of the Son or the Holy Spirit. All three Persons know the same things; They love or hate the same things; They will the same things. So what does the word "person" mean when it is applied to the Trinity?

The ancient Latin word *persona* originally referred to the mask worn by an actor in a play. Afterward, it was applied to the role or part he played. Imagine a play that involves three characters: a father who owns a factory, the owner's son and the plant manager.

- Arianism says, "This play requires three separate individuals to act out the different parts."

- Sabellianism says, "One individual can play all three parts, but he will have to run off stage to change costumes. Just as Superman has to change clothes in order to play Clark Kent, so God can only play one part at a time."

- Trinitarianism says, "God is a great enough Being to play all three parts at once—great enough actually to be three Persons on the stage at the same time." God, of course, is not just acting in a play. He has always been three Persons living out three roles, though He is one God.

What are the roles that the Persons of the Godhead play? How do the three Persons relate to each other? The Bible reveals an eternal ordering among the Persons of the Trinity:

- The Father sent His Son into the world (John 3:16; 4:34; 5:37–38; 1 John 4:9). Since the Father sent the Son, the Father-Son relationship existed before the incarnation, and it must be an indication of what God is like in Himself.

- The Father is the Speaker. The Son is the Word whom the Father speaks (John 1:1–2). Since God is the eternal Speaker, the Word spoken is also eternal.

- The Father is like a bright star. The Son is the Light streaming forth from Him (Heb. 1:3). The star and its light must exist together. If one is eternal, so is the other.

- While He was on earth, Jesus Christ always looked for His Father's direction and did His Father's will (John 5:19–23, 30; 6:38; 8:28).

The church has traditionally recognized the earthly submission of Christ to the Father as an extension of an eternal relationship between them. Some modern theologians suggest that before creation there was no difference between the three Persons of the Godhead and that the Father, Son and Holy Spirit only adopted different roles for the purposes of creation and redemption. If such is the case, then we know nothing about what God is like in Himself, and the submission of Jesus Christ on earth was only a show put on for our benefit. This requires us to imagine that the Trinity drew straws to see which of them would humble Himself through the incarnation and the cross.

The church's historic doctrine of submission and equality in the Trinity provides necessary insights for understanding the statements of Scripture. Though we cannot penetrate the divine nature by our human understanding, we ought to believe what God has revealed about Himself and accept the obedience of Christ as an indication of an eternal relationship among the Persons of the Trinity. The divine nature of the Son does not submit to the divine nature of the Father, because there is only one divine nature. However, the Person of the Son submits to the Person of the Father.[2]

Similarly, the Holy Spirit is dependent on the Father and the Son, for He is both the Spirit of God and the Spirit of Christ (Rom. 8:9). The Father sent the Spirit to the church through the Son (John 14:16; 26; 15:26; 16:7; Acts 2:32–33). With these facts in view, we may speak of the first, second and third Persons of the Trinity not because one is greater than another but because they act together in a certain order. That concept becomes clearer as we consider the various works of the Triune God.

The Works of the Triune God

All three Persons of the Godhead work together in every divine activity, but each Person performs His own particular function in relation to the world and to God's redeemed children. We see this in the following arenas:

Creation. The Father created through the Son (John 1:1–3; Col. 1:15–16). The Son will restore creation to the Father (1 Cor. 15:23–28). The Holy Spirit is intimately involved with creation (Gen. 1:2; 2:7; Job 33:4; Ps. 104:29–30; 139:7–12).

Redemption. The Father planned our salvation (Eph. 1:3–4). The Son purchased our salvation by His blood (1:7). The Holy

Spirit is the chief gift purchased for us by Christ (1:13–14). Christ seals us with the Spirit as letters used to be sealed with an emblem stamped in wax. The Father and the Son dwell in us through the Holy Spirit (John 14:16–17, 23).

Worship. Normally we pray to the Father through the Son and in the Holy Spirit (John 16:23–24; Eph. 2:18; 6:18). The Holy Spirit helps us to pray, while the Son's intercession makes our prayers acceptable to the Father (Rom. 8:26–27, 34). We may also pray directly to the Son (John 14:13–14). Since our fellowship with God involves all three members of the Trinity (2 Cor. 13:14; 1 John 1:3), we may also pray to the Holy Spirit, though this is not the normal pattern.

The distance between us and each Person. The Father is God high above us (Ps. 97:9). The Son is the divine Mediator between the Father and us (1 Tim. 2:5). The Spirit is God up close (John 14:16–17).

This introductory look at the Trinity reveals something of the wonderful harmony that exists between the three members of the Godhead. The biblical doctrine of the Trinity is much richer and more varied than this brief outline suggests, and it has many implications for philosophy, art, science, social structures and interpersonal relationships.

For science and philosophy, the crucial Trinitarian concept is the relationship between the one and the many. If reality consists of only matter, why is the cosmos an integrated whole that evinces purpose and design, as we see in biology, ecology and physics? If reality consists of one undivided spirit as pantheistic philosophy suggests, how is it we perceive ourselves to be discrete individuals? How did the illusion of separateness arise? The doctrine of the Trinity teaches that both unity and plurality are ultimate and that both are essential for understanding our world.

Artists have also struggled with the problem of the one and the many. From ancient Greece up through the post-Renaissance period, artists commonly believed beauty to be a universal category that all people could recognize and appreciate. Flawless marble figures of the Greek gods reflected the conviction that divinity must resemble perfect humanity. Post-renaissance paintings added a note of realism to artistic ideals, for people could be painted (as Oliver Cromwell was) "warts and all." Still, artists strove to bring the diverse elements of their works into a unified, beautiful whole.

Modern artists have largely repudiated that goal. Believing that beauty, truth and goodness are not universal categories, they have stopped trying to portray them. As a consequence, much modern art exhibits brokenness, despair and fragmentation. My hope is that Christian artists, who have a clear understanding of the beauty of the triune God, will bring beauty back into their work even when they are not portraying Christian themes. Such art can be abstract or realistic. It ought not to be merely senti-mental, for our God is the God of truth.

Social structures and human relationships also depend on bringing many individuals into a harmonious unity. They are enhanced by the Trinitarian truth that submission can exist among persons who are equal. The family and larger social struc-tures require submission of some equals to other equals. History abundantly illustrates that when this principle is ignored, some human beings readily turn other human beings into subhuman creatures, either cattle or machines. When people consciously seek to imitate the relationships among the Persons of the Trin-ity, their own relationships become more beautiful.

Edwards on the Trinity

The New Testament frequently refers to Jesus as the Son of God and teaches that Jesus prayed to and obeyed His Father. That kind of language is not hard to understand because good children talk to their parents and follow their parents' instruc-tions. However, to limit discussion of the Trinity to the family metaphor will inevitably lead to thinking of the Father and the Son as two separate individuals. This metaphor—sometimes re-ferred to as the social analogy—leaves us wondering where the

Holy Spirit fits into the family structure. One obvious but mis-
leading suggestion is to regard the Holy Spirit as the Mother
because the mother is often the nurturing family member who
draws the rest of the family together. However, this suggests that
the Son of God is the fruit of the union of the Father-God and
the Mother-Spirit, which is not the case. As we have seen in the
New Testament, the Spirit is sent by the Father and the Son, and
is, in some sense, dependent on them. Therefore, referring to the
Spirit as the divine Mother reverses the biblical relationship of
the members of the Trinity.

We must go beyond the family metaphor to examine other
dimensions of Trinitarian teaching in the New Testament. Jonathan Edwards's exploration of another illustration, the so-called
psychological analogy, affords a number of rich insights into the
inner life of the Triune God.[3]

The psychological analogy. In the fifth century after Christ,
Augustine suggested one of the enduring illustrations of the
Trinity based primarily on three biblical texts:

- "God is love" (1 John 4:8).
- "Then God said, 'Let Us make man in Our image'"
  (Gen. 1:26).
- "In the beginning was the Word, and the Word was with
  God, and the Word was God" (John 1:1).

In his work *On the Trinity,* Augustine constructed the illustration as follows:[4] If God is love, what is the nature of love?
In love "there are three things: he that loves, and that which is
loved, and love. What, then, is love, except a certain life which
couples or seeks to couple together some two things, namely
him that loves, and that which is loved?"[5] God was love before
He made the world, but there was no one for Him to love but
Himself. Therefore, God must contain within Himself a Lover,
a Beloved and the Love that binds them together.

How can such a plurality exist within God who is One? The
first chapter of Genesis provides an important clue. When God

said, "Let Us make man in Our image," the words *Us* and *Our*
appear to refer to the three Persons of the Godhead.[6] Therefore,
the image of God in man must in some way reflect the triper-
sonality of the Trinity. We see this reflection in the mind of a
man who knows and loves himself. Self-knowledge and self-love
differ from each other, but cannot be separated from the mind
in which they reside. In the same way, the Father (the Knower,
or the divine Lover), the Son (the Known, or the divine Beloved)
and the Holy Spirit (the divine self-Love) have one essence.

Augustine strengthens the comparison by noting that when
we know and love something, we express it by a word. Scripture
teaches that Jesus Christ is the Word of God. He is the Father's
eternal self-expression who perfectly represents the Father and
is loved by the Father. This eternal love, says Augustine, is the
Holy Spirit. "And so there is a kind of image of the Trinity in the
mind itself, and the knowledge of it, which is its offspring and
its word concerning itself, and love as a third, and these three are
one, and one substance."[7]

Jonathan Edwards adopts and then transforms the Augustinian psychological analogy of the Trinity by filtering it through
an interesting analysis of how our minds work. Suppose you are
thinking of a conversation you had yesterday. Your memory may
be fuzzy or rather clear. If your powers of visualization are very
good, you may be able, by closing your eyes, to see the speaker
and perhaps even to hear what he is saying. Edwards calls these
sights and sounds in our heads *ideas*. Our ideas are always imperfect, but a perfect idea of an experience would be an exact
replication of the event, including all the smells, tactile informa-
tion and other minute extras lost in even our clearest memories.[8]

Now transfer this definition of "idea" to the way we view
ourselves. We have at best a fuzzy idea of ourselves. I have trouble closing my eyes and recollecting what I saw in the mirror this
morning. I cannot remember very well what I did last week, nor
do I clearly understand the interplay of sinful and holy desires in
my own heart. Nevertheless, if I like what I see in myself—if my

conscience approves of my attitudes and actions—I experience delight or pleasure in myself.

Since God has a perfectly clear idea of Himself, His idea of Himself must be an exact replication of God. God's idea of Himself must be God. As God contemplates this divine Idea, He approves of what He sees, and therefore, He experiences delight or pleasure in Himself. God's delight must be perfect and infinite, and whatever is perfect and infinite must be God. Thus, God's love for Himself makes the third Person of the Trinity. There is an exact parallel between the Son of God and the Spirit of God. The Son is the Word of God; the Spirit is the Love of God. The Son is the Person in whom God knows Himself; the Spirit is the Person by whom God loves Himself.

One might suppose that in this way the number of Persons in the Godhead could be multiplied almost endlessly by positing a different person for each divine attribute. However, all the moral attributes of God are derived from His love. For example, God's wrath is directed toward those who reject the chief object of His love, which is Christ. The nonmoral attributes, such as His eternal nature, His omnipresence and His omnipotence, are all different aspects of His infinity. We end up, then, with three kinds of divine attributes: infinity, intellect and morality. This analysis leads directly to the psychological analogy in which the infinite God knows Himself in the Son and loves Himself by the Holy Spirit.

Edwards argues for the identity of the Son of God with God's idea of Himself:

> It has always been said that God's infinite delight consists in reflecting on Himself and viewing His own perfections, or, which is the same thing, in His own perfect idea of Himself; so that 'tis acknowledged that God's infinite love is to, and His infinite delight [is] in, the perfect image of Himself. But the Scriptures tell us that the Son of God is that image of God which He infinitely loves. [See Colossians 1:15 and Hebrews 1:3.] Nobody will deny this: that God infinitely loves

His Son. [At this point, Edwards quotes or alludes to John 3:35; 5:20; Matthew 3:17; 17:5; Isaiah 42:1; Ephesians 1:6 and Proverbs 8:30.] Now none, I suppose will say that God enjoys infinite happiness in two manners, one in the infinite delight He has in enjoying His Son, His image, and another in the view of Himself different from this. So if not, then these ways wherein God enjoys infinite happiness are both the same; that is, His infinite delight in the idea of Himself is the same with the infinite delight He has in His Son, and if so His Son and that idea He has of Himself are the same. . . .

Lastly, that which is the express image of God, in which He infinitely delights and which is His word and which is the reason or wisdom of God, is God's perfect idea of God. That God's knowledge or reason or wisdom is the same with God's idea, none will deny. . . . But none needs to be told that the Son of God is often called in Scripture by the names of the wisdom and logos of God.[9] Wherefore God Himself has put the matter beyond all debate, whether or no His Son is not the same with His idea of Himself; for it is most certain that His wisdom and knowledge is the very same with His idea of Himself.[10]

Although Edwards couches his argument in philosophical language, he is careful to tie all his conclusions to Scripture. The same is true of His discussion of the Holy Spirit's place within the Trinity. In his *Treatise on Grace*, Edwards carefully draws out the contextual implications of "God is love" (1 John 4:8):

"He that loveth not, knoweth not God; for God is love." So again, ver. 16—"God is love; and he that dwelleth in love, dwelleth in God and God in him." But the Divine essence is thus called in a peculiar manner as breathed forth . . . in the Holy Spirit; as may be seen in the context of these texts, as in the 12th and 13th verses of the same chapter—"No man hath seen God at any time. If we love one another, God dwelleth in us, and His love is perfected in us. Hereby know we that we dwell in Him and He in us, because He hath given us of His Spirit." It is the same argument in both these verses: in the 12th verse the apostle argues that if we have love dwelling in us, we have God dwelling in us; and in the 13th verse he clears the face of the argument by this, that this love which is dwelling in us is God's Spirit. And this shews that the foregoing argument is good, and that if love dwells in us, we know that God dwells in us indeed, for the Apostle supposes it as a thing granted and allowed that God's Spirit is God. The Scripture elsewhere does abundantly teach us that the way in which God dwells in the saints is by His Spirit, by their being the temples of the Holy Ghost. Here this Apostle teaches us the same thing. He says, "We know that He dwelleth in us, that He hath given us His Spirit;" and this is manifestly to explain what is said in the foregoing verse—viz., that God dwells in us, inasmuch as His love dwells in us; which love he had told us before—ver. 8—is God Himself. And afterwards, in the 16th verse, he expresses it more fully, that this is the way that God dwells in the saint—viz., because this love dwells in them, which is God. Again the same is signified in the same manner in the last verses of the foregoing chapter. In the foregoing verses, speaking of love as a true sign of sincerity and our acceptance with God, beginning with the 18th verse, he sums up the argument thus in the last verse: "And hereby we know that He abideth in us, by the Spirit which He hath given us."[11]

What Edwards sees in First John 3 and 4 may be expressed by the following two equations:

- God dwells in us = the Spirit of God dwells in us = Love dwells in us
- We dwell in God = we dwell in Love

Therefore, the Spirit of God is the Love of God.

Edwards's prose is a little dense, but I have quoted two long selections because of the profound impact they had on my understanding of the Trinity. In the writings of C.S. Lewis, I had previously met the Augustinian concept of a divine Lover, a divine Beloved and the divine Love binding them together.[12] Edwards's treatment transformed that concept from a mere illustration or a verbal word play on love into a powerful and moving insight into the dynamic life of God.

The fundamental moral truth about God is that He is love, but His love is not mere sentiment. Love is a Person. God loves whatever participates in the inter-Trinitarian harmony. He hates and rejects whatever does not. This helps us to understand God's holy wrath against sin.

In Romans 5 the apostle Paul explains why Christians are able to rejoice in the midst of tribulations. They test and strengthen the believer's character and deepen his expectant hope of God's ultimate intervention on his behalf. "And hope does not disappoint, because the love of God has been poured out within our hearts through the Holy Spirit who was given to us" (5:5). The love of God—God's own love, not our love for God—is poured out within believers' hearts through the giving of the Holy Spirit. Scripture frequently uses "pouring out" to describe the gift of the Spirit (Isa. 32:15; 44:3; Ezek. 39:29; Joel 2:28; Zech. 12:10; Acts 2:17, 33; 10:45; Titus 3:5–6).

Thus, the divine Love who is poured out is indeed the Person of the Holy Spirit. To make the Holy Spirit merely the delivery boy of divine love and other blessings is greatly to diminish Him. The Spirit does not just produce a feeling of God's love within the believer's heart. When His love is poured out, the Holy Spirit is poured out. So God pours His love into a human heart through the outpouring of His Spirit.

This is consistent with the way other passages describe the work of the Spirit. Love is not just a feeling. It is a rich, harmonious relationship in which both parties find pleasure in contemplating and pleasing one another. Jesus promised His disciples the Holy Spirit would be in them to help them (John 14:16–17). Then He further explained, "If anyone loves Me, he will keep My word; and My Father will love him, and We will come to him and make our abode with him" (14:21) The Spirit of God becomes the Helper of God's children by bringing them into relationship with the Father and Son. The Spirit's presence is the presence of the Father and the Son.

Consider how the Spirit promotes love between Christians. Paul exhorts them to "walk in a manner worthy of the calling with which you have been called, with all humility and gentleness, with patience, showing tolerance for one another in love, being diligent to preserve the unity of the Spirit in the bond of peace. There is one body and one Spirit, just as also you were called in one hope of your calling" (Eph. 4:1–3). The Spirit creates a loving unity among believers by indwelling them. He is in them, so love is in them. Though believers cannot create love, they are responsible to maintain the practical expressions of it.

The Spirit is never just the conduit of divine blessing. He *is* the blessing, and He blesses by wrapping us up in the love relationship of the Triune God. When the New Testament relates the Christian's *inward experience* of divine love to one of the Persons of the Trinity, the Holy Spirit is often prominently in view (Rom. 15:30; Gal. 5:22; Eph. 3:16–19; Phil. 2:1–3; Col. 1:8; Jude 1:19–21). To have love is to have the Spirit; to have the Spirit is to have love. The Father's love for His Son is most fully expressed by pouring into His humanity "the Spirit without measure" (John 4:34–35).

The Beauty of the Triune God. In keeping with Scripture and a theological tradition going back to Augustine, Edwards makes much of the beauty of God. He does not, however, develop his doctrine of divine beauty directly from the psychological analogy, which emphasizes the unity of the divine Mind which knows and approves of Itself. Instead, he turns to the social analogy, which highlights the distinction between the Persons of the Godhead. There must be such a distinction because God is both good and beautiful. No one can be good alone because goodness requires another person to whom one can be good. Danaher summarizes Edwards this way: "As an infinite being, God cannot 'communicate all His goodness to a finite being.' Hence, God 'must have a perfect exercise of His goodness, and therefore must have the fellowship of a Person equal to Himself.' The 'Father's begetting of the Son,' then, 'is a complete communication of His happiness, and so an eternal, adequate and infinite exercise of perfect goodness, that is completely equal to such an inclination in perfection.'[13]

We find a similar argument in Edwards's discussion of beauty. In his notes on "The Mind," he discusses beauty under the heading of "Excellence" or "Excellency." "Excellence," he says, "is that which is beautiful and lovely."[14] Edwards understands beauty in classical terms of harmony, symmetry and proportion.[15] Therefore, beauty necessarily involves more than one element; otherwise there is no harmony.

> One alone, without any reference to any more, cannot be excellent; for in such case there can be no manner of relation no way, and therefore no such thing as Consent. Indeed what we call *One*, may be excellent because of a consent of parts, or some consent of those in that being, that are distinguished into a plurality in some way or other. But in a being that is absolutely without any plurality, there cannot be Excellency, for there can be no such thing as consent or agreement.[16]

In this passage, as he commonly does, Edwards borrows the words "consent" and "agreement" from the sphere of personal relations and applies them to excellence. He does this because the highest kind of excellence is not the symmetry of natural or man-made objects, but rather harmonious relations between persons. Love is the highest form of interpersonal harmony.

> When we spake of Excellence in Bodies, we were obliged to borrow the word *Consent*, from Spiritual things; but Excellence in and among Spirits is, in its prime and proper sense, Being's consent to Being. There is no other proper consent but that of *Minds*, even of their Will; which, when it is of Minds towards Minds, it is *Love*, and when of Minds towards other things, it is *Choice*. Wherefore all the Primary and Original beauty or excellence, that is among Minds, is Love.

Since God is the most excellent Being, the ultimate pattern for agreement and consent must be in God. Therefore, God's Being must encompass a plurality of Persons.

> As to God's Excellence, it is evident it consists in the *Love of Himself*, for He was as excellent before He created the Universe, as He is now. But if the Excellence of Spirits consists in their disposition and action, God could be excellent no other way at that time; for all the exertions of Himself were towards Himself. But He exerts Himself towards Himself, no other way, than in infinitely loving and delighting in Himself; in the mutual love of the Father and the Son. This makes the Third, the Personal Holy Spirit, or the Holiness of God, which is His infinite Beauty; and this is God's Infinite Consent to Being in general. And His love to the creature is His excellence, or the communication of Himself, his complacency in them, according as they partake of more or less of Excellence and beauty, that is, of holiness (which consists in love); that is, according as He communicates more or less of His Holy Spirit.[17]

Several features of this quotation call for comment. First, the Spirit of God is the Beauty of God because without Him there would be no consent or harmony between the Father and the Son. Second, He is the Love of God because He is the eternal act by which the Father and Son give themselves to each other and delight in each other. Third, He is the Holiness of God because love is the sum and substance of God's character and the foundation of all God's actions toward His creatures.

We commonly call beauty, love and holiness attributes of God without considering how all three Persons of the Trinity have them in common. The Persons of the Trinity have the same, identical essence. They permeate one another so thoroughly that they live in each other and have all attributes in common. The Holy Spirit is the Spirit of the Father (Matt. 10:20) and the Spirit of the Son (Gal. 4:6), so He occupies the middle position between the Father and the Son within the Trinity. Since the Spirit provides the bond of love between believers, perhaps the best way to express the Trinitarian relationships is this: The Father loves the Son in and through the Spirit. The Son loves the Father responsively in and through the Spirit. One of the Father's attributes is love, and one of the Son's attributes is love because they share the same Spirit, who is Love.

In summary, through his analysis of love and beauty, Jonathan Edwards brings together two important Trinitarian analogies. "God is love" is the first step in the psychological analogy: God loves Himself as a mind knows and approves of itself. In the social analogy, God loves Himself as one mind consents to and seeks the happiness of another. This inter-Trinitarian consent is the original form of beauty and the source of all loveliness in the created world. As Danaher points out, "The primary form self-love takes in the psychological analogy is *complacence*," that is, the pleasure of the divine Mind contemplating Itself. "In contrast, the social analogy portrays love as the desire to make another happy," which Edwards terms *benevolence*.[18] We must hold on to both analogies at the same time if we want to escape a one-sided and false conception of the Trinity.

The use of the word "analogy" is a concession to traditional theological discourse, but for Edwards these descriptions are not humanly contrived illustrations of the Trinity. They are the closest approach our limited minds and vocabulary can make to comprehending and expressing the inner life of God. As I have meditated on these concepts over the past twenty-five years, they have gripped me repeatedly as no mere illustration has been able to do. The scriptural basis and careful philosophical construction of Edwards's arguments seem intellectually compelling and emotionally satisfying.

At the same time, I admit these are difficult concepts. I have presented them for three reasons. First, to give the Holy Spirit His rightful place in the Trinity. If we only think of Him as the One who brings good things (or even worse, good feelings) from God, we diminish His equality with the Father and the Son. We live in a time when many believers pay scant attention to the Spirit of God. To them He is a vague, shadowy Something. That notion needs to be challenged. Just as the title *Word of God* does not exhaustively describe the Person and work of Christ, so the title *Love of God* does not tell everything we need to know about the Spirit. It does serve, however, to elevate Him to full equality with the Son.

Second, and conversely, many who do exalt the Spirit think of His work primarily in terms of noise and power. Without arguing for or against the permanence of the showier manifestations of the Spirit, it is imperative for the health of the church that Christians recapture supernatural love as the primary sign of the Spirit's presence. Nothing is better suited to this end than to realize that He is the Love of God.

Finally, the skeptic and the believer alike need to catch a glimpse of the incredible richness of the doctrine of the Trinity. A God who does not challenge our minds as well as our hearts easily becomes boring. The inner life of the Triune God is mysterious, but God is never dull. God wants to be sought; He wants to be pursued, so He both reveals and hides Himself. He reveals some of the truth about Himself to all people (Rom. 1:18–2). He reveals the gospel to those He saves (2 Cor. 4:6). But there is always more, so Paul prayed that believers would come to know God better and better (Eph. 1:15–18; 3:14–19). Whatever engages our minds and causes us to think deeply about God enriches our lives, and there is no more noble and engaging occupation for the mind and heart than the contemplation of the Triune God.

Man, as he was first created, was endued with two kinds of principles, natural and spiritual. By natural principles, I mean the principles of human nature, as human nature is in this world—that is, in its animal state, or that belonging to the nature of man as man, or that belonging to his humanity, or that naturally and necessarily flow from the inner human nature. Such is a man's love to his own honour, love of his own pleasure, the natural appetites that he has by means of the body, &c. His spiritual principles were his love to God, and his relish of Divine beauties and enjoyments, &c. These may be called supernatural, because they are no part of human nature. They do not belong to the nature of man as man, nor do they naturally and necessarily flow from the faculties and properties of that nature. Man can be man without them; they did not flow from anything in the human nature, but from the Spirit of God dwelling in man, and exerting [Himself] by man's faculties as a principle of action. . . . But when man fell, then the Spirit of God left him, and so all his spiritual nature or spiritual principles; and then only the flesh was left, or merely the principle of human nature in its animal state. They were now left alone, without spiritual principles to govern and direct them, so that man became wholly carnal, and so wholly corrupt. For the principles of human nature, when alone and left to themselves, are principles of corruption, and there are no other principles of corruption in man but these. Corrupt nature is nothing else but the principle of human nature in its animal state, or the flesh (as it is called in Scripture) left to itself, or not subordinated to spiritual principles; and so far as it is unsubordinate, so far is it corrupt.

—Jonathan Edwards

Does the Trinity Make a Difference in Our Lives Today?

11

I heard once about a young minister who decided to model his pastoral work on the earthly ministry of Jesus Christ. Whenever he encountered a problem, he would look into the New Testament to see what Jesus had done in similar situations. One of his parishioners died halfway through his first week on the job, so the new minister searched the Gospels to see how the Lord handled funerals. The result greatly weakened his resolve to follow Christ's example; every time Jesus attended a funeral, He raised the dead.

The Bible says Jesus is a believer's example for holy living (1 Pet. 2:21), but many Christians may think He cheated. They argue that Jesus is God, so holiness must not have been hard for Him. As the divine Lord, He has the right to tell people *what* to do, but His example does not show them *how* to do it.

The power that beautified the earthly life of the Savior with holiness is available to adorn the lives of the children of God as well. The human life of Christ was beautiful because God gave Him the Spirit without measure. In the same way, Christians' lives begin to be beautiful when they are invaded by the love and beauty of God, that is, by the Holy Spirit.

The Holy Spirit plays a crucial role in the life of Adam, in the life of Christ, and in the lives of God's children.

Adam and the Holy Spirit

The original gift of the Spirit. The Bible indicates that God endowed Adam with a special gift of the Holy Spirit. "Then the LORD God formed man of dust from the ground, and breathed into his nostrils the breath of life; and man became a living being [Hebrew, *nephesh chayah*, a living soul]" (Gen. 2:7). This direct infusion of the divine breath points to a closer relationship between God and man than exists between God and the animals, but it does not prove by itself that the Holy Spirit was the source of Adam's original righteousness. In the words of the Nicene Creed, the Holy Spirit is "the Lord and Giver of life," for the breath or Spirit of God gives life both to people (Job 33:4) and to animals (Ps. 104:27–30). Not only is Adam a nephesh chayah, so are the "living creatures [nephesh chayah]" that fill the waters (Gen. 1:20), and the "living creatures [nephesh chayah]" that inhabit the land (1:24). All living things, all nephesh chayah, receive life from the Spirit of God. There are at least three reasons we can conclude Adam and Eve received a special gift of the Spirit:

First, God made man in His own image and likeness. That image has been terribly marred by sin, but the Holy Spirit is in the process of renewing it in God's children. "Now the Lord is the Spirit, and where the Spirit of the Lord is, there is liberty. But we all, with unveiled face, beholding as in a mirror the glory of the Lord, are being transformed into the same image from glory to glory, just as from the Lord, the Spirit" (2 Cor. 3:17–18). If the Spirit is the One who restores the image of God in us, then it is logical that He is the One who created it in the first place.

Second, consider some elements included in the image of God. Believers in Christ have "laid aside the old self [literally, the old man] with its evil practices, and have put on the new self [literally, the new man] who is being renewed to a true knowledge according to the image of the One who created him" (Col. 3:9–10). They have "put on new the self [the new man], which in the likeness of God has been created in righteousness and holiness of the truth" (Eph. 4:24). Putting these two passages together, we see that the image and likeness of God include the knowledge of God, righteousness and holiness. According to Scripture, the Spirit of God is the source of all three: knowledge (Isa. 11:2); righteousness (Rom. 14:17); and holiness, because the Spirit is the One who sanctifies believers (2 Thess. 2:13; 1 Pet. 1:2). God created Adam in His image, and this image included the knowledge of God, righteousness and holiness. These things are only restored by the Holy Spirit, so He must have imparted them to Adam in the first place.

Third, when Jesus appeared to His apostles on the Sunday evening after His resurrection, "He breathed on them and said to them, 'Receive the Holy Spirit'" (John 20:22). This was either a preliminary infusion of the Spirit prior to Pentecost or a symbol of the Spirit whom He was going to pour out on that wonderful day. In either case, the symbolism came directly from Genesis 2:7—where God breathed into the first man the breath of life. The breath of Jesus restored what God had given to Adam and subsequently removed, that is, the Holy Spirit. (Although the Bible does not specifically say God restored the Holy Spirit to Old Testament believers, we must conclude He did, because no one can repent or please God apart from the Spirit of the Lord. The Spirit takes on added prominence in the New Testament, but He was certainly active in saving and preserving believers in earlier ages.)

The loss of the Spirit. Adam did not lose his basic human nature when he fell; he did not become another sort of creature. Scripture uses the same Hebrew word (*adam*) to denominate man before and after the Fall. The image of God, which makes man a unique creature, is marred but not lost, because possession of the image forms the basis for the death penalty. "Whoever sheds man's blood, by man his blood shall be shed, for in the image of God He made man" (Gen 9:6).

Man still exercises aspects of the image, but in a limited or distorted fashion. He can know and love other persons, but he does not know and love God. He can make moral judgments and perform actions with moral significance, but he cannot keep the law of God that is written on his heart (Rom. 2:12–16). Dominion over the lower creatures appears to be another aspect of the divine image (Gen. 1:26), an aspect human beings may have exercised for ill as often as they have for good.

It has often been said that we all inherit a sin nature from Adam, but this expression raises more questions than it answers. What is that nature—a corrupted spiritual substance passed down to us from Adam and Eve? Perhaps we inherit sinful souls in the same way we inherit blue eyes or black hair. If that is the case, how was Christ born sinless? Perhaps Christ's human nature was pure because the contamination of sin is only passed on to children from their fathers—but children sometimes seem to inherit the sinful tendencies of their mothers. Another suggestion is that each soul is a separate, pure creation from God, but it becomes corrupt when it is united to a fallen physical body. If that were true, we might expect all sins to be linked to bodily appetites, but the Bible condemns pride (a sin of the mind) as severely as it condemns the ungoverned lusts of the flesh.

Jonathan Edwards cuts through all such speculations with a simple biblical observation. Every human being is born without the guiding, governing influence of the Holy Spirit. Unregenerate people are "devoid of the Spirit" (Jude 19). Those who do not have the indwelling Spirit of God do not belong to Christ (Rom. 8:9). Since Adam had the indwelling Holy Spirit when God created him, and we do not possess the Spirit when we are born, the loss of the Spirit for all Adam's descendants must be part of God's just curse on our race.

Since everything God initially created was "very good" (Gen. 1:31), evil has no independent existence. It is only a corruption or twisting of something originally good, as C.S. Lewis has cogently argued:

> Wickedness, when you examine it, turns out to be the pursuit

of some good in the wrong way. You can be good for the mere sake of goodness: you cannot be bad for the mere sake of badness. You can do a kind action when you are not feeling kind and when it gives you no pleasure, simply because kindness is right; but no one ever did a cruel action simply because cruelty is wrong—only because cruelty was pleasant or useful to him. In other words badness cannot succeed even in being bad in the same way in which goodness is good. Goodness is, so to speak, itself: badness is only spoiled goodness.[1]

How does goodness become twisted into something bad? As Augustine said, "Evil has no positive nature; what we call evil is merely the lack of something that is good."[2] The "good" God withdrew from man after the Fall was the Holy Spirit.

Without the Holy Spirit to control our normal human impulses, each of our desires demands to be satisfied. We cannot have everything we want, because not all our desires can be satisfied at the same time. For example, we want the respect of other people, but we soon discover we cannot have it if we insist on stealing their prized possessions. Even within ourselves we find a continual warfare. We cannot sleep as late in the morning as we might like and still earn the wages that pay for our food, clothing and toys. A man cannot enjoy peaceful relations with his wife if he chooses to frequent bars and chase skirts. In the end our stronger desires establish an uneasy hegemony over the weaker ones, without ever producing the beautiful and righteous harmony only the Holy Spirit can give. We are bad because the Holy Spirit, who alone is able to make us good, does not govern us. Many Christians experience a heightening of this inner conflict because the Spirit begins to convict them of sinful desires that had not troubled them before. He does this to lead God's children into increasing submission to their Father.

If God gave Adam the Holy Spirit so that he was able to know, love and obey God, how did Adam fall into sin? Edwards answers in this way:

The first arising or existing of that evil disposition in the heart of *Adam*, was by God's *permission*; who could have prevented it, if he had pleased, by *giving* such influences of his Spirit, as would have been absolutely effectual to hinder it; which, it is plain in fact, he did *withhold*: and whatever mystery may be supposed in the affair, yet no Christian will presume to say, it was not in perfect consistence with God's *holiness* and *righteousness*, notwithstanding Adam had been guilty of no offence before.[3]

The Holy Spirit enabled Adam to have intimate fellowship with God, and the joy of that daily communion must have reinforced the command not to eat the forbidden fruit. Adam was aware that disobedience to God would introduce a detrimental change in his relationship to his Maker. The Bible indicates that Eve was deceived, but Adam ate the fruit with his eyes wide open (1 Tim. 2:14). Though the Holy Spirit enabled Adam to know and love God, the Spirit did not exert the degree of control over Adam that would have kept him from sinning. Therefore, he loved and chose his wife over the Lord.

Christ and the Holy Spirit

How was Christ preserved from the taint of sin even from His birth? The Roman Catholic answer—that His mother was sinless—is wrong, for then we must ask how God protected Mary from contamination. (Were her parents also sinless? The chain would have to continue backward, and there is no scriptural support for this idea.)

Another common error may be illustrated by an old riddle:

Question: What do you get when you cross an elephant and a kangaroo?

Answer: Potholes all over Australia.

The cross between an elephant and a kangaroo would be a *tertium quid*, a third something that is neither one nor the other of its parents. The early church condemned as heresy, in the Council of Chalcedon (AD 451), the view that Christ was a mixture of divine and human natures:

> Therefore, following the holy fathers, we all with one accord teach men to acknowledge one and the same Son, our Lord Jesus Christ, at once complete in Godhead and complete in manhood, truly God and truly man, consisting also of a reasonable soul and body; of one substance with the Father as regards his Godhead, and at the same time of one substance with us as regards his manhood; like us in all respects, apart from sin; as regards his Godhead, begotten of the Father before the ages, but yet as regards his manhood begotten, for us men and for our salvation, of Mary the Virgin, the Godbearer; one and the same Christ, Son, Lord, Only-begotten, recognized in *two natures, without confusion, without change, without division, without separation; the distinction of natures being in no way annulled by the union, but rather the characteristics of each nature being preserved and coming together to form one person and subsistence, not as parted or separated into two persons,* but one and the same Son and Only-begotten God the Word, Lord Jesus Christ; even as the prophets from earliest times spoke of him, and our Lord Jesus Christ himself taught us, and the creed of the fathers has handed down to us.[4]

According to the phrases I have italicized, the human and divine natures of Christ are neither mingled together nor separated into two separate persons.[5]

One modern writer, who appears to have fallen into the error of confusing the natures of Christ, explains the conception of Jesus in this way:

> In that same mysterious moment, an even greater wonder emerged, for the very *DNA of God* joined with this unique seed. And so there joined in this one-cell embryo an unblemished body and soul from the visible realm. And from the invisible realm there was joined in this embryo a living spirit . . . even the very Spirit and life of God. The very essence of all

that God is pulsated deep within that man-child embryo. Behold, the genetics of an unfallen man growing together with the genetics of God.[6]

This DNA analogy is wrong, but it is useful for clarifying what Christ was not.

In Christ there is no mingling of divine and human genes. Jesus is not a semi-divine being, like Hercules whose human mother was impregnated by Zeus. He was and is fully divine and fully human, so His human sinlessness did not result from mixing His two natures together.

Christ's sinlessness from His conception onward was the work of the Holy Spirit. As the angel said to Mary, "The Holy Spirit will come upon you, and the power of the Most High will overshadow you; and for that reason the holy Child shall be called the Son of God" (Luke 1:35). The Child was holy because the Holy Spirit overshadowed Mary's womb. After He was born, "the Child continued to grow and become strong, increasing in wisdom; and the grace of God was upon Him" (2:40).

The Spirit's role in enabling Christ to remain sinless appears at the very beginning of His public ministry. At His baptism "the Holy Spirit descended upon Him in bodily form like a dove, and a voice came out of heaven, 'You are My beloved Son, in You I am well-pleased.' . . . Jesus, full of the Holy Spirit, returned from the Jordan and was led around by the Spirit in the wilderness for forty days, being tempted by the devil. . . . When the devil had finished every temptation, he departed from Him until an opportune time. And Jesus returned to Galilee in the power of the Spirit" (3:22; 4:1–2, 13–14). Although the Spirit of God had been active in Christ's life from the moment of His conception, the Lord received a greater outpouring of the Spirit for two purposes: to enable Him to face the fierce attack of the devil and to enable Him to perform His mighty miracles.

Some theological textbooks point to the miracles of Christ as direct evidence of His deity, but the miracles by themselves do not prove Christ was God. Jesus walked on water; Moses parted the waters. Jesus raised the dead; so did Elijah and Elisha. Jesus exhibited supernatural knowledge of Nathanael's activities and character (John 1:47–50); Elisha did likewise when he gave advance notice to the elders of Israel that the king's messenger was coming "to take away my head" (2 Kings 6:32).

The miracles of the prophets did not prove they were divine, but rather that their messages were from God. Similarly, the miracles of Christ combined with His character prove the message of Jesus was true. Christ's message included statements of His divine identity. As Jesus said to Philip, "Do you not believe that I am in the Father, and the Father is in Me? The words that I say to you I do not speak on My own initiative, but the Father abiding in Me does His works. Believe Me that I am in the Father and the Father is in Me; otherwise believe because of the works themselves" (John 14:10–11). Christ's crowning miracle, His resurrection, was significant both because it happened and because He clearly predicted it in advance.

Scripture consistently points to the power of the Holy Spirit at work in Jesus to perform His miracles. At the synagogue in Nazareth, Jesus claimed He was fulfilling Isaiah's prophecy: "The book of the prophet Isaiah was handed to Him. And He opened the book and found the place where it was written, 'The Spirit of the Lord is upon Me, because He anointed Me to preach the gospel to the poor. He has sent Me to proclaim release to the captives, and recovery of sight to the blind, to set free those who are oppressed'" (Luke 4:17–18).

Jesus healed blind people because God the Father had anointed Him with the Holy Spirit. Likewise, the Lord said, "If I cast out demons by the Spirit of God, then the kingdom of God has come upon you" (Matt. 12:28). In a grand summary of Jesus' ministry, the apostle Peter said, "You know of Jesus of Nazareth, how God anointed Him with the Holy Spirit and with power, and how He went about doing good and healing all who were oppressed by the devil, for God was with Him" (Acts

10:38). The scriptural explanation for Jesus' powerful words and works is contained in one sentence: "For He whom God has sent speaks the words of God; for He gives the Spirit without measure" (John 3:34).

Jesus Christ is a divine Person who possesses both His eternal divine nature and the human nature He received from His mother, Mary. While He walked on earth, the Man Jesus was filled with the Holy Spirit. Relying on the power of the Spirit, He resisted temptation, spoke the words of God and performed mighty miracles. When He addressed the Father, He prayed in the Holy Spirit (Luke 10:21).

In the diagram below several items have been added to the Trinitarian triangle which was shown in chapter 10. The black arrow entering the oval represents the eternal Son of God taking on a human nature in the womb of Mary. The dove represents the Holy Spirit who subdued the human nature of Christ to the will of the Father. At Jesus' conception the human nature was entirely passive and under the Spirit's control, but as He grew to manhood and entered into His ministry, the Lord consciously and continuously submitted His human desires to the will of the Father by the enabling of the Holy Spirit.

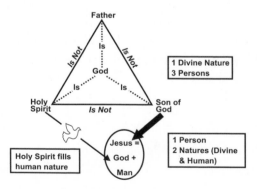

It is impossible to know how all this worked together in the human consciousness of Christ. He was able to recognize

His own deity, yet depended on the power of the Spirit for His mighty works. Scripture provides a few clues to help our feeble understanding. For example, while He was on earth, Jesus did not know the time of His return. He said, "But of that day or hour no one knows, not even the angels in heaven, nor the Son, but the Father alone" (Mark 13:32). Jesus depended on God the Father for direction in His daily activities (John 4:34; 5:19, 36; 8:29). According to His human nature, Jesus knew only the things God the Father wanted Him to know.

Perhaps an illustration will help. When I was a child growing up in California, my telephone number was SHerwood 5–5387. (In those days we used words with two capital letters to indicate our telephone exchange.) I was not consciously thinking of my phone number before deciding to write that sentence, but I was easily able to bring it to mind. The eternal Son of God knows all things, but He chose to bring into His human consciousness only those facts God the Father wanted the Man Jesus to have.

Likewise, Jesus did the miracles the Father wanted Him to perform and relied on the Spirit of His Father to perform them. This follows the normal pattern for God's activity in the world. The Father initiates the works of God; the Son is in the middle position because the Father works through Him; the Spirit is in direct contact with the world, for the Spirit gives and takes life.

Jesus is unique because He is both God and Man. Yet in His humanity He showed believers both what to do and how to do it. The tasks God gives believers are different from the ones He gave Jesus, but like Christ, they must listen to the Father and rely on the Spirit of God.

The Christian and the Holy Spirit

During my senior year in high school, I came under the influence of a man who taught me that the secret to the Christian life is to reckon my old sin nature dead. According to this teaching, the believer's old nature is like a corpse in a coffin. You can shout at it, you can kick it, but it will not move. No matter how many sinful temptations you place in front of a dead body, it will not give in to them. The duty of a Christian is to view his sinful nature like a corpse—dead and unresponsive to sinful desires. I tried diligently to pretend I felt no sinful impulses, but I never succeeded for more than a few minutes at a time. It was a very frustrating period of my life.

John Stott's exposition of Romans 5–8, *Men Made New*, delivered me from those delusions a few years later.[7] I learned that the "old man," who was crucified with Christ (6:6), was not my old nature but my old *self*—my old identity, my former self. At one time I was in Adam and under the curse of the law. Now I am in Christ. When He died to pay the penalty of sin, I died with Him; I am no longer subject to the condemnation of the law. Now I am a new creature in Christ with a new ability to love and obey God. It was a liberating truth.

Through no fault of John Stott, I still tended to think of the Christian life as a struggle between my old nature and my new nature, without clearly understanding what those terms might mean. I read somewhere about an old Native American believer who described his struggles this way: "I have two dogs inside of me, a white dog and a black dog, and they are always fighting." When he was asked which dog won, he replied, "The dog I say, 'Sic 'em' to." While there is a certain amount of truth in this illustration, it does nothing to distinguish between the struggles of Christians and the similar struggles of many non-Christians. Both kinds of people are frequently aware of inner conflicts between their good side and their dark side. The plots of many novels and movies revolve around such ambiguities.

Every human being has a set of normal desires that compete for attention and fulfillment. As long as God does not regulate these desires, they fight against each other and cause conflict between people. "What is the source of quarrels and conflicts among you? Is not the source your pleasures that wage war in your members? You lust and do not have; so you commit murder. You are envious and cannot obtain; so you fight and quarrel" (James 4:1–2).

Treatise on Grace

In what way, then, do the conflicts of a Christian differ from those of a moral unbeliever?

Jonathan Edwards's delightful little book, *Treatise on Grace*, along with the quotation at the head of this chapter, proved to be a turning point for me in understanding my daily struggles over sin. The conflict is not between my two natures but between my untamed human desires, habits and thought patterns (what the Bible calls "the flesh") and the Holy Spirit who lives within me:

> But I say, walk by the Spirit, and you will not carry out the desire of the flesh. For the flesh sets its desire against the Spirit, and the Spirit against the flesh; for these are in opposition to one another, so that you may not do the things that you please. But if the Spirit leads you, you are not under the Law. Now the deeds of the flesh are evident, which are: immorality, impurity, sensuality, idolatry, sorcery, enmities, strife, jealousy, outbursts of anger, disputes, dissensions, factions, envying, drunkenness, carousing, and things like these, of which I forewarn you, just as I have forewarned you, that those who practice such things will not inherit the kingdom of God. But the fruit of the Spirit is love, joy, peace, patience, kindness, goodness, faithfulness, gentleness, self-control; against such things there is no law. (Gal. 5:16–23)

At the risk of flattening Edwards's carefully textured argument, here is a summary, along with some highlights, from his *Treatise on Grace.*

Chapter 1 of the *Treatise* demonstrates that saving grace is entirely different in nature from common grace. (Common grace is a theological term for all the good gifts God gives to humanity at large. It includes the ordinary blessings of rain and sunshine as well as internal gifts such as a conscience and a desire for moral improvement.) God imparts His saving grace through the Holy

Spirit in an operation called the new birth or regeneration (John 3:3–8). Since the unsaved do not have the indwelling Holy Spirit (1 Cor. 2:14; Rom. 8:6–9), they have no saving grace. Therefore, it cannot be accumulated bit by bit as though it were simply a higher degree of moral improvement. Though the preparation for conversion may be gradual, conversion itself is instantaneous. Edwards concludes, "*It is impossible for men to convert themselves* by their own strength and industry, with only a concurring assistance helping in the exercise of their natural abilities."[8]

In chapter 2 Edwards shows that all saving grace may be summed up in love. He quotes Matthew 22 where Jesus declares the foremost commandment is to love God and the second is to love our neighbors as ourselves. "On these two commandments" says Christ, "depend the whole Law and the Prophets" (22:40). He then notes that the virtues listed in First Corinthians 13 are all practical manifestations of love. These are standard observations on the centrality of love. Edwards's subsequent analysis of the nature of love contains some new insights:

> A Christian love to God, and a Christian love to men, are not properly two distinct principles in the heart. These varieties are radically the same; the same principle flowing forth towards different objects, according to the order of their existence. God is the First Cause of all things, and the Fountain and Source of all good; and men are derived from Him, having something of His image, and are the objects of His mercy. So the first and supreme object of Divine Love is God; and men are loved either as the children of God or His creatures, and those that are in His image, and the objects of His mercy, or in some respects related to God, or partakers of His loveliness, or at least capable of happiness.[9]

Although love is something "better felt than defined," Edwards offers a description "to limit the signification of [Divine Love] and distinguish this principle from other things, and to exclude counterfeits."[10]

Divine Love, as it has God for its object, may be thus described. 'Tis the soul's relish of the supreme excellency of the Divine nature, inclining the heart to God as the chief good. . . . When once the soul is brought to relish the excellency of the Divine nature, then it will naturally, and of course, incline to God every way. It will incline to be with Him and to enjoy Him. It will have benevolence to God. It will be glad that He is happy. It will incline that He should be glorified, and that His will should be done in all things. So that the first effect of the power of God in the heart in REGENERATION, is to give the heart a Divine taste or sense; to cause it to have a relish of the loveliness and sweetness of the supreme excellency of the Divine nature; and indeed this is all the immediate effect of the Divine Power that there is, this is all the Spirit of God needs to do, in order to a production of all good effects in the soul.[11]

This description of divine love leads directly to a shocking conclusion: "The main ground of love to God is the excellency of His own nature, and not any benefit we have received, or hope to receive by His goodness to us."[12] Edwards draws a contrast between this conception of love and the more common view that we love God out of gratitude because He has saved us. Although a converted man is grateful for his salvation, "it is possible that natural men, without the addition of any further principle than they have by nature, may be affected with gratitude by some remarkable kindness of God to them, as that they should be so affected with some great act of kindness of a neighbour. A principle of self-love is all that is necessary to both."[13]

The common understanding of our love for God may be expressed thus: "I love God because I'm grateful He saved *me*." Edwards, however, teaches us to say, "Wow! I never imagined God was so amazing. Just look how much He endured to save people who hated Him. Although He is so holy He cannot look at sin, He found a way to pull His enemies out of their filth and turn them into sons and daughters. No other god ever even tried to accomplish such a feat. I can't help loving a God like that. *He is so beautiful.* And this wonderful God even loves me."[14]

Thinking of God in this way transforms one's whole under-standing of the Christian life. Believers obey God not simply because it is a duty or to repay His kindness (which can never be repaid anyway), but because they are overwhelmed by His grace and goodness. They obey Him because they long to be like the most beautiful human being who ever lived—Jesus Christ.

In the third and final chapter, Edwards addresses the ques-tion of how God-hating sinners can come to admire and be at-tracted to the beauty of God. He returns to the Holy Spirit's place in the Trinity. God enables His children to love Him and others by putting His own Love—the Holy Spirit—into them.

The Holy Spirit creates in believers a new sense of the beauty of God and gives them a longing to be like Christ, but He does not stamp it as an indelible brand upon their souls:

> The giving one gracious discovery or act of grace, or a thou-sand, has no proper natural tendency to cause an abiding hab-it of grace for the future; nor any otherwise than by Divine constitution and covenant. But all succeeding acts of grace must be as immediately, and, to all intents and purposes, as much from the immediate acting of the Spirit of God on the soul, as the first; and if God should take away His Spirit out of the soul, all habits and acts of grace would of themselves cease as immediately as light ceases in a room when a candle is carried out. And no man has a habit of grace dwelling in him any otherwise than as he has the Holy Spirit dwelling in him in his temple, and acting in union with his natural faculties, after the manner of a vital principle. . . . Indeed the Spirit of God, united to human faculties, acts very much after the manner of a natural principle or habit. So that one act makes way for another, and so it now settles the soul in a disposition to holy acts; but that it does, so as by grace and covenant, and not from any natural necessity.[15]

As long as I thought of victory over temptation as saying "Sic 'em" to my better nature, I could assume my nature would gradually become more holy. It has not. I have had to learn "that nothing good dwells in me, that is, in my flesh" (Rom. 7:18). My normal human desires will always be unruly and disobedient to my natural—but transient—desires for self-improvement.

But thanks be to God! He has given me His Holy Spirit! Although I cannot store up the Spirit's power from one day to the next, or even from my morning prayers until the afternoon, the Spirit Himself is graciously teaching me to rely on Him. I must meet each temptation or challenge with fresh dependence on the Spirit who lives in me. And what do I need from Him? I need increasingly clear views of the beauty of God in Christ.

The Holy Spirit changes believers by showing them more of the glory of Christ, but they are forgetful sinners who need to see Christ afresh over and over again. So His work is gradual and progressive. "Now the Lord is the Spirit, and where the Spirit of the Lord is, there is liberty. But we all, with unveiled face, beholding as in a mirror the glory of the Lord, are being transformed into the same image from glory to glory, just as from the Lord, the Spirit" (2 Cor. 3:17–18).

Seeing the beauty and glory of Christ does not mean doting on a mental image of Him, for that may easily become idolatry.[16] Rather, Christians see the beauty and glory of Christ as the Holy Spirit opens their minds and hearts to revel in His incarnation, humility, holiness, life, death, resurrection, ascension, offices and return. While He was on earth, Jesus listened to His Father and leaned on the Spirit to resist temptation, speak the words of God and do the works of God.

The Man Jesus is the perfect pattern for Christian living not only because He shows us what to do, but also because He demonstrates how we are to walk with God. Like Him, Christians must *listen* to the Father's voice in the word of God and *lean* on the Spirit in order to receive His strength, wisdom and especially His love. They learn to do so by "*looking* unto Jesus, the author and finisher of our faith" (Heb. 12:2, KJV).

What, then, is the Holy Spirit's role in the life of the Christian? First, the Holy Spirit opens the understanding and renews the affections of a sinner so he sees and is drawn to Christ (2 Cor. 4:3–6). This new sense of the beauty of Christ is the new birth. When the Jewish leader Nicodemus came to see Jesus at night to ask questions, he could not understand or accept what Jesus said because he had not been born again (John 3:1–12). In the new birth the Spirit removes the veil from an unbeliever's eyes. Second, as an immediate result of the new birth, the individual repents of sin, receives Christ and trusts in His atoning death and resurrection (1:12–13). Third, the Holy Spirit enters into a permanent relationship with the believer as the Spirit of adoption (Gal. 3:14; 4:4–6). Fourth, growth in holiness results from increasingly clear views of the glory and beauty of Christ, which come from the indwelling Holy Spirit (2 Cor. 3:17–18).

One day, perhaps not too far off, "the sun of righteousness will arise with healing in its wings" (Mal. 4:2). The voice of Jesus Christ will echo so powerfully throughout the world that the dead will rise. He is able to do this because as God the Father "has life in Himself, even so He gave to the Son also to have life in Himself" (John 5:24–29). The life that reanimates dead believers is not an impersonal power. It is the Holy Spirit. "But if the Spirit of Him who raised Jesus from the dead dwells in you, He who raised Christ Jesus from the dead will also give life to your mortal bodies through His Spirit who dwells in you" (Rom. 8:11).

The Spirit has been slowly effecting the moral and spiritual transformation of God's children. In that moment He will instantaneously complete it. Believers will be like Jesus "because we will see Him just as He is" (1 John 3:2). They will enter, as fully as any created being can, into the love the Father and Son shared before the foundation of the world. As Jesus said, "I have made Your name known to them, and will make it known, so that the love with which You loved Me may be in them, and I in them" (John 17:26). When the Love of God (the Holy Spirit) fills those who believe, then they, who are now still ugly because of sin, will at last be truly beautiful.

If you already know Christ, you will experience this magnificent transformation. If you are a pre-Christian, I urge you to repent of your sin, trust in Christ's death and resurrection and call out to Him to save you (Rom. 10:8–13). If you consider yourself to be an ex-Christian, may you by God's grace become an ex-ex-Christian.

Part 5

SEEING
the Beauty *of* God

All spiritual and gracious affections are attended with, and arise from, some apprehension, idea, or sensation of mind, which is in its whole nature different, yea exceeding [sic] different, from all that is or can be in the mind of a natural man. The natural man discerns nothing of it, (1 Cor. ii.14) any more than a man without the sense of tasting can conceive of the sweet taste of honey; or a man without the sense of hearing can conceive of the melody of a tune; or a man born blind can have a notion of the beauty of the rainbow.

—Jonathan Edwards

Why Are Some Views of God's Glory Spiritually Inadequate?

12

I was mystified when I saw a stage magician sawing a woman in half, but not horrified. I did not expect to see blood spilling out over the floor, because I did not believe what my eyes told me. In spiritual matters too there is a kind of seeing that does not result in true faith. Unconverted men and women can see and experience some things which lead them to assume they have a right relationship with God, but they do not see Christ in a saving way. In their case seeing does not result in believing.

The redeemed see the beauty of the Lord in a special way, and this sight transforms their lives. The unconverted may catch glimpses of God's beauty, but these fleeting looks are different from the way the saved see Christ.

In Second Corinthians 3:18 the apostle Paul writes, "But *we all*, with unveiled face, beholding as in a mirror the glory of the Lord, are being transformed into the same image from glory to glory, just as from the Lord, the Spirit." According to verse 16, "we all" means people who have turned to the Lord. For such people, the veil that hides God's face has been taken away. The lost do not see God's glory in such a way, for "if our gospel is veiled, it is veiled to those who are perishing, in whose case the god of this world has blinded the minds of the unbelieving so that they might not see the light of the gospel of the glory of Christ, who is the image of God" (4:3–4). For believers "God, who said, 'Light shall shine out of darkness,' is the One who has shone in our hearts to give the Light of the knowledge of the glory of God in the face of Christ" (4:6). Many other passages confirm the spiritual darkness and blindness of the lost:

> This is the judgment, that the Light has come into the world, and men loved the darkness rather than the Light, for their deeds were evil. (John 3:19)

> So this I say, and affirm together with the Lord, that you walk no longer just as the Gentiles also walk, in the futility of their mind, being darkened in their understanding, excluded from the life of God because of the ignorance that is in them, because of the hardness of their heart. (Eph. 4:17–18)

> But the one who hates his brother is in the darkness and walks in the darkness, and does not know where he is going because the darkness has blinded his eyes. (1 John 2:11)

Because of their spiritual blindness, human beings frequently interpret certain purely natural experiences as evidence that they are properly related to God. The general rule is that any experience both the lost and the saved may have is not the saving sight of Christ's glory Paul describes in Second Corinthians 3 and 4. There are several kinds of spiritually inadequate views of God's glory. My purpose in this chapter is to examine some views of God's beauty that the unconverted may have and to show that these glimpses of glory are different from those that the saved have of Christ.

Psychologically Induced Visions

A significant number of people report visions, voices and other ecstatic phenomena. According to the Bible, such experiences do not necessarily indicate a saving relationship with God. Careful investigation strongly suggests that a psychological explanation fits most of these cases, even when they occur to genuine Christians.

People in different cultures and religions throughout the

world report hearing voices and seeing images in their minds. Mystical experiences occur among serious followers of Christianity, Islam, Hinduism and Buddhism, to say nothing of the minor cults and religions of the world. Visions and voices are simply interpreted within the religious context of the men and women who experience them. As Evelyn Underhill notes, "The great mystics are faithful sons of the great religions."[1]

The people I know who have reported strong impressions of a supernatural presence, voice or vision have one thing in common: they are sure of their experience. With a perverse twist of logic, people are able to justify their revelation no matter how it may occur. If an impulse, vision or voice comes spontaneously while they are occupied with some other task, they take it as evidence the revelation did not come from their own minds. If, on the other hand, their experience arises during a period of intense prayer or meditation, they assume their holy intentions protect them from delusion. Only rarely can people be led to admit error in their apparently supernatural visitations, even when it is obvious to others.

One exception was Obbe Philips. Around 1560, Philips recorded recollections of his earlier involvement in the radical wing of the Reformation. The believers with whom he associated were certain the time of the end was near.

> Now when these teachings and consolations with all the fantasies, dreams, revelations, and visions daily occurred among the brethren, there was no little joy and expectation among us, hoping all would be true and fulfilled, for we were all unsuspecting, innocent, simple, without guile or cunning, and were not aware of any false visions, prophets, and revelations. We supposed in our simplicity that if we guarded ourselves against the papists, Lutherans, and Zwinglians, then all was well and we need have no cares. Thereby a man's experience brings him great wisdom.[2]

The Lord has called believers to be children in malice, but not to be childish and foolish in their discernment. The Bible says, "In understanding be men" (1 Cor. 14:20, KJV). Earnestness and sincerity are no proof against self-deception.

Any explanation of such mystical experiences ought to cover similar phenomena reported by Christians and non-Christians. It is not very convincing to use one hypothesis for friends and another for adversaries. In addition, the explanation should not question the integrity of everyone who makes such startling claims. There is also a need to account for the errors of fact in the visions of sincere Christians.

While the devil and his minions can give lying visions and prophecies (1 Kings 22), invoking the devil does not help us understand the psychological process at work within the visionary, nor does it explain how sincere Christians can be misled even when they are diligently seeking the Lord.

Jonathan Edwards, who carefully studied mystical experiences during the Great Awakening, offers a compelling explanation. He concluded that visions and voices naturally arise in the imaginations of some people when their minds are greatly excited or disturbed. This mental disruption may come from the devil, from psychological disorders or from the excitement generated during a religious revival. It may also be self-induced in otherwise normal people by various physical, mental or spiritual exertions. When all these avenues have been explored, there remains the possibility that the excitement of the mind has come from genuine contact with God.

When God deals with a person, who then begins to revel in some great scriptural truth, that individual may become wonderfully lifted up in love for God. While the heart is flowing out toward God, purely natural visions may be stimulated in the imagination. At this point such a one needs to heed the warning of Edwards:

Some who are the subjects of [the awakening] have been in a kind of ecstasy, wherein they have been carried beyond themselves, and have had their minds transported into a train of strong and pleasing imaginations, and a kind of visions, as though they were rapt up even to heaven, and there saw glorious sights. I have been acquainted with some such instances, and I see no need of bringing in the help of the devil into the account that we give of these things, nor yet of supposing them to be of the same nature with the visions of the prophets, or St. Paul's rapture into paradise. Human nature, under these intense exercises and affections, is all that need be brought into the account. . . . Some are ready to interpret such things wrong [sic], and to lay too much weight on them, as prophetical visions, divine revelations, and sometimes significations from heaven of what shall come to pass; which the issue, in some instances I have known, has shown to be otherwise. But yet, it appears to me that such things are evidently sometimes from the Spirit of God, though indirectly; that is, their extraordinary frame of mind, and that strong and lively sense of divine things which is the occasion of them, is from His Spirit; and also as the mind continues in its holy frame, and retains a divine sense of the excellency of spiritual things even in its rapture; which holy frame and sense is from the Spirit of God, though the imaginations that attend it are but accidental, and therefore there is commonly something or other in them that is confused, improper, and false.[3]

This psychological explanation of impulses, visions and voices can cover a wide variety of experiences without invalidating the Christian's real fellowship with Christ. At the same time it also gives proper credit to the sincerity of mystics in other religions. Elevated affections in the worship of a false god could easily produce the same sort of effects. Conversely, people who have unusual religious experiences in which Christ is prominent need not be genuine Christians. Emotional distress in their personal lives or the charged atmosphere of a religious revival can easily produce the psychic energy necessary to induce visions and voices in their imaginations.

When the Great Awakening broke out in Scotland in 1742, a small percentage of those affected experienced visions. The pastors kept careful accounts of those awakened. Several years later, they investigated to see who was still persevering in the faith. In 1751 Rev. William McCulloch of Cambuslang wrote that

> the Devil [causes some] to cry out publicly, and to fall down as dead for some time, representing various objects to their fancies, in the air, when they were awake, or when asleep, and suggesting various things to their minds at the same time, urging them afterwards to tell what they saw or heard, as visions, dreams, or revelations from heaven; exciting them to go and join in meetings for prayer; and to hold on in this way under a high profession, some for weeks, some for months, and others for years: and then at length to push them into uncleanness, drunkenness, lying, cheating, and all abominations, even to the throwing off (with some) the very profession of religion; which it is to be wished they had never put on.[4]

The five elders of McCulloch's church signed a statement which concluded, "Though the most of the subjects of the awakening, whose exercise contained a mixture of strong fancy and imagination, are relapsed to their former sinful courses: yet, there are several instances of persons, whose exercises were mixed with fanciful apprehensions; and which they gave out to be real representations of objects and visions, are of the number of those who are persevering in a justifiable christian [sic] profession, and unblemished conversation."[5]

Visions and voices in the minds of religious people provide an inadequate view of God's glory. Any experience common to the converted and the lost is not what Paul intended when he said true believers—and only they—behold "as in a mirror the glory of the Lord."

Supernatural Visions

Scripture records several examples of people who were not saved who saw the glory of the Lord or had a true prophetic vision from God who were not saved. When Moses led Israel out of Egypt, the Lord went before them in a pillar of cloud by day and a pillar of fire by night (Exod. 13:21–22). When Israel set up the tabernacle, the glory of the Lord filled the structure so completely that even Moses could not enter it (40:34–35). When Moses' brother Aaron first placed burnt offerings on the great altar in front of the tabernacle, "Then fire came out from before the LORD and consumed the burnt offering and the portions of fat on the altar; and when all the people saw it, they shouted and fell on their faces" (Lev. 9:24). Something similar occurred at the dedication of Solomon's temple (2 Chron. 7:1–3). On all these occasions believers and unbelievers were present. In spite of seeing such things, a whole generation of Israelite refugees from Egypt died in the wilderness. They are described in Hebrews 3 as unbelievers.

The case of Balaam (Num. 22–24, 31) is even more striking. When a king who hated Israel sent for him and asked him to curse Israel, Balaam consulted God, and He put words in his mouth to speak. Balaam received a number of true prophecies from God, but he was an ungodly man who loved money more than he loved the Lord (Jude 11). This is the introduction to his final recorded prophecy:

> The oracle of Balaam the son of Beor,
>> And the oracle of the man whose eye is opened,
>
> The oracle of him who hears the words of God,
>> And knows the knowledge of the Most High,
>
>> Who sees the vision of the Almighty,
>
>> Falling down, yet having his eyes uncovered.
>
>> (Num. 24:15–16)

Balaam is the most notable example of a general rule the apostle Paul spelled out in First Corinthians 13: "If I speak with the tongues of men and of angels, but do not have love, I have become a noisy gong or a clanging cymbal. If I have the gift of prophecy, and know all mysteries and all knowledge; and if I have all faith, so as to remove mountains, but do not have love, I am nothing" (13:1–2).

In other words, a man can speak in tongues and go to hell. He can give true predictions inspired by the Holy Spirit and go to hell. On the Day of Judgment, many will say to Christ, "Lord, Lord, did we not prophesy in Your name, and in Your name cast out demons, and in Your name perform many miracles?" On that day, even though Jesus may allow their claims to stand, He will say, "I never knew you. Depart from Me, you who practice lawlessness" (Matt. 7:22–23). None of the spectacular gifts of the Spirit, even when genuine, is a sure sign of conversion. Instead, First Corinthians 13 points to love as the best indicator of a right relationship with God.

Natural Beauty

Natural beauty includes all the things we find attractive and can explore with our five senses and our minds without any special assistance from the Holy Spirit. It is distinguished from the supernatural beauty of God Himself and the beauty of the holy angels and the new Jerusalem. We enjoy natural beauty in God's creation, in the arts, in human relationships and in certain intellectual pursuits (such as solving puzzles). How is our experience of natural beauty related to the experience of God's beauty?

Being deeply moved by natural beauty is not the same as seeing God's beauty. Christians and non-Christians alike can lie on their backs and gaze in awe at the immensity of space and the sparkling glory of the stars. A well-crafted story in a book or on film can bring people of all faiths or no faith to tears. A person does not even need to be a believer to be stirred by music with Christian themes. (Johann Sebastian Bach, whose music has been called the fifth gospel, is immensely popular in Japan, one of the most secular nations on earth.)[6] Every Christmas season, lovers of baroque music gather to perform or to listen to Handel's *Messiah.* At the more popular level, believers and non-believers sway and clap their hands in time with popular Christian rock or folk groups.

When Christians sing along enthusiastically with a favorite

praise band, they are not necessarily experiencing the beauty of God. When they listen with great pleasure to an amazing piano-organ duet, their response may be essentially the same as that of their non-Christian neighbors. They may say, "I am worshiping the Lord," when all they mean is "I like this music. It moves me."

People can even be moved in a wholly natural way by a carefully crafted and powerfully presented sermon. Thus, the apostle Paul insisted,

> And when I came to you, brethren, I did not come with superiority of speech or of wisdom, proclaiming to you the testimony of God. For I determined to know nothing among you except Jesus Christ, and Him crucified. I was with you in weakness and in fear and in much trembling, and my message and my preaching were not in persuasive words of wisdom, but in demonstration of the Spirit and of power, so that your faith would not rest on the wisdom of men, but on the power of God. (1 Cor. 2:1–5)

I have heard a man praise an evangelical preacher's message as "well-spoken," but I have no reason to believe the man was converted.

Natural beauty may become a substitute for God's beauty. Whenever secondary beauty draws us away from contemplating and enjoying the primary beauty of God, it becomes an idol.

All the pagan peoples around ancient Israel were involved in nature worship. Sometimes they prostrated themselves before the violent, destructive forces of nature, but just as often their myths deified the impressive and beautiful things their eyes could see. Biblical religion, with its insistence on the unity and sovereignty of the Creator, was profoundly anti-mythical, as we see in the warning of Moses:

> So watch yourselves carefully, since you did not see any form on the day the LORD spoke to you at Horeb from the midst of the fire, so that you do not act corruptly and make a graven image for yourselves in the form of any figure. . . . And

beware not to lift up your eyes to heaven and see the sun and the moon and the stars, all the host of heaven, and be drawn away and worship them and serve them, those which the LORD your God has allotted to all the peoples under the whole heaven. (Deut. 4:15–16, 19)

The ancients worshiped the sun, the moon and the stars as deities. They worshiped the god who throws bolts of lightning and the goddess who brings fertility to families and fields. Lesser gods inhabited trees and rivers. Nature worship has never left us. Many people say they feel closer to God out in the woods or down at the shore than when they are in church or praying on their own. For some this is just a vague sense of enjoying the outdoors more than they enjoy truly spiritual activities. For others, nature as a whole has become divine. Most of the Romantic poets of the late eighteenth and early nineteenth centuries were more in tune with a deified nature than with the God of the Bible. For example, consider "A Thing of Beauty" by John Keats:

A thing of beauty is a joy for ever:
Its loveliness increases; it will never
Pass into nothingness; but still will keep
A bower quiet for us, and a sleep
Full of sweet dreams, and health, and quiet breathing.

When Keats was despondent, what lifted his spirit?

Some shape of beauty moves away the pall
From our dark spirits. Such the sun, the moon,
Trees old, and young, sprouting a shady boon
For simple sheep; and such are daffodils
With the green world they live in; and clear rills
That for themselves a cooling covert make
'Gainst the hot season; the mid-forest brake,
Rich with a sprinkling of fair musk-rose blooms.

We have all been refreshed at one time or another by God's glorious creation, but for many the beauty of the world becomes a replacement for the beauty of God. Some even call themselves pantheists; they are people for whom all nature is divine. The modern ecology movement is often driven by a sense of the sacredness of nature. Biblical ecology teaches that human beings are stewards and caretakers over nature, but nature itself is not divine.

The worship of natural beauty in the form of artistic creativity has also invaded the church. Believers at Corinth lined up behind their favorite preachers because they were focused more on style than on substance (1 Cor. 1:10–13). In our day the arguments usually center on music rather than preachers because music has become more important to many than the sermon.

The church music wars of the past few decades suggest there is a great danger that music will become an idolatrous substitute for God. We are apt to say, "I like *my* music. I don't get anything out of *your* music. I can't worship with *your* music." In church the phrases "my music" and "your music" are fairly sure signs people are mistaking and substituting the beauty of music for the beauty of God.

Natural beauty reflects God's beauty. Certain psalms celebrate the beauty of God's creation:

O Lord, our Lord,
    How majestic is Your name in all the earth,
    Who have displayed Your splendor above the heavens!
From the mouth of infants and nursing babes You have
        established strength
    Because of Your adversaries,
    To make the enemy and the revengeful cease.
When I consider Your heavens, the work of Your fingers,
    The moon and the stars, which You have ordained;
What is man that You take thought of him,
    And the son of man that You care for him?

(Ps. 8:1–4)

God's majesty includes His power, splendor and righteousness. He is an omnipotent, glorious and just King, and the heavens reveal a small portion of His majesty. Job 38–41 turns our attention to the stars, the weather and the animal kingdom. Every living creature is a marvel of complexity, and they are all interlocked like pieces of a gigantic jigsaw puzzle. This amazing balance of nature reveals the orderly intelligence of the one and only awesome God.

Despite the fact that nature tempts human beings to worship it, the Bible presents the world in a very positive light. Creation testifies to the beauty of its Creator in spite of its disfigurement by the fall of Adam.

Natural beauty includes the products of human hands and minds. These also can reflect the supernatural beauty of God, for the Old Testament tabernacle was designed to be "a copy and shadow of the heavenly things" (Heb. 8:5). It was an earthly representation of the heavenly sanctuary where Christ would offer His blood before God as a payment for the sins of His people. Human hands wove the curtains, built the furniture and pounded or molded the gold, silver and brass into shape. These things were artistically beautiful in order to reflect the beauty of God.

God uses natural beauty to increase our enjoyment of His beauty. The proper response to the splendor of the heavens is to reflect on God's greatness and our littleness. The correct response to living things is to marvel at God's knowledge and wisdom.

Solomon's temple was an impressive structure built of massive stones shaped and smoothed at the quarry so no iron tool was heard at the building site. The inner walls of cedar were covered with carvings of cherubim, palm trees and flowers, and then overlaid with pure gold. Large gold cherubim overshadowed the ark Moses had made. The incense altar, the table for bread and the lamp stand were all of gold.

The common people could not see these things; they were visible only to the priests. But the objects outside the temple proper were also impressive. They included two tall bronze pillars, a bronze basin fifteen feet across at the brim resting on the backs of twelve bronze oxen, ten smaller bronze basins on rolling stands and the great altar in front of the temple. All the bronze items were decorated with engravings or castings—lilies, gourds, lions, oxen, cherubim, palm trees and wreaths. The animal figures were not representations of God (as is common in other religions). There were no images or pictures of God, but the beauty of these artistic decorations was intended to help people appreciate the beauty of the Creator.

Music added to the physical beauty of the temple. The Levitical choir sang the psalms accompanied by lyres, harps, cymbals and trumpets. Perhaps the people also joined in at times.

The temple of God and its services were beautiful, but the external beauty was intended to draw worshipers to adore the beauty of the God who dwelt there.

> For great is the LORD and greatly to be praised;
>   He is to be feared above all gods.
> For all the gods of the peoples are idols,
>   But the LORD made the heavens.
> Splendor and majesty are before Him,
>   Strength and beauty are in His sanctuary.
>
> (Ps. 96:4–6)

Strength and beauty were in God's sanctuary because God was there. That is the reason King David sang, "One thing I have asked from the LORD, that I shall seek; that I may dwell in the house of the LORD all the days of my life, to behold the beauty of the LORD and to meditate in His temple" (27:4).

David wrote Psalm 27 before Solomon built the permanent stone temple for God. During David's lifetime, the ark and other sacred objects resided in a tent. The tent was a temple because God dwelt there, but it was not nearly as splendid as the later house of God built by Solomon. What did David see when he went to worship God? How did God reveal His beauty at the tent of worship and, later, at the temple?

The main focus of Old Testament worship was not the pageantry or the singing. Worshipers saw God's beauty in the temple's bloody sacrifices. Israelites journeyed to the temple to offer or observe a sacrifice. The beauty of the temple, the ornate garments of the high priest and the singing of the Levites only served to highlight the beauty of God as revealed by the sacrifices. The bloody offerings on the altar revealed the holiness of God, who hates and must punish sin. They also revealed the mercy and grace of God, who accepts an innocent substitute in place of the guilty sinner. A man who brought a sacrifice placed his hands on the head of his offering and confessed his sins, thus symbolically placing his transgressions of the law onto his substitute.

If a Jewish man killed a sheep for his supper, he might turn up his nose at the blood and entrails he spilled out on the ground. But when he brought a sheep to God as a sacrifice for his sins, he sang and praised the Lord for accepting the animal's blood in place of his own.

God used the beauty of the temple and its services to increase His people's appreciation for the beauty of His holiness and grace, which He demonstrated in the sacrifices. Therefore, while natural beauty can often lead us to a deeper appreciation for God's beauty, appreciating natural beauty is not the same as "beholding as in a mirror the glory of the Lord." The appreciation of natural beauty by itself is an inadequate view of God's glory.

True worship is more than worshipful feelings. It is common for people to fall in love with their feelings and mistakenly think their lives have been invaded by the love of God in the Person of the Holy Spirit.

Seeing—and even being thrilled—by natural beauty is not the same as believing on the Lord Jesus Christ. Whoever has not seen the beauty of His sacrificial death and glorious resurrection is still walking in the darkness.

And that a true and saving belief of the truth of religion is that which arises from such a discovery, is also what the Scripture teaches. As John vi.40. "And this is the will of Him that sent me, that every one who seeth the Son, and believeth on Him, may have everlasting life;" where it is plain that a true faith is what arises from a spiritual sight of Christ.

—Jonathan Edwards

13 How Can We Recognize the True Glory of God?

Saving faith is a direct result of seeing the glory and beauty of Christ. "And even if our gospel is veiled, it is veiled to those who are perishing, in whose case the god of this world has blinded the minds of the unbelieving so that they might not see the light of the gospel of the glory of Christ, who is the image of God. . . . For God, who said, 'Light shall shine out of darkness,' is the One who has shone in our hearts to give the Light of the knowledge of the glory of God in the face of Christ" (2 Cor. 4:3–4, 6).

If people do not believe in Christ when they hear about Him, the devil has blinded their minds. When God shines the light of the gospel into a human heart, that person comes to know Christ as Lord and Savior. John 6:40 reinforces the connection between seeing and believing: "Everyone who beholds the Son and believes in Him will have eternal life." So does John 12:44–45: "And Jesus cried out and said, 'He who believes in Me, does not believe in Me but in Him who sent Me. He who sees Me sees the One who sent Me.'"

Jesus was speaking about a spiritual way of seeing because many who saw Him in the flesh did not perceive God acting and speaking before their eyes. Although some glimpses of God and His glory do not lead to faith, there is a kind of seeing that automatically entails believing. Without such sight there is no

263

faith. With it, faith is inevitable. How do the redeemed see the glory of the Lord in a way the lost do not?

Seeing the Beauty of Christ in the Gospel

In the Old Testament the most profound revelation of God's beauty was not in the starry sky or the elaborately decorated temple. It was in a bloody carcass on the altar, for there God displayed the glory of His mercy in the forgiveness of sinners. This foreshadowed the far more astounding sacrifice of Christ.

The redeemed see "the light of the gospel of the glory of Christ, who is the image of God" (2 Cor. 4:4). This sight of Christ is not an image of Him in the mind; both the redeemed and the lost may have that kind of experience. This sight is a new way of experiencing the truth of the gospel.

The gospel in its simplest form is that Jesus died in the place of sinners. He rose again from the dead, demonstrating that God had accepted His sacrifice. Those who repent of sin and trust in Christ will receive the forgiveness of sins and live forever with God (1 Cor. 15:1–4). This is what a person must see in order to be saved.

If a saving sight of Christ is a new way of seeing the gospel, then it does not entail private revelation of any truth not contained in the Bible. For example, at the emotional high point of the Great Awakening in the 1740s, two young women became "exceedingly filled with zeal" at a prayer meeting and were "in some degree depriv'd of their bodily strength." They exhorted those who were present, particularly those they supposed to be unconverted. The next evening they were so overcome "that they fell down unable to walk, and so continued for some Time, lying in the Street like Persons dead or asleep." They were brought into a nearby house where they continued for some time in a state of ecstasy, delivering supposed revelations and messages to a number of people who came to see them. They claimed that *they had been to Heaven, had seen the Book of Life, the Names of many Persons of their Acquaintance wrote in it; that they had seen the Seats of the Blessed, and their own Seats empty,* and the like."[1] Neither salvation nor a reasonable assurance of salvation rests on a personal revelation of one's redemption because even unconverted persons may have such experiences.

Since a saving sight of Christ is a new way of apprehending the gospel, no revelation going beyond the gospel can contribute to salvation: "But even if we, or an angel from heaven, should preach to you a gospel contrary to what we have preached to you, he is to be accursed!" (Gal. 1:8). "To be accursed" means the person will be damned by God and go to hell. That is the Bible's verdict on people like Muhammad and Joseph Smith whose revelations contradict the gospel of Jesus Christ.

God's redeemed people see the glory of Christ in the old-time gospel preached by Matthew, Mark, Luke, John, Paul, Peter, Jude, James and the author of Hebrews. How do they see the gospel?

Seeing the Beauty of Christ by the Illumination of God's Spirit

In Second Corinthians 3:17–18 a saving glimpse of God's glory is ascribed to the Holy Spirit: "Now the Lord is the Spirit, and where the Spirit of the Lord is, there is liberty. But we all, with unveiled face, beholding as in a mirror the glory of the Lord, are being transformed into the same image from glory to glory, just as from the Lord, the Spirit."

The Holy Spirit is the Lord. He is God, and only God can show us the glory of God. Theologians use the word "illumination" to distinguish this work of the Holy Spirit from His work of revealing new truth to the apostles and prophets. He does not give us new truth; He turns on the light in our minds to see the old truth of the gospel in a new light.

We need to differentiate the saving work of the Spirit from His more ordinary activity in the minds and hearts of all people. Job 32:8 says, "But it is a spirit in man, and the breath of the Almighty gives them understanding." The "breath of the Almighty" is a designation for the Holy Spirit. "The Spirit of

God has made me, and the breath of the Almighty gives me life" (33:4). The Holy Spirit gives human beings the intellectual and moral capacities that distinguish them from animals. He also informs the conscience. Although people can become hardened through obstinate disobedience, the Spirit convicts "the world concerning sin and righteousness and judgment" (John 16:8). Even in its weakened state, the conscience is adequate to show sinners on the Day of Judgment that they have deliberately disobeyed the law of God (Rom. 2:14–16).

People often feel guilty without any saving light in their souls. Their conscience strikes them, and they may even become frightened, as the Roman governor Felix did under the soul-searching preaching of Paul (Acts 24:24–25). Trembling at the thought of God's holiness and His just judgment is not a sign a person has seen the beauty of Christ. Every person professing conversion with tears and evident sorrow is not necessarily in a good spiritual state. There is, after all, a "sorrow of the world" that only "produces death" (2 Cor. 7:10).

Seeing Christ in Order to Trust Him Alone for Salvation

The theme of Second Corinthians 3 and 4 is the glory of the gospel. These chapters exalt Christ and the gospel over the fading glory of the Mosaic Law. Those who trust in the Law and seek to be justified by keeping the Law do not see Christ. Therefore, Paul writes about the glory of Christ so his readers may trust in Christ alone and not in their obedience to the Law.

Justification by faith rather than by legal obedience is one of Paul's chief concerns throughout his writings. In Philippians 3 he used his own experience to stress this crucial difference. After listing his Jewish pedigree and his pharisaic zeal for God, He explained what was truly important:

> But whatever things were gain to me, those things I have counted as loss for the sake of Christ. More than that, I count all things to be loss in view of the surpassing value of knowing Christ Jesus my Lord, for whom I have suffered the loss of all

things, and count them but rubbish so that I may gain Christ, and may be found in Him, not having a righteousness of my own derived from the Law, but that which is through faith in Christ, the righteousness which comes from God on the basis of faith, that I may know Him and the power of His resurrection and the fellowship of His sufferings, being conformed to His death; in order that I may attain to the resurrection from the dead. (Phil. 3:7–11)

The apostle's great goal in life was to *know Christ*. In Second Corinthians 4:6 Paul indicated that people are converted when God shines the "Light of the *knowledge* of the glory of God in the face of Christ" into their hearts. Philippians 3 tells us what must take place in our lives if we want to have this knowledge, which is a divine and supernatural light in the soul.

To see and know Christ, people must renounce the value of their own self-effort. Those who are notorious sinners usually have no trouble with this. They know they have nothing of value to offer to God. Ordinary people who are moderately successful in life frequently have great difficulty saying, "Whatever things were gain to me, those things I have counted as loss for Christ," because we tend to overvalue our own work.

From time to time, I do things around the church that are not normally included in a pastor's job description. Sometimes I do them without much reflection; other times my attitude may swing in one of two directions. I may grumble inwardly, *Why am I doing this? Somebody else should be doing it. I have more important things to do.* On the other hand, I may start patting myself on the back: *Here I am doing this thing that is beneath me. I'm a pretty good fellow, after all, because I don't really mind doing it. I'm not grumbling or complaining, even though I shouldn't have to do this.* Both reactions are filled with pride in the value of *my* time and *my* work.

When a person carries such an attitude into his relationship with God, he cuts himself off from seeing the beauty of Christ and the gospel. For example, if you sit in the park with your hands over your eyes, you cannot see the beautiful flowers and trees. In the same way, if you hold the labors of your hands up in front of your face, you cannot see the beauty of Christ. It is necessary to renounce the value of your self-effort in order to have a saving sight and knowledge of Christ. Only after the apostle Paul had set aside his own righteousness derived from the Law was he able to receive the righteousness of God, which comes through faith in Christ. The same is true for us as well.

The glory and beauty of the gospel is that God saves undeserving sinners by giving them a righteousness they have not earned. This righteousness does not come gift-wrapped in a box. It comes in a Person—Jesus Christ—who is God and man together. If Christ is not sufficient to save sinners, the gospel is not glorious. If He is sufficient and sinners refuse to cast themselves on Christ alone, then they have not really seen the beauty and glory of the gospel.

Finding Christ and the Gospel Amazing and Attractive

The most common word for "glory" in the Old Testament is *kavod*, which refers to something weighty or impressive. God reveals His kavod both in redemption (Isa. 60:1–2) and in judgment (Ezek. 39:17–21). Other Old Testament words for "glory" refer to the attractiveness of God rather than His impressiveness. They are sometimes translated "beauty." One example is *tiphrah*. "No longer will you have the sun for light by day, nor for brightness will the moon give you light; but you will have the LORD for an everlasting light, and your God for your glory [tiphrah]" (Isa. 60:19). This beautiful aspect of God's glory is what Paul has in mind when he refers to the "glory of God in the face of Christ" (2 Cor. 4:6).

Believers in Jesus Christ see Him as a wonderful and amazing person because He is the image of the invisible God. He is God and man together. Believers also see the gospel as wonderful, amazing good news. It is too good to be true, and yet it is. It is better news than winning the lottery or having the doctor say he made a mistake—you are not going to die in three weeks after all.

Atheists tend not to see things this way, but what is the problem when professing Christians do not bow in awe at the glory of Christ and the gospel? There are several possibilities:

Professing Christians who are not gripped by the gospel may have never seen Christ. Suppose a certain young man has heard that Susie Q is the most beautiful girl in the world. Perhaps he has received this report from several of his friends, both male and female. He will probably believe Susie is very attractive, but he will not feel the pull of her attractiveness.

Thus it is with many people in church. They have often heard that Christ and the gospel are wonderful, so they believe it to be the case. They have an opinion that the gospel is true, but they have never felt for themselves how glorious it is that God would become a man to die for sinners and rise again to give them new life. Though they believe the facts, the truth has never gripped them. They have not seen the glory of Christ; they are not saved. A person can attend church regularly and not be a Christian just as he can sit in the garden and not be a daisy.

The redeemed who are not gripped by the gospel may have a stagnant knowledge of Christ. Sometimes genuine children of God—those who have truly glimpsed the glory of Christ—begin to forget what they have seen. Christ and the gospel may be good news but old news, and old news is not very interesting. Second Corinthians 4:6 speaks of "the *knowledge* of the glory of God." In order for the beauty of Christ and the gospel to remain fresh in their hearts, Christians must keep growing in their knowledge of the Lord:

> And this I pray, that your love may abound still more and more in real knowledge and all discernment, so that you may approve the things that are excellent, in order to be sincere and blameless until the day of Christ. (Phil. 1:9–10)

> Grow in the grace and knowledge of our Lord and Savior Jesus Christ. (2 Pet. 3:18)

When a Christian's knowledge of Christ and the gospel are not growing, fascination with Christ will dim, and boredom will set in. Then the stunted believer begins looking somewhere else for excitement. Many young people graduate from the high-school department of their Sunday schools with a third-grade understanding of God and His Word. When they go to college, they are exposed to a wealth of knowledge and ideas that have never occurred to them before, and the gospel seems suddenly passé.

Head knowledge does not automatically translate to heart knowledge—but an empty head can never produce a full heart. Empty-headed Christians quickly lose sight of the beauty of Christ and the gospel.

The redeemed who are not gripped by the gospel may be tolerating disobedience to Christ. Israel reeled under the threat of foreign invasion seven hundred years before Christ. When the people complained that God was distant and not paying attention to their troubles, Isaiah the prophet replied:

> Behold, the LORD's hand is not so short
>   That it cannot save;
>   Nor is His ear so dull
>   That it cannot hear.
> But your iniquities have made a separation
>   between you and your God,
> And your sins have hidden His face from you
>   so that He does not hear.
>
>   (Isa. 59:1–2)

This passage illustrates two deadly effects of sin. One is that God does not listen to people who refuse to repent. The other is that sin puts a dark cloud or veil over God's face so His people cannot see Him. When a Christian clutches some favorite sin and refuses to let it go, his spiritual vision becomes dim.

If you are wearing a large diamond, you cannot cover your hands with gooey, rotten garbage and expect it to sparkle in the sun. The sinful pleasures of this world attract us because they appeal to some good, though perverted, desire of our created humanity. When we cling to favorite sins, their perverted natural goodness hides the pure spiritual goodness of the gospel.

The redeemed who are not gripped by the gospel may not be spending much time with Christ. There is no substitute for spending time with Christ. Our culture has fallen prey to the myth of *quality time.* Parents claim that though they do not have much time with their children, what they do have is quality time. Husbands say the same thing when they neglect their wives for work or golf. In order to have *quality* time, there must also be *quantity* time.

Veteran amateur astronomers know it takes time to see what the eyepieces of their telescopes reveal. The longer they look at a faint, fuzzy galaxy, the more detail they are able to see. The more often they look at the planet Jupiter, the more easily they distinguish changes in its colored bands. The same is true in a Christian's relationship to Christ. A believer can read the Bible and not see Christ. We can say our prayers without looking at the Savior. But we cannot see Christ apart from seeking Him in the Word of God and in prayer.

Some people have jobs that do not demand all their attention, so they are able to pray frequently throughout the day. But a factory worker whose attention lapses for a moment may lose a finger. God does not withhold a satisfying vision of Christ from those to whom He has allotted little time. A woman caring for five preschool children and an infirm grandmother may see more of Christ than her pastor does if she uses the *quantity of time* God gives her to develop a *quality* relationship with her Lord.

The redeemed may lose sight of Christ on dark days. Godly men and women sometimes pass through dark and doubting times. There is, however, a very great difference between a godly person's darkness and the darkness of an unconverted person or an unrepentant child of God.

Unconverted sinners do not realize they are walking in spiritual darkness unless the Holy Spirit begins to show them their condition. They do not have a desire to see the spiritual glory of Christ, because they have no concept of a spiritual sense beyond and above their natural human abilities.

When a believer has a dim or darkened view of Christ because he is clinging to some sin, he is normally very uncomfortable at first. King David said, "When I kept silent about my sin, my body wasted away through my groaning all day long. For day and night Your hand was heavy upon me; my vitality was drained away as with the fever heat of summer" (Ps. 32:3–4). Fresh joy only returned when he confessed his sin to God.

The case of a godly man or woman who is walking through dark days is far different.

> (A Psalm of David, when he was in the wilderness of Judah.)
>
> O God, You are my God; I shall seek You earnestly;
>   My soul thirsts for You, my flesh yearns for You,
>   In a dry and weary land where there is no water.
> Thus I have seen You in the sanctuary,
>   To see Your power and Your glory.
> Because Your lovingkindness is better than life,
>   My lips will praise You.
>
> (63:1–3)

In this case David was not involved in sinful behavior. He was fleeing for his life from King Saul. Though his world seemed dark and he did not have a clear vision of God, the Lord was still attractive to him. He hungered and thirsted for more of Him.

This, then, is the great difference: for the godly person in great distress, the world and the Lord seem dark, but the believer desires the Lord more than the world. For the ungodly person the Lord is dark, and the visible world is bright and greatly desirable.

The Holy Spirit Transforms Lives through the Glory of Christ

The conclusive test of whether professing Christians have really seen Christ is that the Holy Spirit is transforming their lives and making them over into the image of Christ (2 Cor. 3:17–18). Transformation by the Spirit is gradual and progressive. All believers are *being transformed*. The Spirit of God does not make the children of God perfect and sinless in this life, but He does make a difference. The Spirit performs this transforming work by showing believers more and more of Christ.

When Moses came down from Mount Sinai (Exod. 34), his face shone because he had seen a little bit of God's glory. Believers in Christ will experience a similar, though far more extensive, transformation when they see Christ at His second coming. "When He appears we will be like Him, because we will see Him just as He is" (1 John 3:2). The present gradual transformation of believers comes from the same source as their final glorification—from seeing the glory and beauty of Christ.

As believers are waiting for Christ to return, they need to ask themselves whether they are experiencing ongoing transformation by the Spirit. This leads us to two questions.

First, am I fighting sin by the Spirit? Near the end of Romans 7, the apostle Paul describes his ongoing battle against sin. "For the good that I want, I do not do, but I practice the very evil that I do not want" (7:19). Every Christian can identify with Paul's frustration, but the battle is not hopeless—the Holy Spirit really does enable us to say no to temptation when we consciously lean on His strength.

> So then, brethren, we are under obligation, not to the flesh, to live according to the flesh—for if you are living according to the flesh, you must die; but if by the Spirit you are putting to death the deeds of the body, you will live. For all who are being led by the Spirit of God, these are sons of God. (Rom. 8:12–14)

> But I say, walk by the Spirit, and you will not carry out the desire of the flesh. For the flesh sets its desire against the Spirit, and the Spirit against the flesh; for these are in opposition to one another, so that you may not do the things that you please. (Gal. 5:16–17)

The Galatians passage goes on to say that people who consistently manifest the deeds of the flesh "will not inherit the kingdom of God." So although the flesh often prevents believers from doing God's will, it does not have the final say. The Holy Spirit is at work in all of God's children in a lifelong project to subdue the unruly flesh.

Professing Christians should ask themselves whether they know some measure of victory in their struggle against sin. If so, they will have experienced the Holy Spirit coming to their rescue when they are struggling against temptation and turn to the Lord asking Him for relief. Jesus lifts the pressure of temptation for a time when God's children ask Him to strengthen them by His Spirit.

 Second, Am I bearing fruit by the Spirit? In opposition to the deeds of the flesh (Gal. 5:19–21), "the fruit of the Spirit is love, joy, peace, patience, kindness, goodness, faithfulness, gentleness, self-control" (5:22–23). This list of character qualities is similar to the characteristics of love found in First Corinthians 13. All of God's commands are summed up in love (Matt. 22:37–40); the fruit of the Spirit is the outworking of love in the life of the believer.

Since the Holy Spirit is the personal Love of God, the presence of the Spirit in a believer's life is an invasion of Love. If, over a period of time, the divine Love has not made His presence known in a professing Christian's life by beginning to produce the fruit of the Spirit, there is real reason to question whether that person has seen Christ. A believer should have a good answer to the question, "So, how is your love life?" The Spirit of God sometimes takes believers out of their comfort zones and enables them to love the people they do not like. He makes them more gentle and patient, and increases their devotion to the Lord Jesus Christ.

If these marks of genuine conversion are not in some measure true of you, then I, as a servant of Jesus and a minister of the gospel, urge you to go to the Lord. Beg Him to give you a new transforming sense of Christ's beauty so you will be able first to trust Him as Savior and then to grow into His likeness. You cannot give yourself a saving sight of Christ; only He can work this miracle of grace within your heart. When He does, your stubborn resistance to the Lordship of Christ will crumble.

Every one must be sensible that this was a great trial to Mr. Edwards. He had been nearly twenty-four years among that people; and his labours had been, to all appearance, from time to time greatly blessed among them: and a great number looked on him as their spiritual father. . . . Now to have this people turn against him, and thrust him out from among them, stopping their ears, and running upon him with furious zeal, not allowing him to defend himself by giving him a fair hearing . . . surely this must come very near to him, and try his spirit. . . . Let us therefore now *behold the man*!—The calm sedateness of his mind; his meekness and humility in great and violent opposition, and injurious treatment; his resolution and steady conduct through all this dark and terrible storm; were truly wonderful, and cannot be set in so beautiful and affecting a light by any description, as they appeared in to his friends, who were eyewitnesses.

—Samuel Hopkins
Describing the dismissal of Jonathan Edwards by his church

Conclusion

Beauty for Brokenness

Christians need to gaze on the beauty of God in Christ in order to live well in a broken world. God's people can bear trials and tribulations with grace, peace and strength if they fix their hearts on Christ. I write with the hope that Christian readers will live out the beauty of Christ and that non-Christians will begin to seek His beauty for themselves.

Jonathan Edwards is arguably America's best expositor of God's beauty. But was he a man devoted to a theory that had no bearing on how he lived? How did he fare in the storms of life?

The quotation at the head of this chapter by one of his closest friends describes Edwards's response to the greatest crisis of his life and ministry. His devotion to a beautiful, sovereign God stood him in good stead when the people who had once loved and praised him turned against him.

In addition to Samuel Hopkins's eyewitness testimony, we also have several of Edwards's letters from this period to his correspondents in Scotland. The letters describe the controversy at his church in general terms without ever descending into vitriol, self-pity, slander or self-justification. To the Rev. Mr. M'Culloch, he wrote:

> I am now separated from the people between whom and me there was once the greatest union. Remarkable is the providence of God in this matter. In this event we have a striking

instance of the instability and uncertainty of all things here below. The dispensation is indeed awful in many respects, calling for serious reflection and deep humiliation in me and my people. The enemy, far and near, will now triumph; but God can overrule all for His own glory. I have now nothing visible to depend upon for my future usefulness, or the subsistence of my numerous family. But I hope we have an all-sufficient, faithful, covenant God, to depend upon. I desire that I may ever submit to him, walk humbly before him, and put my trust wholly in him.[1]

Would that all God's people might walk through the storms of life with such calm submission to His will. Edwards's ability to stand tall under pressure was in large part the result of gazing on the beauty and glory of God throughout his life. In his *Personal Narrative* (found among his papers after his death) Edwards wrote:

The first instance that I remember of that sort of inward, sweet delight in God and divine things that I have lived much in since, was on reading those words, I Tim. i.17. *Now unto the King eternal, immortal, invisible, the only wise God, be honour and glory for ever and ever. Amen.* As I read the words, there came into my soul, and was as it were diffused through it, a sense of the glory of the Divine Being; a new sense, quite different from any thing I ever experienced before. Never any words of scripture seemed to me as these words did. I thought with myself, how excellent a Being that was, and how happy I should be, if I might enjoy that God, and be rapt up to Him in heaven, and be as it were swallowed up in Him for ever! I kept saying, and as it were singing, over these words of scripture to myself; and went to pray to God that I might enjoy Him; and prayed in a manner quite different from what I used to do, with a new sort of affection.[2]

Our desperate need for beauty is not always obvious. When we consider the suffering and injustice in the world, the pursuit of beauty can seem a bit irrelevant, like an artist with his easel set up on the railroad tracks, painting a gorgeous sunset while oblivious to the train racing toward him at seventy miles an hour.

What is the use of beauty in a hard and hostile world? The answer lies in a simple phrase that occurs twice in Second Corinthians 4: "Therefore, we do not lose heart."

> But we all, with unveiled face, beholding as in a mirror the glory of the Lord, are being transformed into the same image from glory to glory, just as from the Lord, the Spirit. *Therefore*, since we have this ministry, as we received mercy, *we do not lose heart*. (3:18–4:1)

> *Therefore we do not lose heart*, but though our outer man is decaying, yet our inner man is being renewed day by day. For momentary, light affliction is producing for us an eternal weight of glory far beyond all comparison, while we look not at the things which are seen, but at the things which are not seen; for the things which are seen are temporal, but the things which are not seen are eternal. (4:16–18)

In both instances the victorious assertion "We do not lose heart" depends on looking steadfastly at unseen but eternal glory. The glory of the Lord that enables us to keep our hearts—rather than losing them in a muddy pit of despair—is not the dreadful glory of God's fierce wrath or even the glory of God's splendor in the starry sky. It is the beautiful glory of His grace in Christ.

The Pressures of a Hostile World

We live in a world that is broken because of sin, a world hostile to God and to the servants of God. The apostle Paul found meditation on the glory and beauty of Christ to be indispensable in his trials and troubles:

> We are afflicted in every way, but not crushed; perplexed, but not despairing; persecuted, but not forsaken; struck down, but not destroyed; always carrying about in the body the dying of Jesus, so that the life of Jesus also may be manifested in our body. For we who live are constantly being delivered over

to death for Jesus' sake, so that the life of Jesus also may be manifested in our mortal flesh. (2 Cor. 4:8–11)

Paul says he was *afflicted*. On his missionary journeys he was shipwrecked at least four times. He mentions three shipwrecks in Second Corinthians (11:25), all of which occurred before the famous one of Acts 27. He was often hungry, thirsty, cold and without adequate clothing (11:27). In addition, he had a "thorn in the flesh" (12:7–10), probably some kind of recurrent physical ailment or permanent disability.

Paul was also *perplexed*. Elsewhere in this epistle, he says he faced such "conflicts without, fears within" that he became depressed and needed both divine and human comfort (7:5–6). He felt the weight of his concern for all the churches he had founded (11:28). Sometimes he was afraid he would be humiliated before God by the failures of his disciples (12:20–21).

Paul was *persecuted*. He had to flee for his life from the majority of the cities where he preached. Five times he received thirty-nine lashes with a whip from the Jews, the maximum number permitted by their law. He was beaten three times with rods, probably by Roman authorities (11:24–25). Paul was intimately familiar with the Roman jails of Philippi, Jerusalem, Caesarea and Rome.

Paul says he was *struck down*. This is probably a general metaphorical description of his troubles, but on at least one occasion, it was literally true. At Lystra an angry crowd stoned him, dragged his body outside the city and left him for dead. This less-than-favorable welcome did not prevent him from returning to Lystra to encourage the disciples by saying, "Through many tribulations we must enter the kingdom of God" (Acts 14:19–22).

Finally, Paul was "constantly being *delivered over to death* for Jesus' sake." Every day his life was in danger, and he was exposed to difficulties and hardships that might have led to his premature demise. Apostleship was not a cushy job.

In sum, the pressures Paul faced were physical, emotional, relational and spiritual. To that extent they were like the trials God's people still face. Christians in Muslim countries, North Korea and elsewhere can identify point-for-point with Paul's tribulations. Believers in North America and Europe generally cannot, but they are still able to learn from his example.

The Bible never makes light of the sufferings God's people have to endure. It never tells them to put on a happy face and to pretend everything is wonderful. In spite of his difficulties, Paul was not *crushed*, *despairing*, *forsaken* or *destroyed*. To the extent that God's children keep their eyes on the glory of Christ and on the gospel, they too can learn to face trials realistically, yet without moaning and complaining.

The picture of Paul we see in Second Corinthians is different from, yet consistent with, the view we have of him in Philippians. Second Corinthians reveals the ragged edge of Paul's emotions. He is down, then up, but always looking at Christ. Philippians was written a few years later and is the most joy-filled book in the New Testament, yet when Paul wrote it, he was a prisoner in Rome. Philippians shows Paul's happiness in Christ, but Paul also indicates that it took him some time to learn the art of Christian contentment (Phil. 4:6–13). That is an encouraging note for those who struggle. Even an apostle had to practice the presence of Christ in order to cope with the rocky roads of life.

God's Provision for His Suffering Children

God's most important provision for distressed believers is neither the psychiatrist's couch nor the counselor's office. Wise counselors can help people see and change faulty patterns of behavior. Drugs may help to stabilize the mind and emotions. But people have a deeper need than these gifts of God's common grace can supply. His fundamental provision for His children in crisis is to point them to the glory and beauty of Christ. In times of trouble we need above all to be "fixing [our] eyes on Jesus, the author and perfecter of faith" (Heb. 12:2).

Second Corinthians 4 helps us to see the beauty of Christ in three ways:

We gaze at the beauty of Christ in the gospel. Believers "see the light of the gospel of the glory of Christ" when God shines in their hearts "to give the light of the knowledge of the glory of God in the face of Christ" (2 Cor. 4:4, 6). Gazing at this light carried Paul through his trials.

The gospel can be looked at narrowly or broadly. Paul wrote to the Corinthians, "I determined to know nothing among you except Jesus Christ, and Him crucified" (1 Cor. 2:2). Then again, he reminded the elders of the church at Ephesus, "I did not shrink from declaring to you the whole counsel of God" (Acts 20:27, ESV). How can we harmonize these descriptions of his preaching? Did he have a short, simple message for the Corinthians and a longer, more elaborate one for the Ephesians?

If we look at Paul's letters, the answer is plain: Paul preached all the great doctrines and stories of the Bible from a Christ-centered perspective. He taught about Abraham and Sarah, the Exodus from Egypt, predestination, the Trinity, the church, faith versus works, the Spirit-filled life, the end of the age and eternal judgment—always with his eyes focused on Christ. He proclaimed the whole counsel of God, and at the same time, he preached only Christ.

When people first become Christians, they see the beauty of the simple gospel: hell-bound sinners can have eternal life through faith in the death and resurrection of Jesus Christ. As they grow in Christ, believers need an expanded view of the glory of God in predestination, the Trinity, final judgment and the rest of God's whole counsel. They need to see that the gospel is central to every major doctrine of the Bible and that the story line of the Bible leads straight to Christ crucified. Meditation on these truths helps believers to become more firmly grounded and stable in the midst of life's storms.

We gaze at the beauty of Christ manifested in our weakness. The apostle Paul was fully aware that he did not have the strength to bear up under his trials:

> But we have this treasure in earthen vessels, so that the sur-passing greatness of the power will be of God and not from ourselves; . . . always carrying about in the body the dying of Jesus, so that the life of Jesus also may be manifested in our body. For we who live are constantly being delivered over to death for Jesus' sake, so that the life of Jesus also may be manifested in our mortal flesh (2 Cor. 4:7, 10–11).

Sometimes God protects and preserves His people from danger and disaster, but quite often He deliberately sends them through the fires and floods of life (Isa. 43:2). Why does He do this? One reason is to demonstrate the difference between His children and the children of the devil. He wants to manifest the power of Christ in human weakness.

This is a testimony first to believers themselves and then to others. When God carries a Christian through tribulation, the believer says, "God has helped me. The Spirit of Christ in me has enabled me to go through this difficulty." At the same time, the world looks on and says, "This man is different. This woman is special."

God takes His children through trials in two ways. First, He sustains us when we do not feel His nearness. In Psalm 22 King David cried out, "My God, my God, why have You forsaken me?" On the cross King Jesus uttered those same words in a far deeper sense than His famous ancestor had. Both were sustained by the eternal Spirit (Ps. 22:24; Heb. 9:14). We often feel deserted by God, even in this present gospel age. When we cry out to the Lord, He holds us up by His indwelling Spirit. In our darkest hours we may not sense the presence of the Spirit or be able to see the beauty of Christ, but after we have gone through the trial, we realize who has carried us, and we confess with gratitude the glory of God's grace.

The second way God sustains His children through trials

and troubles is by pouring out His Holy Spirit in a sensible way so that we feel overwhelmed by the love of our Father rather than by our difficulties. "And not only this, but we also exult in our tribulations, knowing that tribulation brings about persever-ance; and perseverance, proven character; and proven character, hope; and hope does not disappoint, because the love of God has been poured out within our hearts through the Holy Spirit who was given to us" (Rom. 5:3–5).

Since the Spirit is the Love of God, as Jesus is the Word of God, the Father pours out His Love for us by pouring His Spirit into us. As God's children, we ought to seek a fresh outpouring of His Spirit in our hour of need, as Jesus encouraged us to do when He said, "If you then, being evil, know how to give good gifts to your children, how much more will your heavenly Father give the Holy Spirit to those who ask Him?" (Luke 11:13).

If you are a believer and are going through a dry and difficult time, lay hold of God as Jacob did (Gen. 32:24–32). Wrestle in prayer with Him; plead with confidence for an outpouring of His Love into your heart. He may give it early, or He may give it late. He may wait to see how earnestly you want more of Him, but persevere in asking the Lord to fill you with more of Him-self. Remember and trust in His promise: "If anyone is thirsty, let him come to Me and drink. He who believes in Me, as the Scripture said, 'From his innermost being will flow rivers of liv-ing water'" (John 7:37–38).

We gaze at the beauty of Christ in our future. Like Paul, we need to look steadfastly at the "eternal weight of glory" that lies ahead of us. We see it not with our physical eyes nor as an image in our minds, but only with the new eyes God gives us at conver-sion. With these we are able to "look not at the things which are seen, but at the things which are not seen; for the things which are seen are temporal, but the things which are not seen are eter-nal" (2 Cor. 4:17–18).

There are many things we cannot see clearly now, but even a dim view of eternal glory enables us to say, "We do not lose heart" (4:16). When people are young, they sometimes make the mistake of thinking that heaven is for old people. Young men and women tend to be captivated by the here and now. Life is exciting: falling in love, finding a mate, searching for a calling—all of these can make heaven appear as wispy as a morning fog. Older Christians, on the other hand, and believers who have a terminal illness tend to think more of heaven. The nearer they draw to heaven's shores, the brighter its glory appears, and the dimmer this world and its attractions become.

Such a change in perspective is normal, but it is not best. Meditation on the eternal glory of heaven is profitable and life-changing for all of God's children. What is the chief charm of our eternal home? Is it the streets of gold, or perhaps access to the tree of life? No. God is going to catch us up into the life of the holy Trinity. We shall experience love, beauty, holiness and glory with an intensity impossible for us to fathom as long as we live in these houses of clay. Such is the destiny that God has foreordained for all His elect children. The more we look at the place we are headed (even while we are young), the better we will walk on the pilgrim pathway we must tread to get there.

Our Perseverance until the End

We have already seen that gazing on the glory and beauty of Christ enables believers to persevere in holiness. The Spirit is at work in all God's children to transform us into the image of Christ, and He will finish that work at the resurrection.

Another aspect of perseverance relates to ministry. While God enables all His elect to persevere in faith until the end, He does not guarantee that we will all finish well the tasks He has set before us. The only way for us to fulfill our mission with confidence and joy is by steadfastly looking at the glory and beauty of Christ.

As he contemplated the assignment God had given him, the apostle Paul exclaimed, "And who is adequate for these things?" (2 Cor. 2:16). A few sentences later he answered his own question: "Such confidence we have through Christ toward God. Not that we are adequate in ourselves to consider anything as coming from ourselves, but our adequacy is from God, who also made us adequate as servants of a new covenant" (3:4–6).

Throughout Second Corinthians Paul defended his ministry from the slanders of certain "false apostles" (11:13). Apparently these were Judaizers—people who tried to smuggle the Mosaic Law into the gospel and add its burdens to freedom in Christ. In chapter 3 Paul showed that the permanent glory of the gospel outshines the transient glory of the Law, which was symbolized by the fading glow on Moses' face after he came down from conversing with God on Mount Sinai. How was Paul able to conduct his ministry with sincerity and singleness of purpose? His focus on the glory of the gospel enabled him to be clear and true to his calling:

> But we all, with unveiled face, beholding as in a mirror the glory of the Lord, are being transformed into the same image from glory to glory, just as from the Lord, the Spirit. There-fore, since we have this ministry, as we received mercy, we do not lose heart, but we have renounced the things hidden be-cause of shame, not walking in craftiness or adulterating the word of God, but by the manifestation of truth commend-ing ourselves to every man's conscience in the sight of God. (3:18–4:2)

He did not engage in the tricky, deceitful tactics of his adver-saries in order to gain converts. He was enamored with the naked gospel—which is "the power of God unto salvation" (Rom. 1:16).

The work God gives us to do would be completely over-whelming apart from Christ. He has designed it that way in order to manifest His power in us. Feeling like a helpless failure can actually provide a firm foundation for further usefulness. We cannot begin to be fruitful until we feel our own inability. That is when we need to turn away from ourselves and gaze on the face of Christ.

Our mission in life may involve serving many people or only a few. Our commission from Christ may be a very visible and public one, or it may be obscure. But no matter how competent a person may be in the ordinary affairs of life, no one can accomplish God's work in God's way with God's blessing except through God's power. And this power comes from "beholding as in a mirror the glory of the Lord" (2 Cor 3:18).

In the midst of difficulties and disappointments, Paul did not despair over the eventual outcome of his ministry. He looked forward with expectation, having the hope "that the grace which is spreading to more and more people may cause the giving of thanks to abound to the glory of God" (4:15). The apostle might have been suffering, but he was not moaning and groaning. He was depressed at times, but he did not allow himself to wallow. When life was hard, he looked forward to God's being glorified in his sufferings, and was glad.

When God puts us through difficulties that seem impossible to bear, we need to remember that He will be glorified through our pains and problems. He will get praise and glory for Himself, and He will share that praise and glory with us. So we can be thankful not for the trials themselves but for the promised outcome of them. With that kind of focus, we can finish our course with joy.

When Christians think about finishing their course joyfully, they may envision some grand project or great endeavor, like planting a church among headhunters or speaking before presidents and kings. God's assignment for most believers is to walk in the fullness of Christ through the very ordinary responsibilities of life. Most of us know what God wants us to do; the crucial matter is the motivation behind our obedience. Does our obedience flow out of a sense of duty alone, or does it come from the devotion of our hearts?

Duty looks at the law of God and sees a list of obligations: Do this and this; don't do that or the other thing. It is quite clear from the Bible that we all have certain duties. God is the

Lawgiver, and His laws have absolute and binding authority over us. But duty alone is not enough. The law is a heavy burden, a backbreaking load no one can bear. To live under a constant sense of duty causes us to become "weary in well doing" (Gal. 6:9, KJV). We may often become discouraged at our inability to perform our duties perfectly. If, however, we do have some measure of success, we tend to congratulate ourselves rather than giving glory to God. Duty is a man buying his wife an expensive birthday present to make up for his lack of love for her. It can be an external show to disguise an internal deficiency.

Devotion, however, looks at the law and sees a list of ways to express love for God. Devotion is a man doing some household chore because he enjoys pleasing his wife. Devotion is a woman fixing a special meal for her husband because she knows he will appreciate it and because his smile over the dinner table makes her feel warm and loved.

What is the source of devotion to Christ? Is it simply gratitude? No. Where does a wife's devotion to her husband come from? Is it simply based on the fact that he bought her a ring, gave her his last name and his children, and provides her with a house and money to buy groceries? Not at all. Her devotion to her husband rests on certain qualities that she sees in him. She is in love with the kind of man he is.

In the same way, devotion to Christ comes from seeing Him for who He is. When we see the glory and beauty of Christ in the gospel, we obey Him because we want to express our love for Him. That is how Christ's beauty becomes the motivation for our perseverance. When we look on His face, His Spirit gives us fresh energy to see our appointed task through to the end.

Beauty for Brokenness

We live in a world filled with suffering and sorrow, a world that often seems dark and difficult. As I conclude these meditations on the beauty of God, I want to speak to the different kinds of situations in which may find yourselves.

Are you hostile to the God of the Bible? Maybe the church and its representatives have done you a great harm. Perhaps you have found Christianity to be intellectually stifling and emotionally unsatisfying. You may be overwhelmed by the suffering of the world and resentful of a God who claims to be in charge of this mess. Even more personally, perhaps you or your loved ones have been crushed by unimaginable pain. Whatever the case, beauty is not a word you readily apply to God.

I cannot give you new eyes by arguing with you, but I hope I have caused you to think more deeply about the nature of God and His work in the world. Perhaps your mind is entertaining a new possibility that Jesus Christ may be God and that He is attractive. Pray to the God whose existence you doubt, and call out to Him, "If you are real, please show me Your beauty." Pain may awaken you to your need, but only a new sense of the beauty and glory of God will draw you to the Savior.

Are you a Christian whose faith in Christ has become dry and stale? At one time your heart was deeply stirred by the gospel, and you loved to read God's word and sing His praise. But that is all in the past. You are going through the motions of being a Christian, but your heart is not really engaged. As King David said to his son, "The LORD searches all hearts, and understands every intent of the thoughts. If you seek Him, He will let you find Him; but if you forsake Him, He will reject you forever" (1 Chron. 28:9).

The Lord wants to be pursued. He wants us to seek Him diligently with all our heart, soul, mind and strength (Mark 12:30). He does not reveal the glories of His grace to the casual observer. Bend your mind toward understanding the beauty of God, and bare your heart in an earnest prayer, "Lord, please show me Your beauty." The better you see Him, the more you will love Him, and the more satisfying to your heart He will be.

Are you struggling against temptation? All of us face this challenge. The things that tempt us are things we find attractive. They lure us and draw us in as a wriggling night crawler attracts a trout. Sometimes a fish will feel the hook in its lip and shake it out as it steals the bait. But a few minutes later it might bite again and be fatally hooked.

That is how we respond to sin. We feel the hook. We know the attraction may be fatal, but we keep on biting anyway. As long as sin is attractive, mere will power is ineffective.[3] The will weakens before the onslaught of things that appeal to our untamed natural desires. You may dream of sexual indulgence, sweet revenge, winning the lottery, impressing your friends with your sarcastic wit or being the tragic victim. It does not matter what your besetting sin may be. Your only hope is to find something else more attractive that is also good (Phil. 4:8). That is the reason meditating on the sufferings and the glory of Christ is essential for our spiritual well-being (Col. 3:1–11; Heb. 12:1–2).

Or are you suffering what Hamlet called "the slings and arrows of outrageous fortune"? Your once-bright hopes have been dimmed or dashed by death, divorce, desertion or disaster. Remember, what we call ill fortune is actually the hand of a loving Father. After God informed Habakkuk that the Chaldeans were going to devastate his homeland and massacre his people, the prophet responded with these amazing words:

> Though the fig tree should not blossom
>   And there be no fruit on the vines,
>   Though the yield of the olive should fail
>   And the fields produce no food,
>   Though the flock should be cut off from the fold
>   And there be no cattle in the stalls,
> Yet I will exult in the LORD,
>   I will rejoice in the God of my salvation.
> The Lord GOD is my strength,
>   And He has made my feet like hinds' feet,
>   And makes me walk on my high places.
>
> (Hab. 3:17–19)

God granted Habakkuk such a vision of His greatness, goodness and glory that his aching heart was more than satisfied. To skip like the deer on the mountains when all you hold dear on this earth has been taken away is incomprehensible to the heart that has not seen the Lord. Scripture does not trivialize the pain of loss in using the image of a running deer. God's people have often found that pain and God's peace, grief and God's gladness can exist together in their hearts. Paul Tournier, the famous Swiss Christian psychiatrist, captured the thought well when he wrote after the death of his wife, "I can truly say that I have a great grief and that I am a happy man."[4]

Jonathan Edwards and his wife Sarah discovered the same truth in 1748 when their daughter, Jerusha, died after a brief illness. Jonathan described their bereavement in a letter to his friend John Erskine:

> It has pleased God, since I wrote my last to you, sorely to afflict this family, by taking away by death, the last February, my second daughter, in the eighteenth year of her age; a very pleasant and useful member of this family, and one that was esteemed the flower of the family. Herein we have a great loss; but the remembrance of the remarkable appearances of piety in her, from her childhood, in life, and also at her death, are very comfortable to us, and give us great reason to mingle thanksgiving with our mourning. I desire your prayers, dear Sir, that God would make up our great loss to us in himself.[5]

Jerusha herself knew the "peace of God which surpasses all comprehension" (Phil.4:7). On her deathbed she told her parents that "she had not seen one minute, for several years, wherein she desired to live one minute longer, for the sake of any other good in life, but doing good, living to God, and doing what might be for his glory."[6]

We are broken people living in a broken world. When that world comes crashing down around you, pray earnestly, "Lord, show *me* Your beauty."

APPENDIX 1

An Ex-Christian Critique and My Response

The following note comes from a thoughtful and articulate ex-Christian named Jeffrey Purdon, who kindly consented to read the manuscript of this book. It is a sample of the hostility one sometimes encounters toward the gospel:

> I'd like to comment on the main argument that God as presented in the Bible can be understood as a good character. If I follow things correctly, in the beginning there was God and Jesus. God loved Jesus so much that He wanted to have more creatures to love. He created the angels who seemed to be perfect in every way, but somehow God was unable to love the angels as much as He loved Jesus. And so God devised a scheme by which mankind would be imperfect and sinful, but would strive to redeem themselves to God. Sin and redemption apparently please God and make mankind as lovable as Jesus is. But in order to have a system of sin and redemption, there needs to be a real hell, and people really need to go to it. Therefore, enough people have to go to hell so that just enough people can go to heaven and become loved like Jesus. God shares His love as much as possible, and all is good.
>
> Maybe I've simplified things a bit, but I hope that just in my paraphrasing you can see that I don't agree that this makes the literary character of God a good person, or even a particularly understandable person. It makes God out to be selfish, a bit deranged and certainly uncaring. Try to compare the character of God above to a human person doing similar things. Let's say that I have a son, and I want another son that I can love like the first. At first I have a daughter, which just isn't the same, so I am sad. Then I have another son, but for whatever reason this son isn't very lovable. I need him to fail and be miserable and then find some true love from me because of the ordeal. I make up rules and regulations that this son, and all my future sons, must follow. And if they don't

follow them, or don't repent when they break a rule, I eventually . . . shoot them?[1]

Response to Jeffrey: A Parable

The kingdom of heaven is like a wealthy philanthropist who built a lovely apartment complex for the indigent. The rooms were tastefully furnished. Flowers and shrubs adorned the walkways between the buildings, and a waterfall in the central square splashed over boulders into a shallow goldfish pond.

The entrance requirements for inhabitants were simple: no criminal activity and a signed agreement to maintain the individual apartments along with the common space. The monthly rent was far below the cost of the hovels from which the poor had come.

Within a short time the tenants turned the philanthropist's gift into a wasteland. Trash accumulated in the central square. The goldfish died, and the pond stank. The residents ripped out all the copper wires they could find to sell for drug money. Robberies and rapes became common, and the people cursed their benefactor for his failure to take care of them.

The philanthropist sent a representative each month to collect the rents, but soon one, then another, then all the tenants refused to pay. They slammed their doors in his face and openly scorned his requests. On one occasion they stoned the representative so he barely escaped with his life. When the police arrived to investigate the incident, nobody knew anything. Nobody had seen anything.

Finally, the philanthropist sent his only son to investigate the situation. Like a pack of rabid wolves foaming at the mouth, the people poured out of their apartments into the central square and stoned the young man to death. Recently installed security cameras recorded the brutal murder and revealed that every resident had been involved. All were found guilty at the trial. Some were sentenced to death and others to extended prison sentences.

But then the father of the murdered man intervened. He chose half a dozen of the worst offenders and pled with the governor of the state to commute their sentences so he could adopt them. When the governor agreed, the philanthropist bulldozed the apartment complex and erected a gorgeous new mansion on the site where he lived with his newly adopted sons and daughters.

*   *   *   *   *

I made four observations concerning God in this parable when I wrote to Jeffrey:

First, God the Father is the philanthropist, the judge and the governor combined.

Second, God could have forestalled mankind's rebellion, but He chose to permit it—even though our sin would cost Him so much grief—because He wanted an opportunity to exercise His outrageously generous lovingkindness. The authors of the New Testament saw their sins in light of God's holiness; they were overwhelmed by the greatness of God's love, grace and mercy. The apostle Paul initially persecuted the earliest Christians. He was in hearty agreement with the stoning of the first Christian martyr. To the end of his life, he remained amazed at the astounding kindness of God:

> I thank Christ Jesus our Lord, who has strengthened me, because He considered me faithful, putting me into service, even though I was formerly a blasphemer and a persecutor and a violent aggressor. Yet I was shown mercy because I acted ignorantly in unbelief; and the grace of our Lord was more than abundant, with the faith and love which are found in Christ Jesus. It is a trustworthy statement, deserving full acceptance, that Christ Jesus came into the world to save sinners, among whom I am foremost of all. Yet for this reason I found mercy, so that in me as the foremost, Jesus Christ might demonstrate His perfect patience as an example for those who would believe in Him for eternal life. Now to the

King eternal, immortal, invisible, the only God, be honor and glory forever and ever. Amen. (1 Tim. 1:12–17)

Third, the philanthropist in the parable could not assume that his adopted children would behave any better than they had before, but God sends His Spirit into the hearts of His adopted children to transform their whole outlook on life:

> However, you are not in the flesh but in the Spirit, if indeed the Spirit of God dwells in you. But if anyone does not have the Spirit of Christ, he does not belong to Him. . . . So then, brethren, we are under obligation, not to the flesh, to live according to the flesh—for if you are living according to the flesh, you must die; but if by the Spirit you are putting to death the deeds of the body, you will live. For all who are being led by the Spirit of God, these are sons of God. For you have not received a spirit of slavery leading to fear again, but you have received a spirit of adoption as sons by which we cry out, "Abba! Father!" The Spirit Himself testifies with our spirit that we are children of God, and if children, heirs also, heirs of God and fellow heirs with Christ, if indeed we suffer with Him so that we may also be glorified with Him. (Rom. 8:9–17)

And fourth, someone might charge God with doing evil in order to bring about good. God never does evil, but He chose before the foundation of the world to permit evil in order to bring about good. The good He chose to produce involved the greatest possible outpouring of His love by redeeming His enemies from the greatest possible disaster, at the greatest possible cost to Himself, for the greatest possible creaturely happiness in fellowship with Himself

I have had only occasional e-mail contact with Jeffrey since this correspondence. We have never met, but I pray for him regularly. I plan to give him a copy of this book.

Show Me Your Beauty

John K. LaShell, 1986

arr. by Bethany S. LeBedz

Chorus

Show me Your beau - ty in the stars and in the trees.

Tenor Harmony

Show me Your beau - ty in the ho - ly Tri - ni - ty.

Show me Your beau - ty in the gos - pel of grace.

I want to hear Your voice and see Your face.

2. The Father, Son and blessed Holy Spirit,
        Forever one yet in Their Persons three,
    Before the world began They dwelt in glory,
        Complete in love and perfect harmony.

3. The glorious gospel of our Lord and Savior
        Outshines the beams of any earthly light.
    It scatters clouds of sin and wrath against us,
        Dispels our fear and banishes our night.

4. Beholding now His glory in a mirror,
        Transformed into His likeness by His grace.
    I long to be perfected at His coming,
        To be like Jesus when I see His face.

A Visual Summary of God's Plan for Creation

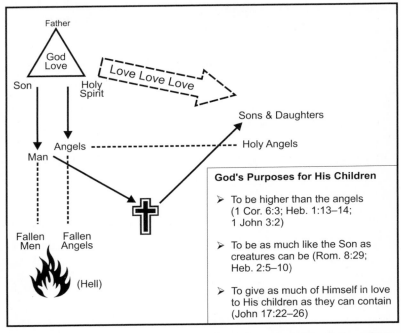

The beauty of God's plan needs to be viewed in light of His stated objective. Some people think God's goal should be to eliminate all suffering for all people immediately. Others think God's goal should be to save everybody eventually—or if His power is limited, His goal should be to save as many as He can. The Bible declares God's goal is to "bring many sons [and daughters] into glory" (Heb. 2:10) and to pour out His love on them in the greatest possible way. Viewed in light of God's ultimate goal, the beauty of God's plan lies in several things: the wisdom with which God is accomplishing His intention; the fairness and justice according to which He deals with rebels; and the great love (Eph. 2:4) He is thereby able to express.

Trinitarian Relationships

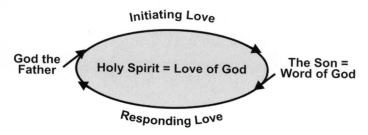

The standard Trinitarian triangle shown in chapter 10 is a visual representation of the defining statements of the basic doctrine of the Trinity. It stresses the unity of the divine nature and the distinction between the three Persons of the Godhead.

The diagram above is an attempt to represent visually the relationships among the three Persons.

- The Father, Son and Holy Spirit share the identical divine nature and are equal in every divine attribute. For that reason I have put them on the same horizontal line rather than arranging them vertically.
- The Son is the Word, the eternal self-expression of God the Father. To use Edwards's terminology, He is God's idea of Himself. The Father loves what He sees in the Son.
- The Person of the Father is in some nontemporal sense prior to the Person of the Son, so I have called the Father's love for the Son *initiating* love. I have called the Son's love for the Father *responding* love.

The Holy Spirit, as the Love of God, is not the love of the Father alone nor of the Son alone. Rather He is the bond of love between them. This is in accord with the Western version of the Nicene Creed, which states that the Holy Spirit proceeds from the Father and the Son.

God's Love In Us

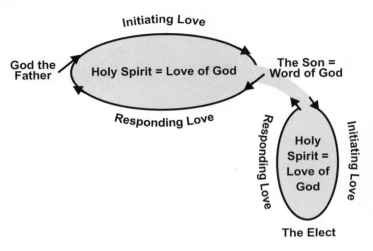

This diagram builds on the diagram on the previous page. It is an attempt to portray visually the grand truths of John 17:22–26 where Jesus prays:

> The glory which You have given Me I have given to them, that they may be one, just as We are one; I in them and You in Me, that they may be perfected in unity, so that the world may know that You sent Me, and loved them, even as You have loved Me. Father, I desire that they also, whom You have given Me, be with Me where I am, so that they may see My glory which You have given Me, for You loved Me before the foundation of the world. O righteous Father, although the world has not known You, yet I have known You; and these have known that You sent Me; and I have made Your name known to them, and will make it known, so that the love with which You loved Me may be in them, and I in them.

Note particularly: First, the very same Love that unites the Father and the Son, that is, the Holy Spirit, is in the elect. And second, the gift of the Spirit comes through Christ (Acts 2:33). Similarly, our responsive worship and fellowship with the Father are through Christ and in the Holy Spirit (Eph. 2:18).

ABBREVIATIONS
for the Works of Jonathan Edwards

End of Creation	*A Dissertation concerning the End for Which God Created the World* in *Works*, vol. 1
Original Sin	*The Great Christian Doctrine of Original Sin Defended* in *Works*, vol. 1
Controversies	*Remarks on Important Theological Controversies* in *Works*, vol. 2
Religious Affections	*A Treatise concerning Religious Affections* in *Works*, vol. 1
Treatise on Grace	*Treatise on Grace* in *Unpublished Writings*
True Virtue	*A Dissertation concerning the Nature of True Virtue* in *Works*, vol. 1
Unpublished Writings	*Selections from the Unpublished Writings of Jonathan Edwards, of America.* Edited by Alexander B. Grosart (Edinburgh: privately printed, 1865)
Works	*The Works of Jonathan Edwards, with a Memoir by Sereno E. Dwight.* Edited by Edward Hickman. 2 vols (Edinburgh: Banner of Truth 1979)

ENDNOTES

Introduction: The Challenge

Epigraph. Edwards, "God Glorified in Man's Dependence" in *Works* 1.5.

1. Conrad Cherry, *The Theology of Jonathan Edwards: A Reappraisal* (Gloucester, MA: Peter Smith, 1974), 1.

Chapter 1: Why Did God Create the World?

Epigraph. Edwards, *True Virtue* in *Works* 1.125.

1. Aristotle, *The Nicomachean Ethics*, bks. 8–9.

2. For a simple proof that some infinites are larger than others, see George Gamow, *One, Two, Three . . . Infinity: Facts & Speculations of Science* (New York: Viking Press, 1962),14–23.

3. Edwards explains the distinction between primary and secondary beauty in chapter 3 of *True Virtue* in *Works* 1.127–30.

4. The distinction between delight and benevolence is common, but I learned it from Edwards. (Edwards often uses *complacence* as a synonym for *delight.*) God's delight in Himself and our delight in God figure largely in his works. For Edwards's definitions of delight and benevolence see *True Virtue* in *Works* 1.123.

5. The NASB text of Matthew 17:5 has "with whom" instead

of "in whom," but the Greek is the same in both cases. Either is an acceptable translation. Second Peter 1:17 refers to the same event in almost identical language.

6. In *End of Creation*, 2.3, Edwards gives an extensive list of Scriptures that show that God's glory is the ultimate end of creation. See *Works* 1.107–12.

7. When I say that the communication of God's love to His children is the grand goal of creation, I am not undermining the truth that God created all things for His glory, because these two ends are actually one. "It comes to the same thing. God's respect to the creature's good, and His respect to Himself, is not a divided respect; but both are united in one, as the happiness of the creature aimed at is happiness in union with Himself [i.e. God]" (*End of Creation*, 2.7, in *Works* 1.120).

8. The heavens declare the glory of God (Ps. 19:1), as do the animals (Isa. 43:20) as well as God's judgments (Ezek. 28:22). God made all His other works, however, for the sake of His redeemed children. Therefore, God's communicating Himself to His people is the highest expression of His glory and the fullest manifestation of His beauty.

Chapter 2: Does Science Reveal a Designer in Nature?

Epigraph. Edwards, *True Virtue* in *Works* 1.128.

1. Edwards, *True Virtue* in *Works* 1.127. Edwards's definition of beauty is unremarkable. Many philosophers of an earlier time and most ordinary people of all times would probably agree with him. Philosophers infected with diseases such as linguistic analysis, existentialism and postmodernism have given up trying to find a universal definition of beauty.

2. Shankara's philosophy is, ironically, beautifully expressed in his "Crest-Jewel of Discrimination." The excerpt from which I have summarized his fundamental idea is found in Gary Kessler, *Voices of Wisdom: A Multicultural Philosophy Reader* (Belmont, CA: Wadsworth/Thompson Learning, 2004), 385–93.

3. For the sake of simplicity, I have labeled Shankara's system

"monism," even though he preferred the term "non-dualism."

4. Edwards, *True Virtue* in *Works* 1.127.

5. Michael J. Behe, *Darwin's Black Box: The Biochemical Challenge to Evolution* (New York: The Free Press, 1996), 74–97. Behe has been soundly criticized by his professional peers for his attack on blind evolution. In my view he has provided reasonable responses to his critics, so his research continues to provide strong evidence that these systems were designed. However, my purpose in this chapter is not to prove the existence of a Designer—that is what I am assuming—but to foster an appreciation for the beauty of well-designed biological systems.

6. Hugh Ross, *The Fingerprint of God* (New Kensington, PA: Whitaker, 1989), 119–38. See also Ross, "Big Bang Model Refined by Fire" in *Mere Creation: Science, Faith & Intelligent Design*, William A. Dembski, ed. (Downers Grove, IL: InterVarsity, 1998), 363–84. In addition to the fine-tuning of fundamental constants, Ross includes numerous other examples of fine-tuning for life on earth. For more on the fine-tuning argument, search the Internet or physics and astronomy publications under the heading "anthropic principle" or "fine-tuning of the universe."

7. Dan Falk, "The Anthropic Principle's Surprising Resurgence," *Sky and Telescope*, March 2004, 43–47.

8. Ross, *Fingerprint of God*, 134.

9. Sir Isaac Newton in John Polkinghorne, *Science and Creation: The Search for Understanding* (Boston: New Science Library, Shambhala, 1989), 26.

10. Richard Dawkins, *The God Delusion* (New York: Houghton Mifflin, 2006), 111–59.

Chapter 3: Where Is God in the Brutality and Inefficiency of Nature?

Epigraph. Edwards in Wallace E. Anderson, ed., "Of Insects" in *Works of Jonathan Edwards, Volume 6, Scientific and Philosophical Writings* (New Haven, CT: Yale University Press, 1980), 154, 158, 161.

1. "Ravine," also spelled "ravin," refers to a violent act of seizure—in this case, a predator seizing its prey.

2. Alfred, Lord Tennyson, *In Memoriam,* 56. Tennyson was not an atheist, but these lines echo the despair he felt as he worked through the pain of his friend's death.

3. Sam Harris, *Letter to a Christian Nation* (New York: Alfred A. Knopf, 2006), 75. This book is not so much a careful argument against theism as it is a series of hit-and-run attacks, more liberally laced with sarcasm than with logic.

4. Ibid., 77.

5. "Analogous and Homologous Structures," *Microsoft Encarta* 2006. © 1993–2005 Microsoft Corporation. All rights reserved.

6. Wayne Grudem, *Systematic Theology: An Introduction to Biblical Doctrine* (Grand Rapids: Zondervan, 1994), 317.

7. Ibid., 319.

8. Augustine in Vernon J. Bourke, ed., *The City of God* (New York: Image Books, 1958), 11.22

9. Cicero in C.D. Yonge, trans., *Cicero's Tusculan Disputations; Also, Treatises on The Nature of the Gods, and on The Commonwealth* (New York: Harper & Brothers, 1877).

10. Cicero, *The Nature of the Gods*, 2.5–6, 51–53.

11. Stephen Charles Neill, *Christian Faith and Other Faiths: The Christian Dialogue with Other Religions* (London: Oxford University Press, 1968), 132. Wilhelm Schmidt has collected many examples of this widespread belief. These are conveniently summarized in his *The Origin and Growth of Religion: Facts and Theories* (New York: Cooper Square, 1972), 261–71. Don Richardson has popularized a number of accounts of "the Vague God" in *Eternity in Their Hearts* (Ventura, CA: Regal Books, 1981).

12. Sigmund Freud in James Strachey, trans., *Civilization and Its Discontents* (New York: W.W. Norton, 1961), 62–64.

13. There are extensive treatments of the relationship between

Christianity and modern science in R.J. Hooykaas, *Religion and the Rise of Modern Science* (Grand Rapids: Eerdmans, 1972) and in Christopher B. Kaiser, *Creation and the History of Science* (Grand Rapids: Eerdmans, 1991).

Chapter 4: What Was Jesus' Appeal to His Contemporaries?

Epigraph. Edwards, "The Excellency of Christ" in *Works* 1.680. The basic idea for the present chapter comes from this sermon. Edwards's text is Revelation 5:5–6, where Christ is represented under the contrary figures of a lion and a lamb.

1. Edwards, *True Virtue* in *Works* 1.127.

2. The tractate *Sanhedrin* (43a) of the Babylonian Talmud in Everett F. Harrison, *A Short Life of Christ* (Grand Rapids: Eerdmans, 1968), 15.

3. Ibid., 16.

4. Flavius Josephus in William Whiston, trans., *The Antiquities of the Jews,* 8.2.5, in *The Life and Works of Flavius Josephus* (Philadelphia: John C. Winston Company, n.d.).

5. Aristotle, *Nicomachean Ethics*, 4.3.

6. Albert Orsborn, "Let the Beauty of Jesus Be Seen," ca. 1916.

Chapter 5: Is Christianity a Unique Religion?

Epigraph. Edwards, "Ruth's Resolution," in *Works* 1.665.

1. John Wesley's, *Letters,* 6.123, in John N. Oswalt, *The Book of Isaiah, Chapters 1–39* (Grand Rapids: Eerdmans, 1986), 203. A similar statement has often been mistakenly ascribed to G.K. Chesterton. The "Quotemeister" section of the American Chesterton Society website traces it to Emile Cammaert's apparent elaboration of Chesterton's ideas.

2. Augustine, *City of God*, 6.1.

3. J.P. Holding, "Mighty Mithraic Madness: Did the Mithraic Mysteries Influence Christianity?" *Tekton: Building Blocks for Christian Faith.* Online at http://www.tektonics.org/copycat/mithra.html. Accessed on November 7, 2007. This article is accompanied by a detailed bibliography.

4. "Mithraism," *Encyclopedia Britannica* (CD-ROM, 2003).

5. Andrew J. McLean provides an excellent summary of neopagan beliefs and practices in "Neo-Paganism: Is Dialogue Possible?" *Apologetics Index.* Online at http://www.apologeticsindex.org/313-neo-paganism-dialogue. Accessed on November 7, 2007. The article was originally published in the *Lutheran Theological Journal*, 36.3, December 2002, 112–25. For another overview of the movement, see "Neopaganism," online at http://www.Wikipedia: en.wikipedia.org/wiki/Neo-paganism (November 7, 2007).

6. "Kali: The Dark Mother." Online at http://www.hinduism.about.com/library/weekly/aa051202a.htm. Accessed on November 7, 2007.

7. *Magick* is the spelling preferred by many who distinguish their serious interest in the occult from the illusions of an entertainer.

8. Anton Szandor LaVey, "The Eleven Satanic Rules of the Earth," *The Church of Satan.* Online at http://www.churchofsatan.com/Pages/Eleven.html. Accessed on November 7, 2007.

9. Microsoft Encarta 2006. © 1993–2005 Microsoft Corporation. All rights reserved.

10. Plato in Francis MacDonald, Cornford, trans., *The Republic of Plato* (New York: Oxford University Press, 1965), 46–47.

11. In spite of the pains of the cross, God's essential and eternal happiness remains undiminished, for the Bible describes Him as the blessed God, that is, the supremely happy God (1 Tim. 1:11; 6:15). God's eternal and unchangeable nature cannot suffer pain at the hands of His creatures. He takes delight in His own divinely difficult work of salvation, so the cost of our salvation does not diminish His happiness.

12. Freud in James Strachey, trans., *Civilization and Its Discontents* (New York: W.W. Norton, 1961), 64.

13. Münster Gesangbuch, Joseph A. Seiss, trans., "Fairest Lord Jesus," 1873.

Chapter 6: What Did Jesus' Dying on the Cross Achieve?

Epigraph. Edwards, "Justification by Faith Alone" in *Works*, vol. 1. Quotations are from pp. 624–27. Edwards taught me the reason that sinners are justified by faith alone, but I later learned about other aspects of our union with Christ from John Owen's *Meditations and Discourses on the Glory of Christ* in *The Works of John Owen* (Edinburgh: Banner of Truth, 1965), 1.352–59. This chapter is largely a reworking of concepts from those two sources.

1. Cyprian in John F. McNeill, ed., Ford Lewis Battles, trans., *Calvin: Institutes of the Christian Religion* in *The Library of Christian Classics* (Philadelphia: Westminster, 1960), 1012, fn. 3.

2. John Calvin, *Institutes of the Christian Religion*, 1.4.1.

3. Several passages in the Old Testament refer to the angel of the Lord in such a way that He appears to be more than a messenger of the Almighty. He appears to be Yahweh Himself. See, for example, Exodus 3:2–4. John 1:18 leads us to conclude that these were appearances of the pre-incarnate Christ.

4. For a defense of baptism in the Holy Spirit occurring at salvation, see John R.W. Stott, *Baptism and Fullness: The Work of the Holy Spirit Today* (Downers Grove, IL: InterVarsity, 1975), 19–46.

5. John Owen, *The Glory of Christ*, 354.

Chapter 7: How Can Predestination Be Fair?

Epigraph. Edwards, "Personal Narrative" in *Works* 1.xii–xiii. Edwards wrote this piece for his own private benefit. It was found among his papers after his death.

1. Edwards provides a penetrating philosophical and psychological critique of natural human goodness in *True Virtue* in *Works* 1.122–42.

2. Some theologians, who wish to be called evangelicals, even deny that God is able to know the future. For a refutation

of this unwholesome and unbiblical doctrine, see Bruce A. Ware, *God's Lesser Glory: The Diminished God of Open Theism* (Wheaton, IL: Crossway Books, 2000). For a striking example of God's knowledge of future events, compare First Kings 13:1–2 with Second Kings 23:15–18; God gave the detailed prophecy about three hundred years before its fulfillment.

3.   Unfortunately, some translations obscure the clear parallel between "foreknowledge" in First Peter 1:2 and "foreknown" in First Peter 1:20. The NIV has "foreknowledge" in verse 2 and "chosen" in verse 20. The NKJV has "foreknowledge" in verse 2 and "foreordained" in verse 20.

4.   "Besides, unjustifiable partiality is not imputable to a sovereign distributing his favours, though ever so unequally, unless it be done unwisely, and so as to infringe the common good" (Edwards, "Concerning the Divine Decrees in General and Election in Particular," *Controversies* in *Works* 2.540).

5.   Since God is eternal and since time did not exist until He created the universe, the order of His decrees is logical rather than temporal.

6.   Martin Luther in J.I. Packer and O.R. Johnston, trans., *The Bondage of the Will* (Grand Rapids: Revell, 1957), 207.

7.   Mark Galli, "The Man Who Wouldn't Give Up," *Christian History* 1992, no. 4, 11.

8.   For a classic refutation of the notion that the doctrine of God's sovereignty discourages evangelism, see J.I. Packer, *Evangelism and the Sovereignty of God* (Chicago: InterVarsity, 1961). See also Iain H. Murray, *Revival and Revivalism: The Making and Marring of American Evangelicalism 1750–1858* (Carlisle, PA: Banner of Truth, 1994). Murray demonstrates the historical inaccuracy of Charles Finney's charge that Calvinism is hostile to evangelism.

9.   The concluding section of this chapter was written by John LaShell and first published in *The Morning Call* (Allentown, PA), October 24, 2009, GO 9. Used by permission.

Chapter 8: Why Would a Good God Allow Suffering?

Epigraph. Edwards, "Concerning the Endless Punishment of Those Who Die Impenitent," *Controversies* in *Works* 2.518

1. Thomas Hobbes, *Leviathan; or, The Matter, Form, and Power of a Commonwealth Ecclesiastical and Civil* (first published in 1651), chap. 13.

2. Many of the concepts in this chapter are dependent on "Concerning the Divine Decrees in General, and Election in Particular," *Controversies* in *Works* 2.525–43.

3. Edwards, "The Eternity of Hell Torments" in *Works* 2.87.

4. Traditionally, the phrase "Today I have begotten You" has been interpreted to mean that God the Father begot the Son in the day of eternity past. In other words, the Father-Son relationship between the first and second Persons of the Trinity is eternal. This is also the traditional interpretation of the phrase "only begotten Son" in John 3:16. More recently it has been suggested that "Today I have begotten You" refers to the day of Jesus' coronation after His resurrection (see Acts 13:33–34).

5. Along with many other theologians, I distinguish the moral law from the ceremonial law, which prefigured Christ and the New Covenant; I distinquish it also from the civil law, which prescribed specific punishments for infractions of the moral law in the theocratic state of Israel under the Old Covenant. The shadowy ceremonial law is no longer in effect, because reality has come in Christ (Col. 2:16–17). The civil aspects of the law ceased to be in effect with the ending of the theocracy. The moral law continues to be an expression of God's will for mankind.

6. Evangelical feminists have disputed the idea that headship implies submission to authority, but see Thomas R. Schreiner, "Head Coverings, Prophecies and the Trinity: 1 Corinthians 11:2–16" and Grudem, "The meaning of *Kephalē* ('Head'): A Response to Recent Studies," in John Piper and Grudem, eds., *Recovering Biblical Manhood and*

Womanhood: A Response to Evangelical Feminism (Wheaton, IL: Crossway Books, 1991), 124–39, 425–68.

7. Jonathan Edwards thoroughly explores this idea in "Concerning the Endless Punishment of Those Who Die Impenitent," Controversies in Works 2.515-525

8. My inspiration for using the Star Trek episode as an image of the lost probably comes from C.S. Lewis, "The Weight of Glory" in *Screwtape Proposes a Toast and Other Pieces* (London: Collins, Fontana Books, 1965), 109.

9. David Bentley Hart, *The Beauty of the Infinite: The Aesthetics of Christian Faith* (Grand Rapids: Eerdmans, 2003), 272, 399.

10. Timothy Keller, *The Reason for God: Belief in an Age of Skepticism* (New York: Dutton, 2008), 278.

11. Johnson Oatman Jr., "Holy, Holy, Is What the Angels Sing," 1894.

Chapter 9: How Could a Good God Command Ethnic Cleansing?

Epigraph. Edwards, *A History of the Work of Redemption* in *Works* 1.543.

1. Christ instituted the New Covenant by shedding His blood for our sins (Luke 22:20). Hebrews 8–10 draws on the New Covenant promise of Jeremiah 31 to explain why the New Covenant is superior to the Old.

2. Hadith 9:45; 84.2.57 in George W. Braswell Jr., *Islam: Its Prophet, Peoples, Politics and Power* (Nashville: Broadman & Holman, 1996), 73–74.

3. Quotations from the Qur'an are from *The Koran*, translated with notes by N.J. Dawood (New York: Penguin, 1999).

4. This summary of Kelsay is from Braswell, *Islam*, 144.

5. Braswell, *Islam*, 144–146, has a good discussion of how Muslim scholars believe the West has a distorted understanding of Islam.

6. While Edwards believed in Adam's representative union

with (or federal headship over) his posterity, he buttressed his position with a unique theory of identity, which few since him have adopted. He suggested that God preserves the world by a process of continual creation. According to this theory, I am the same person as I was a moment ago not because I have existed from that moment to this, but because God keeps recreating me anew every moment. In that case I am only the same person as I was because God has willed it to be so. Therefore, according to Edwards, our identity with Adam rests on the same foundation as our own continuing identity, that is, the sovereign will of God, who makes us one with Adam in the same way as He makes us one with ourselves. See Edwards, *Original Sin,* 4.3, in *Works* 1.223–25. For a thorough refutation of this view, see Charles Hodge, *Systematic Theology* (Grand Rapids: Eerdmans, 1981), 1.577–81, 2.217–21.

7. See Ecclesiastes 9:2–6. In Ecclesiastes God reveals the despair of a man who is trying to figure out the meaning of life on his own.

8. If even the land was defiled by the sin of the Canaanites, then surely their offspring were also regarded as unclean (Lev. 18:24–25).

9. Hodge, *Systematic Theology,* 1:26–27.

10. In John 5 and several other passages, good deeds are the evidence of true conversion. It is not reasonable to draw from such texts a doctrine of salvation by works. Such a conclusion goes contrary to Paul's argument in Romans 1–5 that we are saved by faith alone. Likewise, John 5:24 clearly teaches that salvation is by faith and that through faith we can escape the final judgment.

11. Edwards, *True Virtue* in *Works* 1.129.

12. The salvation of Adam and Eve is implied by the animal-skin clothing God gave them to cover their nakedness (Gen. 3:21). Throughout the Bible the garments God gives to people are symbols of the righteousness He grants to cover their sin. See, for example, Zechariah 3:1–5.

Chapter 10: Is the Trinity Nonsense?

Epigraph. Edwards in Harvey G. Townsend, ed., *The Philosophy of Jonathan Edwards* (Eugene, OR: University of Oregon, 1955), Miscellany 94, 252–53.

1. Some theologians use the word "person" both to refer to the three members of the Godhead and to refer to the one Triune God. However, this entails using person in two different ways, and it introduces a confusion we can avoid by using person in only one sense.

2. Jehovah's Witnesses insist that since Christ prayed to His Father and obeyed His Father, He must not be equal with God. Although I have spoken to many Jehovah's Witnesses, I have never had the happy privilege of having one actually listen to me well enough to understand that the earthly submission of Christ is an important part of Trinitarian doctrine. Other common objections to the doctrine of the Trinity by Jehovah's Witnesses include Revelation 3:14, which describes Christ as "the Beginning of the creation of God" and Colossians 1:15 in which He is the "firstborn of all creation." Christ is the Beginning of creation not because He was the first-created being, but because He is the One through whom creation began. God created all things through Him (John 1:1–3; Col. 1:16). He is the "firstborn of all creation" because He is the heir of all creation. In Jewish law the firstborn was the chief heir and head of the family after the father's death. For that reason God called the whole nation of Israel His firstborn in order to emphasize Israel's privileged position (Exod. 4:22). Jesus is the firstborn because as the Messiah, He has the exalted position of God's chief heir. See also Psalm 89:20–29, where the Lord calls King David His firstborn.

3. For a lucid and thorough study of how Edwards employs the psychological and social analogies to the Trinity, see William Danaher Jr., *The Trinitarian Ethics of Jonathan Edwards* (Louisville, KY: Westminster John Knox Press, 2004), especially chapters 1 and 2.

4. The following discussion is a summary of Augustine, *On the Holy Trinity*, Book 9 in *A Select Library of the Nicene and Post-Nicene Fathers of the Christian Church*, Philip Schaff, ed. (Grand Rapids: Eerdmans, 1980), vol. 3.

5. Augustine, *On the Trinity*, 8.10.

6. "Us" and "Our" in Genesis 1:26 have been interpreted in three ways: as referring to God and the angels; as a plural of majesty (kings say "we" when they mean "I"); as a hint of the plurality of Persons in the godhead. The third option was the almost unanimous opinion of the early church, and it still has much to commend it. The first alternative cannot be correct because Genesis 1, and indeed the whole Bible, pictures God as the sole Creator. The second is suspect because no biblical king employs a plural of majesty in his speeches.

7. Augustine, *On the Trinity*, 9.12.

8. For a full discussion of this concept, see Danaher, *Trinitarian Ethics*, 19–26.

9. The word *logos*, which is translated "Word" in John 1:1 and 14, signifies more than a single spoken or written word. Its meanings include "discourse" and "reason." First century Jewish-Hellenistic writers appropriated the term to describe God's wisdom by which He made the world (Prov. 8:31). The Gospel of John draws from, but transforms that tradition, when it describes Christ as "the Word." Edwards employs the same thought connections in His description of Christ as the idea, the wisdom and the Word of God.

10. Edwards in Townsend, *Philosophy*, Miscellany 94, 254–55.

11. Edwards, *Treatise on Grace* in *Unpublished Writings*, 43–44.

12. Lewis, *Mere Christianity* (New York: MacMillan, 1958), 135–36.

13. Danaher, *Trinitarian Ethics*, 69, summarizing from Edwards's Miscellanies 96 and 97.

14. Edwards, "The Mind" in *Works* 1.ccxxix.

15. For example, consider this definition from Thomas

Aquinas in the high Middle Ages: "For beauty includes three conditions, 'integrity' or 'perfection' since those things which are impaired are by the very fact ugly; due 'proportion' or 'harmony'; and lastly, 'brightness' or 'clarity,' whence things are called beautiful which have a bright color" (*Summa Theologica*, part 1, question 39, answer 8 in *The Ages Digital Library* [Albany, NY: AGES Software, 1997]).

16. Edwards, "The Mind" in *Works* 1.ccxxix.

17. Ibid., *Works* 1.ccxxxi.

18. Danaher, *Trinitarian Ethics*, 71.

Chapter 11: Does the Trinity Make a Difference in Our Lives Today?

Epigraph. From an annotation in Edwards's interleaved Bible on Galatians 5:17 in *Unpublished Writings*, 163–64.

1. Lewis, *Mere Christianity* (New York: Macmillan, 1958), 35.

2. Augustine in Vernon J. Bourke, ed., *The City of God* (New York: Image Books, 1958), 11.9.

3. Edwards, *The Great Christian Doctrine of Original Sin* in *Works* 1.221. Augustine gave the same reason for the fall of the devil and his angels. They rebelled because God did not give them the same measure of grace as He gave to the elect angels (*City of God*, 11.11, 13).

4. This translation of the creed is online at http://www.reformed. org. The English is a little clearer than the commonly quoted version found in Schaff, *The Creeds of Christendom*.

5. The standard theological texts give a thorough defense of Christ's two natures united, but not mingled, in one Person. See, for example, Hodge, *Systematic Theology* (Grand Rapids: Eerdmans, 1981), 2. 378–454; L. Berkhof, *Systematic Theology* (Grand Rapids: Eerdmans, 1941), 315–30; Millard J. Erickson, *Christian Theology* (Grand Rapids: Baker, 1985), 683–738; and Grudem, *Systematic Theology: An Introduction to Biblical Doctrine* (Grand Rapids: Zondervan, 1994, 2000), 529–67.

6. Gene Edwards, *The Birth* (Carol Stream, IL: Tyndale, 1990),
    46. Gene Edwards may not have intended to mingle the
    divine and human natures of Christ in such a way as to
    blend their characteristics, but his reference to God's DNA
    is misleading.

7. Stott, *Men Made New: An Exposition of Romans* 5–8
    (Chicago: InterVarsity, 1966), 37–48.

8. Edwards, *Treatise on Grace*, 28.

9. Ibid., 35–36.

10. Ibid., 36.

11. Ibid., 36–37.

12. Ibid., 37.

13. Ibid., 37–38.

14. Edwards replaced *gratitude to God* with *delight in God* as the
    primary aspect of the saints' love for God. Some might object
    to this reversal on the basis of First John 4:19, "We love
    because He first loved us." Edwards responds, "The saints'
    love to God is the *fruit* of God's love to them, as it is the *gift*
    of that love. God gave them a spirit of love to him, because
    he loved them from eternity." In addition, the manifestation
    of God's love in the work of redemption excites the
    admiration and affection of angels and men, so that the
    saints' delight in God rests on the prior exercise of His love
    toward fallen human beings (Edwards, *Religious Affections* in
    Works 1.277).

15. Edwards, *Treatise on Grace*, 55. The second commandment,
    "You shall not make for yourself an idol," prohibits fashioning
    images of the true God or of false gods, as Moses' commentary
    on the giving of the Law makes clear. In Deuteronomy
    4:10–20 he reminds the Israelites that they did not see any
    form of God when He spoke to them from Sinai. For that
    reason they were not to make a graven image or worship
    God under the form of any created thing. The *Westminster
    Larger Catechism* says that the sins forbidden in the second
    commandment include "the making any representation of

God, of all or any of the three persons, either inwardly in our mind, or outwardly in any kind of image or likeness of any creature whatsoever; all worshiping of it, or God in it or by it" (answer to Question 109). I dealt with physical images of God in "Images of the Lord: A Travesty of Deity" (MA thesis, Talbot Theological Seminary, 1976). My "Imaginary Ideas of Christ: A Scottish American Debate" (PhD dissertation, Westminster Theological Seminary, 1985) dealt with the mental images of Christ some converts experienced during the Great Awakening. Some of the findings of that study are summarized in my "Imagination and Idol: A Puritan Tension," *Westminster Theological Journal* 49 (1987), 305–34.

Chapter 12: Why Are Some Views of God's Glory Spiritually Inadequate?

Epigraph. Edwards, *Religious Affections* in *Works* 1.267.

1. Evelyn Underhill, *Mysticism: A Study in the Nature and Development of Man's Spiritual Consciousness* (New York: E.P. Dutton, 1961), 291.

2. George Huntston Williams and Angel M. Mergal, eds., *Spiritual and Anabaptist Writers*, The Library of Christian Classics (Philadelphia: Westminster, 1957), 213.

3. Edwards, *Distinguishing Marks of a Work of the Spirit of God* in *Works* 1.263.

4. James Robe, *Narratives of the Extraordinary Work of the Spirit of God, at Cambuslang, Kilsyth, &c. Begun in 1742* (Glasgow, Scotland: David Niven, 1790), 307.

5. Ibid., 319.

6. Uwe Siemon-Netto, "Bach in Japan," *Christian History and Biography*, summer 2007, 42.

Chapter 13: How Can We Recognize the True Glory of God?

Epigraph. Edwards, "A Divine and Supernatural Light, Immediately Imparted to the Soul, by the Spirit of God, Shown to Be Both a Scriptural and Rational Doctrine" in *Works* 2.15.

1. Charles Chauncy, *Seasonable Thoughts on the State of Religion in New England* (Hicksville, New York: Regina Press, 1975), 128–29.

Conclusion: Beauty for Brokenness

Epigraph. Samuel Hopkins in Dwight, *Memoirs of Jonathan Edwards* in *Works* 1.cxxiii–cxxiv.

1. Edwards, *Memoirs* in *Works* 1.cxxii.

2. Edwards, *Works* 1.xiii.

3. Actually, "will power" is a misnomer. The will has no independent power. As Edwards clearly showed in *Original Sin*, the will always follows the inclination that is strongest at the moment of choosing.

4. Paul Tournier, "The Blessings of a Deep Loss," *Christianity Today*, November 23, 1984.

5. Edwards, *Memoirs* in *Works* 1.xciv.

6. Ibid., 1.xcv.

Appendix 1

1. E-mail, September 8, 2008. Used by permission.

This book was produced by CLC Publications. We hope it has been life-changing and has given you a fresh experience of God.through the work of the Holy Spirit. CLC Publications is an outreach of CLC Ministries International, a global literature mission with work in over fifty countries. If you would like to know more about us or are interested in opportunities to serve with a faith mission, we invite you to contact us at:

CLC Ministries International
PO Box 1449
Fort Washington, PA 19034

Phone: 215-542-1242
E-mail: orders@clcpublications.com
Website: www.clcpublications.com

- - - - - - - - - - - - - - - - - -

DO YOU LOVE GOOD CHRISTIAN BOOKS?
Do you have a heart for worldwide missions?

You can receive a FREE subscription to
CLC's newsletter on global literature missions
Order by e-mail at:

clcworld@clcusa.org

Or fill in the coupon below and mail to:

PO Box 1449
Fort Washington, PA 19034

FREE *CLC WORLD* SUBSCRIPTION!

Name: _____

Address:_____

_____

Phone: _____ E-mail:_____

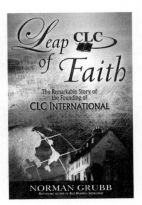

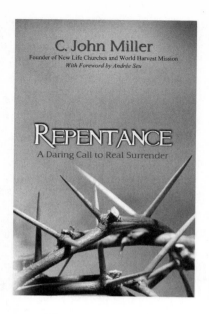

Repentance

C. John Miller

Repentance starts at conversion—but it doesn't stop there. It's an ongoing attitude for daily living in Christ. True repentance puts us in right relationship with the Lord and enables us to walk in the fullness of His Spirit, growing and being used in His purpose for us.

ISBN-13: 978-0-87508-979-9